LIFESTREAMS

LIFESTREAMS

An Introduction to Biosynthesis

DAVID BOADELLA

ROUTLEDGE & KEGAN PAUL
LONDON AND NEW YORK

First published in 1987 by
Routledge & Kegan Paul Ltd
11 New Fetter Lane, London EC4P 4EE

Published in the USA by
Routledge & Kegan Paul Inc.
in association with Methuen Inc.
29 West 35th Street, New York, NY 10001

Set in 11 on 13 point Baskerville
by Witwell Ltd, Liverpool
and printed in Great Britain
by The Guernsey Press Co. Ltd,
Guernsey, Channel Islands

Library of Congress Cataloging in Publication Data

Boadella, David.
Lifestreams: an introduction to biosynthesis.

Bibliography: p.
Includes index.
1. Mind and body.   2. Psychology.
3. Psychotherapy.   I. Title.
BF161.B54   1987   150.19'5   86-31592

British Library CIP Data also available
ISBN 0-7102-1145-7

To Stanley Keleman, who taught me both to follow and guide the formative process.

Illustration by Michael Chaitow

CONTENTS

CONTENTS

ILLUSTRATIONS

ACKNOWLEDGMENT

I wish to thank Courtenay Young for his invaluable help in editing and preparing the manuscript of this book and for his active advice and encouragement at many stages of its growth.

INTRODUCTION

Freud believed that one day psychoanalysis would discover its organic functions. In my book on Wilhelm Reich[1] I showed how Reich's consistent development from character-analysis, through to what he called 'vegeto-therapy', a therapy working with the physiological roots of neurosis in the body, provided these organic foundations.

Reich laid the first basis for a somatic psychology. Today we can see Reich as the godfather of all present therapies working with the emotional life of the body. Gestalt therapy originated with Fritz Perls who was both a patient and student of Reich's. Bioenergetic analysis, based in New York, was co-founded in 1956 by Alexander Lowen and John Pierrakos, two doctors trained by Reich. Gerda Boyesen founded her Centre for Biodynamic Psychology in London in 1970. She has developed the therapeutic work that Reich had initiated in Scandinavia.

Today somatic psychology has grown from many roots beyond those developed by Reich. Stanley Keleman, a senior trainer in bio-energetics, created the Centre for Energetic Studies in 1970 and developed a rich theory and practice of somatic processes, linking the understanding of muscle tone and tissue pulsation with the biology of dreaming and the poetry of embodiment.

I began my therapeutic work on the basis of Reich's bio-energetic approach; the word 'bio-energetic', for me, is descriptive of all the life processes in the body. After twenty-five years of work in this field, I began to use the word 'biosynthesis' to describe my particular therapeutic approach.

Biosynthesis means the integration of life. The term was first used by Francis Mott, an Englishman who developed a method of configurational psychology based on depth studies of life in the womb. Since 1975 I have been developing an approach to therapy founded on an understanding derived from embryology.

The central concept in biosynthesis is that there are three fundamental energetic currents or lifestreams flowing in the body, associated with the cellular germ-layers (ectoderm, endoderm and mesoderm) in the fertilised egg out of which the distinctive organ systems are formed. These streams express themselves as a flow of movement throughout the muscle pathways; a flow of perceptions, thoughts and images through the neuro-sensory system; and a flow of emotional life in the core of the body through the deep organs of the trunk. Stress before birth or during infancy and in later life breaks up the integration of these three streams.

In biosynthesis the therapeutic re-integration works with breath-release and emotional *centring*; with re-toning the muscles and the *grounding* of posture; and with the *facing* and shaping of experience through eye-contact and voice communication.

The embryological understanding has been greatly deepened by knowledge gained from Francis Mott's *Configurational Psychology*, Frank Lake's *Clinical Theology* and Otto Hartmann's *Dynamic Morphology*.

The work of integrating action, feeling and thought forms the outer ground of biosynthesis. There is an inner ground which underlies this and which expresses the essence or spirit of each person. Robert Moore's work in Denmark on psychic centring through imagery of the breath and re-balancing of the energy field of the body has been one of the most recent influences on this direction.

In biosynthesis I have developed a theory of the therapeutic work of re-integration that shows it to be an expression of two fundamental themes which are deeper than either psychology or biology. Indeed they appear to be basic themes which underlie the emergence of matter and of life, as well as the integrity of the body and the formation of the self. These themes are as follows.

1 The formative process in nature. The emergence of higher from lower levels of order is a basic natural law in an open system. The self-healing principle, which is the core of therapy, is an expression of this law.

2 The organising field. The formative process has to be potentiated by an appropriate set of conditions. Without these, self-organisation does not take place. Healthy child-development needs the presence of contactful parents to provide the 'biological organiser' (Mahler) for normal growth. In work on transforming blocked patterns of feeling and expression, the most essential tool is the responsive life of another human being. Reich called this 'vegetative identification', the ability to sense in our own body the blocked patterns of expression that are constricting another. Stanley Keleman used the term 'somatic resonance' for the biological rapport between two people. The somatic resonance of the therapist's hands, voice and presence, is the organising field in which the formative process of reintegrating body, mind and spirit takes place.

I have worked as a therapist with a background linked to these traditions of understanding the dynamics of the body for the past thirty years. In the following pages I have tried to set out some of the principles of my practice.

I have tried, throughout the text, to avoid an overuse of the masculine pronoun and the 'convention' that this pronoun stands for both sexes. It is unfortunate that I find most of the alternatives clumsy or unacceptable. I hope that the reader does not assume that I am referring to men, male development or masculine principles if I happen to refer to a person as 'he', for nothing of the sort is intended.

David Boadella
Centre for Biosynthesis
BCM Chesil
London WC1N 3XX

CHAPTER 1

EMOTIONAL EXPRESSION AND THE BODY

The language of bio-energy

It must be recognised at the outset that it is impossible for an individual not to communicate. Even total silence tells us something about a person and the way in which he or she meets the world. The focus on neurotic *symptoms* as related in *words* by a disturbed person is complemented in bio-energetic therapy by a focus on the *signs* of emotional stress and expressive disturbance as revealed by the *non-verbal* aspects of a patient.

The first scientist to put whole-hearted stress on non-verbal means of communication as being of fundamental importance was Charles Darwin in his remarkable book, *The Expression of the Emotions in Man and Animals*, which must be looked on as a basic primer of psychology as well as of ethology.

I should like to give a brief quotation from what Darwin said, because this helps to set the framework of reference for the work I shall be describing.

> The movements of expression in the face and body are of much importance for our welfare. They serve as the first means of communication between mother and her infant; she smiles approval or frowns disapproval, and thus encourages her child on the right path ... The movements of expression give vividness and energy to our spoken words; they may, and often do, reveal the

thoughts more truely than do words, which may be falsified. The free expression by outward signs of an emotion intensifies it. Passions can be produced by putting people into appropriate attitudes. On the other hand the repression of all outward signs softens our emotion.[1]

All this was written in 1872, a quarter of a century before Freud began to unravel the unconscious. There is also much evidence in the early history of psychoanalysis[2] that Freud discovered the fundamental principle which Darwin here described. For instance, Freud recognised quite early on that remembering forgotten childhood experiences had no curative effect unless the buried emotion was also recovered. He tried through his verbal techniques to encourage affective memories, but many of his patients were unable to experience their long-withheld emotions. Something seemed to get in the way. In Freudian terminology, one talks of the 'resistance' to getting well; the resistance to facing what a friend of mine once called 'the supreme crisis of being helped'.

One of the earliest workers in the psychoanalytic framework of reference, who began to understand what it was that got in the way, was Wilhelm Reich. He is well known to some for his classic book on *Character Analysis*.[3] In this book he provided the first detailed map of the elaborate defence systems which neurotic patients construct to protect themselves both from the outside world and from the impact of their own feelings. Reich founded bio-energetic theory because he did not rest content with this major achievement of insight into the workings of the neurotic personality. He went much further. From 1935 onwards he began a close investigation of the muscular tensions in the bodies of his patients.

It is true that, independently of Reich, people like Jacobsen and Schulze had published books on systems of relaxation. Also, Rudolf Laban[4] had developed a whole system of expressive movements which led to a revitalisation of dance training, of occupational rhythm and of physical education principles in schools. In 1966 the Laban Institute convened their first conference on 'Movement as Therapy' (Senate House, London) in which the possibility of movement therapy with emotionally disturbed children and adults was explored.

Reich's approach was deeper and more dynamic, precisely because of his psychiatric orientation. Reich was concerned with the fact that his patients behaved as though they were half-dead and that their normal functioning at every level was blocked. He realised that they were disturbed sexually; they were disturbed in their work function; their bodily processes lacked rhythm; their breathing was uncoordinated. In other words, Reich began to study and approach his patients in the way Darwin had advocated, as *organisms* first and foremost, whose *total behaviour* was involved in their neurotic difficulty.

Reich's approach was little understood because the therapeutic schools of that time lacked an orientation in this framework of references. Ethology, the systematic study of human character, had barely begun. The mind was still considered as some kind of separate compartment from the body. Reich's emphasis on bodily expression diverged so much from the prevailing practice of other analysts that it was regarded as eccentric heresy and many thought that Reich had gone astray.

At this point I would like to refer briefly to the four people who have done most to continue Reich's system of therapy, to teach it and to train others in it. In Scandinavia, where Reich first developed this work, Dr Ola Raknes was engaged in this form of therapy for over 35 years.[5] Dr Nic Waal, who held many prominent positions in psychiatry in both Norway and Denmark and who was the director of the Institut for Psykiatri in Oslo, was trained by Reich and, in turn, trained many groups in this bio-energetic approach.[6] One of the many offshoots of her work is the school of 'movement therapists' who are working in Holland in psychiatric hospitals with severely disturbed psychotics.

In America, where Reich moved from Scandinavia, Dr Elsworth Baker has been responsible for training a younger generation of therapists in the methods which he learnt from Reich.[7] Finally Dr Alexander Lowen has extended and developed Reich's work in many radical ways and is the founder of the Institute for Bio-Energetic Analysis in New York.[8] Through his influence, knowledge of bio-energetic principles and practice has been diffused widely in the United States and elsewhere.

To call such therapies 'bio-energetic' indicates that we are dealing with powerful emotional reactions. The capacity of emotion to mobilise or paralyse the body is well known. Furthermore, it can be said fairly generally that every neurotic or psychotic person has lost part of the full range of human emotional expression. Such a person has lost, or never developed, the full range of movement possibilities of which any healthy child is capable. In some degree or other *motility* is disturbed. A neurosis then is equivalent to a system of blockages which prevent the free flow of feelings through the body. The aim of bio-energetic therapy is, therefore, to overcome the blockages and restore the free flow.

Before describing in detail some of the blockages we deal with and the means used to free them, I must make clear that, in this work, emotion is defined rather literally as a 'movement out'. In this sense it is a fundamental expression of all life forms. Even one-celled animals show a simple function of expansion and contraction of protoplasm in response to stimuli.

We can look on this as the prototype of what we recognise in higher animals as reaching out towards the environment in pleasurable anticipation or shrinking away in pain from unpleasant situations. The term 'flow' has literal meaning for such protoplasmic reactions. In higher organisms the processes of expansion and contraction are mediated through the two branches of the autonomic nervous system, impulses from which pass to all the organs and muscles of the body. These impulses regulate the energy metabolism of the body and control such basic functions as circulation and heart beat, digestive processes, breathing, sexuality and orgasm. In a state of health, or of mature functioning, all these processes occur rhythmically. Humans, who can verbalise their emotions, describe the experience of these rhythmic processes in their bodies as pleasurable. In all neuroses and psychoses these free-flowing rhythmic processes are considerably disturbed.

If an animal is threatened by some event or object in its environment, a state of tension is created and it reacts to the threat as to an emergency. When the body is mobilised by the nervous system to cope with emergencies there are normally two possible reactions, which we can summarise as 'fight' or 'flight'. If the animal has succeeded in ridding itself of what threatens it by attack or by escape, it has coped successfully with the emergency and can return to its normal rhythmic state afterwards; thus the disturbance was temporary and acute. The exception is in certain domestic or experimental animals, subject to human treatment (or perhaps we should say inhuman treatment), who may be kept permanently in situations from which they can neither attack nor escape. Such animals become neurotic and show psychosomatic symptoms like the ulcers developed by monkeys who are repeatedly put in stress situations which they cannot avoid.

When we look at human existence, we see that nearly every maladjusted person lives as though permanently in a state of emergency. Thus tension-states, and the over-activity of the sympathetic nervous system which maintains them, have become chronic. At this point, we find that the normal, built-in, self-regulatory processes have ceased to function and outside help or stimuli are required. It is only by dissolving the blockages which prevent the free-flowing movements that we can restore to people the ability to approach their environment rationally and healthily.

What these people need, more than anything, is to be able to relax, which is precisely what they cannot do. If persons who have bottled up their feelings of rage (say) for years are asked to relax, they cannot do so. They must brace themselves

5

to contain their anger. If a child cannot release the tensions of inescapable stress by crying, then it must continue to hold itself in tension as if the state of emergency still exists. If it can, then the stress is more bearable.

So, in bio-energetic therapy people are helped to experience their underlying rage, sorrow, anxiety and longings and to express these in the fullest possible way within the sessions. Only after the body has given in to its blocked impulses is it able to begin to recover a true capacity for joy and for rhythmic and pleasurable vital functioning. The understanding of how a tension-state can begin and be re-inforced until it builds up into a chronic situation, incapable of release, is basic to somatic therapy. This understanding, essentially from one's own experience, eliminates any form of judgment of neuroses and is thus a necessary and desirable prerequisite to being a therapist.

I should now like to go more specifically into the details of some of these muscular blockages and to describe some of the changes noticed when they are dissolved. The description of bodily tension-patterns can be attempted in one or two ways. I can either discuss the different segments of the body, putting before you the principal immobilities that are found and relating them to the underlying blockage in expression; or alternatively I could take the different character-patterns and attempt to show you how they vary in the nature of the tension-systems which underlie them. The second approach is by far the more subtle and discriminating,[9] but it would require far too much detail. Furthermore, no particular individual necessarily suffers from all of this at the same time.

Reverting thus to the former method, we can view the tensions of the body as a series of constrictions, created in a situation of emergency, the purpose and effect of which are to limit movement, breathing and feeling as the only available alternative to effective action. Each constriction divides the body into separate segments, in the way that a tight ring of pressure would split up the flowing movement of a snake into two disjoint halves. Reich described a number of body segments, proceeding longitudinally down the body from head to toe.

If we concentrate for a moment on the upper half of the face, the therapist is interested immediately in the expression of the eyes. A patient may look at the therapist with studied seriousness or with an anxious shifting glance, or may have a superior stare or a worried frown. The schizoid person has a characteristic vacant look, as though gazing into the distance; Reich called it the 'faraway' look. These different expressions reflect how these people meet the world; they contain also, in locked-up form, their own story of how the early relationships with parents and siblings were experienced.

The tension patterns of the body can be looked on as a person's frozen history. It is in the face that the truth of this can first be seen. The vital importance of eye-contact in the treatment of autistic children has been demonstrated[6] and its importance in treatment lies in the fact that these children show a massive immobility and blockage in this particular area. All neurotic people tend to show some degree of disturbance in the eye area, which we can visualise as extending from the eyes themselves through the forehead and across the large muscles of the scalp to where they insert in the neck. The inhibition of weeping, fright or anger can set up very severe tensions in the scalp and muscles at the base of the skull. These tensions are the physiological basis for the severe headaches that are prevalent in certain kinds of character.

To mobilise this area, it is necessary to encourage scalp movements and the opening wide of the eyes. There is also much room for work in developing awareness of the ways in which the patient's eyes react, or don't react, to the therapist. Emotions that need to be released from this area, before healthy seeing and looking with full contact can be restored, can include panicky flight, buried suspicion, murderous rage expressed in the eyes, and crying, which is bound up particularly in the muscles between the eyes.

This should give an indication of the type of tensions, the emotions behind them, and a taste of how they can be

7

released. Obviously a full treatise on this would be a biosynthesis training manual, which is not the object here. However, I hope that this, and what follows, serves to introduce and illustrate some of the basics.

Naturally each area of the body is linked up with the next, and the divisions are somewhat arbitrary. The tensions of the upper half of the face are functionally related to the lower half of the face, centred round the mouth and jaws. Patients come with fixed grins or with the down-turned mouth of despair. The compulsive character is nearly always saddled with a stiff upper lip. There are tight jaws, weak chins and gaunt cheeks, all expressing the use which the patient has learned to make of the facial muscles. The healthy child or adult has muscles which can express the full range of emotions according to the requirements of the occasion. Such a person is mobile and acceptable. The tense person is restricted and limited to a narrow range of facial expressions which was acquired in order to deal with stress. This person cannot consciously alter these expressions easily; they will change fundamentally only when the emotion behind the facial tensions can be released.

Such emotions, when they emerge in a session, are naturally infantile, since it is in infants that the first blockages of emotional expression usually take place. In therapy it is possible to release repressed impulses to bite, suck, cry and grimace from these areas of the face. With each such affective outburst and release, the patient often recovers the memory of some traumatic childhood experience; but the recovery of such memories is not essential for improvement. What is essential is the release of the bound emotion from the tensions which blocked its expression. The face is then able to relax properly, for the first time perhaps since the early trauma, and the patient is more able to face the world without the crippling limitations of the past which have been literally embodied.

The neck is one of two major constrictions in the framework of the body, the other being the waist. The neck can be viewed as a conducting tube linking the head to the rest of the body. Tensions in this area are particularly common.

They have been described independently of Reich by both Feldenkrais[10] and Alexander[11] and they serve to separate the head from the feeling of connection with the body. Many people feel identified with their heads and cut off from their bodies. In contrast, some schizophrenics suffer from such intolerable pressure in their heads, due to the pressures induced by these constrictions, that they identify with their body and feel their head as alien, even wishing it could be taken away and replaced with a new head. The feeling of identification is found to be proportional to the capacity of a person to be aware of what is felt in the body.

The main emotions held down in the throat area tend to be the noisy expressions of sobbing, shouting and screaming. In our culture, children are not supposed to make too much noise. But what else is an infant to do in intolerable situations of stress? It can only learn how to swallow down its anger and choke over its sorrows. Years later, in therapy, these unexpressed and held-down feelings can be elicited, with their original strength, by stimulation of the muscles in the throat and neck. It is remarkable to witness the changes of body-colour between the face and the trunk as the emotions are released. Patients experience a sense of 'clearing' in the head. A sense of unity between the head and the trunk develops. They begin to experience a feeling of coordination and grace, which a person free of such tensions is fortunate to take for granted.

Anger held back in the neck is connected to tensions in the muscles of the shoulders, which includes large areas of the back. It is astonishing how much rage is contained in some people's backs. Of course, it is dead rage, leading to rigid backs and stiff shoulders, as well as to unfeeling arms with poor circulation in many cases. The only way to restore mobility in this area is to provide opportunities in a controlled situation for the safe discharge of this anger in the form of violent movements of the arms and fists. With special arrangements in the treatment room it is possible to provide such a safe outlet for impulses, like hitting and striking, in

9

which the whole back can be involved. Naturally very good rapport has to exist between therapist and patient. However it is perfectly possible, at one and the same time, to be giving vent to old rage in this way and yet to be aware of the present-day situation and the need to avoid damaging either the room or the therapist. Judging the right conditions for releasing rage in this way is one of the skills required of a bio-energetic therapist.

After the neck constriction, one comes to the trunk segment. This contains one of the key indicators in this type of therapy, the breathing. Because breathing is so basic to life and to emotional expression in any form, the work on breathing is basic to this therapy. It underlies and accompanies all the work on specific tensions in particular parts of the body.

The entire trunk of the body, in a state of health, can be seen to pulsate gently, in a wavelike movement, during breathing. If we watch any healthy animal or child while it is breathing, we see that the breathing involves full mobility in the chest and abdomen. One of the first things that a child learns, however, when it seeks to suppress a feeling, is how to control its breathing. This control serves to subdue the processes of the body to the purposes of the mind, which here seeks to avoid the conflicts which open expression of feeling must involve in suppressive homes.

We find that all neurotics show disturbances in their breathing, of which there are two extreme forms: the high chest and sucked-in abdomen of the characteristic military posture, which was criticised by Mathias Alexander in his books on coordination and posture; and a generally deficient respiration, where a minimum of air is taken into the lungs. Schizoid people, and particularly some hysterics, soon become dizzy if their breathing deepens; getting such people to accept a fuller form of breathing is comparable to acclimatisation – it must be carried out gradually so that they learn to tolerate a higher level of vitality.

At the end of the trunk we find a further constriction – the waist. This is linked to tensions in the lower abdomen, in the small of the back and in the muscles of the pelvic floor, all of which serve to constrict the pelvis, which in many neurotics is held fixed in a retracted position. The immobility of the pelvis leads naturally to sexual difficulties, but the sexual problems cannot be seen as confined to this area in a dissociated way. To function well sexually involves a full expression of the personality. Reich's explicit description of disturbances in orgasm were sometimes misunderstood by those who thought he offered a sort of sexual panacea. Nothing could be further from the truth. The ability to surrender oneself wholly to an experience is one and indivisible, whether that experience be commitment to work, a reaction to a piece of music or a painting, a sincere dramatic performance, a deep involvement in a close relation with another person, or any other fundamental life experience. Hypertension in any part of the body will subtract from the experience.

The pelvis leads naturally into the legs, which are the main supports of the body. Tensions in the legs lead to a disturbance in one's contact with the ground. The expression held down in the legs is principally kicking, both aggressive and pleasurable. Lowen, in particular, and Keleman have stressed the importance of establishing a free flow of feeling in the legs, so as to bring about a sensation of being 'grounded'. If we look at some of the more common disturbances, it is easy to see what is meant by this term. Many people quite literally feel that they do not belong on the ground, while some schizoid people may even have a sense of floating. Weakness in the joints is a characteristic of the schizoid disturbance. Legs which are over-rigid may provide firm support, but prevent flexibility. The absence of spring in the legs is related to the loss of joy in life. Watch any child dancing for joy and you must know what I mean.

When the main tensions in the body are overcome by special forms of massage and postural movements, eliciting fundamental body expressions, the patient experiences his or her body in a new way. They value themselves and their world differently. The word 'value' comes from the Latin root *valere*, to be well. To be well in bio-energetic terms is to be free to function rhythmically without blockages due to chronic muscle tensions. It was Reich's distinction to discover the subtle relationships between the defences of the body and the emotional vitality they contained and hence to devise ways of altering the balance of forces in the direction of health. Such health is both psychic and physical at the same time.

There is a quotation from D. H. Lawrence which sums this theme up.

> The body's life is the life of sensations and emotions.
> The body feels real hunger, real thirst, real joy in the
> sun or the snow, real pleasure in the smell of roses or
> the look of a lilac bush; real anger, real sorrow, real
> tenderness, real warmth, real passion, real hate, real
> grief. All the emotions belong to the body and are only
> recognised by the mind.[12]

CHAPTER 2

CENTRING, GROUNDING AND FACING

Embryology and therapy

In my development of body-centred therapy, which I label as biosynthesis, I work with the assumption that there are three primary modes of therapy, which I call centring, grounding and facing. Each of these is linked to the harmonious functioning of the organ-systems which are derived from the primary cell layers in the embryological organisation of the foetus. Excessive stress, whether before, during or after birth, breaks up the cooperation and integration between the realms of these three cell layers. Therapy can be defined as a way of seeking to restore that integration.

The inside layer of the foetal body (the endoderm) produces tissues that metabolise energy. They provide the lining of the intestinal tubing, all the digestive organs and the tissues of the lungs. The energy level of a person is dependent on the efficient mobilisation of energy and this metabolism is most powerfully influenced by emotion. This is obvious if we see a person who is emotionally depressed. The whole metabolism of the body is slowed, appetite is lost and breathing drastically reduced.

The emotional balance of a person is mediated by the two great branches of the vegetative nervous system, the sympathetic and the parasympathetic systems. The sympathetic system prepares us for emergency action, fight or flight, and is associated with the emotions of anger and fear. The parasympathetic system prepares us to give up fighting or running away: it is associated with another contrasted pair of emotions, pleasurable relaxation and the letting go into sadness and grief.

Both halves of the vegetative nervous system send branches to all the internal organs that metabolise energy. Both the contraction and expansion of the lungs in breathing and the peristaltic movements of the intestines in digestion respond to the signals of the vegetative nerves. This rhythm of expansion and contraction is one of the most fundamental rhythms of life. It is found in primitive unicellular organisms, long before the evolution of a central nervous system.

The therapeutic work of *centring* is concerned with re-establishing a functioning rhythm in the flow of metabolic energy and the balance between the two halves of the vegetative nervous system. In practice this means help towards recovering emotional balance and harmonious breathing. What this looks like in practice will be described in detail in Chapter 6 'Waves of breath: Rhythms of respiration and feeling'.

The middle cellular layer in the foetus (the mesoderm) forms itself into the muscular system, the bony skeleton and the blood vessels and heart. It is a system for movement and action. The heart and the smooth muscle sheets are regulated by the vegetative nerves, like the other internal organs. The skeletal muscular system, on the other hand, has three different forms of control: cortical, sub-cortical and spinal. Cortical control is through the main voluntary nerve pathways (the pyramidal system). Sub-cortical control is through a special nervous system linked to the basal ganglia, the mid-brain and the cerebellum, called the extra-pyramidal system. It is responsible for balance, for the preparation of muscle tone and for posture. The third form of control is in the spinal reflex pathways. Everyone is familiar with the instantaneous response of jerking the hand away from a hot object. Such reflexes exist throughout the whole body and can be found occurring in the movements of birth (birth reflex), many of the early infant reflex patterns (tonic neck reflex,

Babinsky reflex, etc.) and in the orgasm reflex in sexuality. The interaction between these three systems will be explored more fully later.

The therapeutic work of *grounding* is concerned with establishing a good relationship between the voluntary, semi-voluntary and involuntary modes of movement and with re-creating a more appropriate muscle tone. Muscle tone can be unbalanced in two directions. Hypertonus is an excess of tension, more than is required for a particular action; the muscles feel tense, knotted and rigid. Hypotonus is a deficiency of tonus, less than is necessary for a particular action; the muscles feel slack, spongy and over-sluggish.

To be well grounded is to be in an appropriate state of tonus for a particular set of conditions. A sailor on a ship's deck is well grounded; he can continually adapt his posture to the shifting conditions of the 'ground'. A person sleeping needs to relax his muscle tone from the action of the day; he is well grounded in bed when he has the appropriate muscle tone for bed. A person who stiffens in water is an incompetent swimmer; he is badly grounded in the water. To be grounded on earth is to have a good muscle tonus in the legs, without a tendency to over-stiffen or over-collapse. The training in the martial arts, emphasising dynamic balance and relaxed attention with no wastage of energy, shows an excellent understanding of the principles of grounding.

Patients who come for therapy show excesses or deficiencies in muscle tonus. These are expressed in disturbances of posture that are reflected in the somatic expression of character-structure. How we hold ourselves reveals something of how we stand in the world, how we feel and who we are. Changing posture involves the possibilities of strong emotional reaction and the uncovering of deeply ingrained character attitudes.

The third cellular layer of the foetus is the outermost layer, the ectoderm. It forms all the nervous tissues in the body and the sense organs, including the skin. It is a system designed for gathering and integrating information about the world. The nervous system deals with three kinds of perception: perception drawn from the internal organs (interoception); perception drawn from the muscular system (proprioception); and perception drawn from the five sense organs (exteroception). We can see this division as a division within the sensory system that reflects the tripartite organisation of the body, nerves bringing information from the endoderm, from the mesoderm and from the ectoderm.

The way we receive information is channelled through the eyes, the ears and the sense of touch, primarily, and the specialised sense of smell and taste to a secondary degree. The way we think is grounded in these sensory channels. We think in visual patterns, in auditory patterns (speech), or in tactile patterns.

The typical imbalances found in the ectoderm are patterns of over-sensitivity and under-sensitivity. The over-sensitive person has a low threshold for excitation; small signals easily trigger him into stress. The under-sensitive person has a high threshold to excitation and blocks out a lot: he has eyes but doesn't look; ears but doesn't listen. The low-threshold person is under-bounded, thin-skinned, easily threatened and invaded by a harsh look, a loud noise or a sudden touch. The high threshold person is over-bounded, thicker-skinned and well defended against invasion.

Thus, the therapeutic work of *facing* is work with eye contact, voice contact and with the integration of language and perception with feeling. It will be described in more detail in Chapter 8, 'Facing and sounding: Eye contact, voice and language'.

The realms of experience founded in the embryonic cell layers are the realms of breathing and feeling, of action and movement, of thought and sensation. Just as high levels of stress break up the integration of feeling, movement and thinking, so we find that therapeutic systems themselves tend to reflect this splitting. Thus there are therapies that concentrate on emotional release, or liberating breathing, with little or no understanding of posture, movement or the subtleties of language. There are other therapies specialised in remedial movement and the correction of posture which neglect emotional life and concept formation. A third group of therapies are rich in skills for the analysis of thought patterns, memories and spoken experience, but are blind to the organic foundation of experience in vegetative rhythms and postural adaptation.

The three psychoanalytic terms for the psychic structures of the mind, the id, ego and super-ego, have corresponding organic foundations. The id, that reservoir of primitive feelings, corresponds to the charge of emotional energy associated with the deep organ systems of the endoderm. When anger boils up in the intestine and fear clutches us in the solar plexus, the id has us in its grip.

The ego has two main divisions: a perceptual division and a motor division. The sensory ego makes sense of perception. It organises a thought-picture of the world, a mental map. The other branch of the ego, the motor ego, coordinates movements into effective action. The sensory ego is closely linked to the ectoderm while the motor ego is expressed through the mesoderm. Both are linked to the spine, which can be thought of as the 'ego-canal'. Thus we see the three-fold pattern again, linking psychoanalysis and embryology.

The concept of the super-ego is a sociological concept with no direct foundation or origin in the embryonic layers. The super-ego is something over and above the ego. It corresponds to the internalised parent, the voice of how we should be, which becomes physiologically embedded in what Reich called 'armouring'. This is a system of strains and tensions designed to achieve what is expected or demanded from outside, rather than respond to the inner feelings and wishes of the self.

The super-ego becomes a policeman standing over us with a club. My therapeutic work is seeking to reduce the influence of this policeman so as to expand the territory of the ego as the best regulator of the energies of the id. The integration of the id with the two branches of the ego corresponds to the

17

harmonious coordination of the three embryonic realms.

If we return to the embryology of the body, we find there are three streams of affect associated with the three cell layers. There is an affect over the surface of the skin which Francis Mott called 'foetal skin affect'.[1] It is experienced as waves of pleasure or displeasure on the skin in response to touch; thus it has a positive and a negative form which itself reflects how the infant was handled. In the use of therapeutic touch in different forms of massage, we need to be aware of what kind of affect stream is present. Since the eye and ear are specialised forms of development from the (ectodermal) skin, the response of the eye to light and the ear to sound (also with their positive and negative forms) are equally expressions of 'foetal skin affect'. So we can wash the eyes with colour in colour therapy and wash the ears with sound in music therapy.

Kinaesthetic affect is the flow of feeling associated with movements. Graceful and joyful movements carry a pleasurable and positive kinaesthetic affect; tense and constricted movements will carry a painful and negative kinaesthetic affect. Spontaneous movements have a dance-like quality of effortless coordination. The foetal swimming movements, the joyful kicking of a baby, the pleasure of running and jumping, the coordinated actions of the athlete and the sportsman are high in kinaesthetic affect. Thus this affect is related to the mesodermal layer.

Umbilical affect is the flow of feeling associated with the sense of life and energy being pumped into the centre of one's body through the umbilical cord (endodermal). Positive umbilical affect carries a sense of well-being and vitality, a golden glow in the pit of the stomach. Negative umbilical affect carries a sense of malaise, anxiety, despair and loss of well-being; it is a dark sense of being poisoned or blackened at the source of life.

Once the child is born and the cord is cut, the umbilical affect remains as a somatic memory that can powerfully affect the quality of feeling and distribution of energy in the abdomen. The way a child digests food is related to how he digests feelings. Gerda Boyesen developed this connection in her theory of psychoperistalsis.[2]

The flow of affect in the abdomen is also regulated by the way we breathe and by the activity of the diaphragm. At the inception of psychoanalysis, Freud's colleague Josef Breuer described three channels of excitement which bear a close relationship to the three embryonic lifestreams. A description of his work gives some historical root to the tripartite view of therapy developed here (see Appendix 1).

The embryological view of therapy can be seen to have a most comprehensive way of understanding somatic organisation. This will be developed more fully in the chapter on the design of the body (Chapter 5). In its understanding of the organic roots of the id and the two branches of the ego and through its links to the energetic concepts of Breuer, it can illuminate the understanding of the psyche. There is, therefore, one more connection that needs exploring.

Psychics who study the energy field (or aura) find that it has a vital, emotional and mental component. The vital component can be related to the charge of blood and through this to the mesoderm. The emotional field likewise can be linked to the endoderm, and the mental field to the ectoderm. The healer who seeks to balance the energy in these three fields and to help them function in an integrated way is doing, at the subtle level, what the work with centring, grounding and facing is doing at the organic level. So we can look at the cell layers as generating the three energy fields, or at the three interacting fields as organising the embryonic layers.

The healer can affect the somatic energy through his work with the life force and the somatic therapist can affect the subtle energy of the life-fields through his work on breathing, movements and perception. The embryological approach to understanding somatic and psychic organisation is the taproot of biosynthesis.

CHAPTER 3

EMBODIMENT BEFORE BIRTH

Life in the womb

Because embryological insights are basic to my therapeutic approach, a clear understanding of the development in the womb and the transition to life outside it provides an essential background against which to comprehend not only neurotic conflicts, but also the earliest emotional history of the body and its organisational plan. Therefore, this chapter and the following one are devoted to a description of these earliest developmental processes.

When a patient comes to a therapist for help, he or she brings problems that have an emotional history. The symptoms that are presented can be seen as the tip of an iceberg. The part of the iceberg that is invisible to the patient is his or her own character-structure which generates the symptoms. Reich saw a person's character-structure as their frozen history.

Psychoanalysis took memories back to the beginning of language. Melanie Klein traced the origins of some neuroses more definitely to the first year of life. Otto Rank saw the trauma of birth as the central generator of emotional stress. Frank Lake and a whole school of pre-natal psychologists have gone back to the time *in utero* to study the roots of emotional problems. Thus, in presenting my understanding of the relationship between energy and character, I will now give an inside view of life in the womb.

To form the body of a new person the germ cells which are

embedded in the tissues of the parents have first to be released and allowed to become free-floating. These are explosive and climactic events. Ovulation, filmed using fibre-optic techniques, is a spectacular and breath-taking process; the sight of the ripe follicle bursting to expel the future ovum brings gasps of amazement and awe from those who see it. The orgasm itself, during which the sperm are flung by the pulses of ejaculation many thousands of times their own length to begin their journey, is capable of spreading a shock wave of excitement through all the tissues of the body.

The sperm and the ovum, microscopic specks of germ plasm with a prehistoric history, begin to move towards each other. The ovum floats down the canal of the oviduct and is carried along by peristaltic waves and the beating of the cilia lining the Fallopian tube. Four hundred million sperm swim against the current, like miniature salmon forcing their way upstream, running the gauntlet of the molecular patterns in the mucus, which are at maximum density during ovulation. Their crystalline patterns, under a microscope, look like fern leaves, coral branches or fragments of snow flakes. This is described beautifully by Lennard Nilsson in his book *The Everyday Miracle*.

> They are constantly oscillating and the bindings
> sometimes come loosened for a moment. Then a sperm
> can take the opportunity to swim forward in free space
> as far as possible. It is rather like running the gauntlet.
> When one is as small as a sperm, one has to pay
> attention to molecules and their position. The
> penetration of the sperm in the cervical mucus is very
> much like the progress of a fleet of boats up a river full
> of invisible logs.[1]

The mucus stream which carries this fantastic shoal of sperm not only nourishes them; it appears to appetise them. Some quality in the secretions energises them and attracts them towards the ovum. The first one to make contact with the gelatinous membrane of the ovum excites a response from the membrane. The membrane appears to form a cone and to soften enough to allow the leading sperm to pass into the inner fluid of the cell. As soon as it has passed, the membrane becomes impermeable to all the remaining sperm which are nosing into it on all sides.

The free-floating, but now fertilised, zygote continues its slow voyage down the oviduct. By the end of about 30 hours it will have achieved its first division into two cells. As Stanley Keleman wrote:

> If you watch a cell divide, first you see that the cell is excited, vibrating. You see the forming of two poles, two areas of intense internal activity. You can actually see the radiation between one pole and the other and the lining-up of chromosome bodies within that field. The radiating between the two poles intensifies until it becomes a pulsation and then a streaming. The streaming communicates the deepest information about life – as we do when we communicate with each other. We are all, for better or worse, attuned to such intensely human patterns of excitement.[2]

After six or seven divisions, the week-old cell-clump fastens itself to the wall of the womb and undergoes its first experience of embeddedness. On film, implantation resembles a moon landing. R. D. Laing gave a great deal of emphasis to the importance of this transition in a talk entitled 'Life before birth'. He suggests that implantation is the equivalent of adoption and that the embedding cell-body is, in some way, sensitised to the receptivity of the womb. The free-floating state of awareness, familiar in some mystical and dissociated conditions, carries with it a fear of being washed away. Myths of the hero who, very early in his existence, is put into a container and allowed to drift down the river until he lands at a suitable place, correspond, Laing suggests, to this time of journeying down the Fallopian canal. If the uterus is felt to be unreceptive, then fantasies or nightmares of being embedded in quicksand may haunt later awareness. If the uterus is receptive, the cell-mass effectively puts out roots into fertile soil.

For the rest of its life in the womb the growing organism will remain rooted, like a plant, until the final severance of this root connection during the third stage of labour. By this time the new-born baby should have already established itself on the stomach or at the breast of the mother. Premature cutting of the umbilical cord can lead to a state of disconnection or rootlessness.

In Laing's fertile imagery, the wall of the womb is the soil; the embryo is the seed; the villi of the chorion are the primal roots; the developing umbilicus is the stem; and the foetus is the developing fruit of the plant. He writes:

> Before implantation, the secretions of the uterine tube may be calm or stormy ... plentiful or a drought; one may spin, revolve, float, fly; be dashed against rocks; be washed ashore and be washed away again, before journey's end. Before eventual definitive implantation there may be many adventures. This journey to implantation may form a template for subsequent patterns. An implantation may be mapped onto birth...
>
> Birth is implantation in reverse and the reception one receives from the post-natal world generates a sympathetic resonance in us to our first adoption by our pre-natal world.[3]

In the next two weeks this clump of about 100 cells will grow a thousand-fold into an elongated disc with a head end and a tail end that already consist of three layers: a back, middle and front layer. In this period of maximum growth, it also rolls itself into a series of tubes. You need to be a three-dimensional geometer to follow the topological transformations of this period, but this basic embryology is essential to an understanding of later energy flows.

One and the same egg-cell will give rise to nerve cells, muscle cells, blood cells and bone cells at this stage. Cells are originally 'totipotent', in that they all have the same potential to generate any part of the body. Somehow they are 'guided' to act on only part of their total genetic blueprint. 'Signals' from the environment of the dividing cell can activate or inhibit a given daughter-cell to develop in the direction of nose or finger, lung or kidney. It is only at this division into embryological layers that they really begin to specialise. Morphogenesis – the origin of form – and what controls it is not understood. What biologists describe is a process of protoplasmic directional movement, as individual cells begin to migrate and re-position themselves in the body of the elongating and invaginating cell-mass. This process, called 'morphogenetic streaming', suggests that there is communication between the cells through contact as they flow along bio-electrical and chemical gradients into organised functional locations in the body. As they divide, they differentiate. We can only marvel at this process of self-formation.

The embryo is built from the outside inwards. Otto Hartmann has described how the three embryological layers or discs are formed,[4] and it is necessary to dwell on these details here in order to gain a full understanding of the differences in these layers (see Figure 3.1).

Two hollow elliptical cell-bubbles form – the amniotic sac and the yolk sac. Packing cells of magma occupy the space between. There is nothing like an organism yet, just two sacs swimming in magma inside the peripheral boundary of the zygote. But, from the cells lining the lower surface of the amniotic sac, the ectoderm develops, which later becomes the outer layer of the body. From the cells lining the upper surface of the yolk sac develops the endoderm, the inner lining of the body. The magma cells form into the mesoderm, the packing material of the body.

The three layers of the original disc – outer (ecto), middle (meso) and inner (endo) – each have an associated tube system. Along the back of the outer ectodermic layer a groove forms and the edges fold in to enclose the neural canal, a sealed tube full of fluid that will soon swell out at the head end into three bulges. We are watching the emergence of what will become

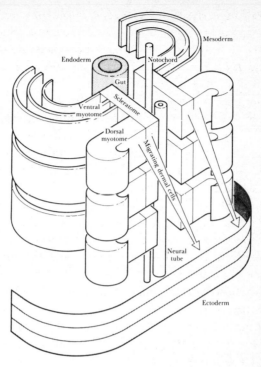

Figure 3.1   The formation of the three embryological layers

the three parts of the brain – forebrain, midbrain and hindbrain. The whole three-layered disc then folds down and rolls in to form a long, curved, triple cylinder. The innermost tube (endodermic) becomes the gut. All the organs of digestion will bud out from this in due course, differentiating into stomach, liver, pancreas, etc. The lungs will also bud out from the front end, like two little pods, which then will subdivide and ramify into the tree-like patterning of the bronchial tubes. Out of the middle (mesodermic) layer cells stream from both sides towards the centre to form the two halves of a third tube which will fuse into the primitive heart. By twenty-five days, in an organism weighing less than a thousandth of a gram, that heart will have started to beat; the tube pulsates spontaneously.

Theodore Schwenk sensitively describes this chaos in terms of rhythms.

> The digestive tract as a whole, starting at the lips, is not simply a cylindrical pipe, but a rhythmically articulated structure dividing the process of metabolism in space and time into several main parts, in expansion and contraction. It is as though this rhythm has become a form and superimposed on it is the peristalsis of the intestine which is still purely movement.
>
> The whole function and form of the heart is a reflection of the streaming processes of water, where, in its movements of expansion and contraction, it is as though separate spaces were continually being formed ... the organ pulsates in the rhythm of the stream of liquid out of which it has been shaped, thus simply making this rhythm visible.[5]

Only after the first three weeks is this set of tubes termed an embryo; in the next five weeks all the fundamental structures of the human body will be laid down. Rivers of cells will flow out to form flesh, muscle and, some time later, bone. Nerves will grow out from the primitive spinal column like delicate roots towards the organs they will communicate with. Blood islands appear and elongate, joining like raindrops to form rivulets, as the vascular system forms. Paired outgrowths from the brain grow out to meet paired depressions in the outer skin as the two halves of the eyes make contact. Somewhere between the heart and mouth, buds of flesh are pushing out to become stumps and then arms, which will grow hands that will open into blunt stars that become fingers. A little later the leg buds will follow a similar course of development.

> Along the sides of the trunk, cells are moving in twelve horizontal currents which will give rise to ribs. They meet in the midline on the breast where they help form the sternum. Between the ribs and in the trunk wall beneath the chest, future muscle cells are migrating.

And just beneath the surface the skin is taking shape.[1]

The form of inner organs, and the outer sheathing of flesh that encloses them, reflects the meandering and migratory movements of the primitive cell streams; just as vulcanised rock preserves the flow-lines of molten magma and glass retains the flowing shapes it was blown into. Schwenk again describes this.

> Through the limbs whole systems of currents stream
> and the muscles more or less follow them. Both muscles
> and vessels speak of the same thing: streaming
> movement in spiralling forms. This movement runs
> through the sinews into the bones. The bone has raised
> a monument of stone to the flowing movement from
> which it originates: indeed one might say that the
> liquid has 'expressed itself' in the bone.[5]

The period of organ-formation and tissue development is over after a 100 days. In the remaining seven months of pregnancy the foetus will grow some 600 times in size, but will lay down no basically new structures.

Developmental biologists, struggling to form a language to express this organisation and synchronisation, a million times more complex in timing than the launching of any moon rocket, are driven to adopt terms which sound amazingly psychological. They talk of 'competence' and 'commitment', 'attraction' and 'contact', 'guidance', 'information', 'organisation', 'determination' and 'strategy'.

At what stage in this emergence of a forming body can we speak of experience, sensitivity and primitive memory? The ears can hear before the face has finished forming, six weeks after conception. Thumb-sucking may occur before half-term, when the fingers are still boneless. It is around this time that the mother, noticing the more vigorous movements inside her womb as the foetus treads water, recognises what is called 'the quickening'. The primitive swimming movements of the foetus are prototypes for the movements it will make in post-natal life when it learns to resist gravity. They are the biological foundations for aggression (in the sense of a moving forwards), which is based on the mobilisation of the spinal muscles. A. W. Liley describes early foetal movements using the long spinal reflexes, observed at twenty-six weeks.[6] The point is made that 'a trick which is simple in a state of neutral bouyancy becomes difficult under the newfound tyranny of gravity', to the extent that these movements are not seen after birth until the baby is fourteen to twenty weeks old.

Now, most people's earliest conscious memory is around two. Psychoanalysis never penetrated before that age because its tool was language. A child of two has already had thirty-four months of bodily experience, ten months of it in the womb. Are we to believe that this rich primordial time, when the organism grows faster than in any other phase of its life, leaves no trace in the tissues? In many forms of therapy – hypnotherapy, primal therapy, Reichian therapy, LSD therapy – people claim to remember and re-experience earlier events that are pre-verbal and pre-natal. There is mounting evidence that the excitation patterns of the foetus, both pleasurable and unpleasurable, and the reflexive movement patterns associated with these, are retained in some form that may be recoverable. If this is so, then it is legitimate to assume that the laying-down process of the memories of these experiences will also shape and direct the organism.

We do not need to limit memory, in this sense, to the brain. Organisms without brain tissue or nervous systems, have experiences. They are sensitive and they respond to the environment and act upon it. Some system of primitive recall of past organismic states seems the property of even single cells.

Many who have read accounts of early pre-verbal states, or seen such states being apparently re-lived, will accept the reality of pre-natal memories. However there are even earlier claims. Under LSD, people have claimed to experience even pre-embryonic states and conceptual states. Some of the events 'apparantly' remembered could not have happened in the womb. Denys Kelsey and Joan Grant wrote a book called *Many Lives* in which they claimed to recover memories of previous deaths and experiences in earlier lives. There are other similar claims.[7]

I do not wish to enter here into controversies over pre-incarnation, the nature of consciousness and whether it can exist as an entity separate from the body. I am therefore beginning with conception. It does not matter whether one thinks of the accounts that follow as 'memories', 'fantasies' or 'imaginative reconstructions'. They were profound experiences affecting the consciousness, and often subsequent lives, of those who underwent them. They are the closest we shall ever get to recovering our subjective origins. The first I call the 'sperm-dream', which was an experience related by a psychiatrist after a training session on LSD.

> I started experiencing a strange excitement that was dissimilar to anything I have ever felt in my life. The middle part of my back was generating rhythmical impulses, and I had the feeling of being propelled through space and time towards some unknown goal; I had a very vague awareness of the final destination, but the mission appeared to be of the utmost importance. After some time I was able to recognise to my great surprise that I was a spermatozoid and the explosive regular impulses were generated by a biological pace-maker and transmitted to a long flagella flashing in vibratory movements. In spite of the fact that this whole scene seemed absurd and ridiculous to my sober scientific mind, I could not resist the temptation to get involved in this race with all seriousness and full expenditure of energy.
>
> Experiencing myself as a spermatozoid competing for the egg, I was conscious of all the process involved. What was happening had the basic characteristics of the physiological event as it is taught in medical schools; there were, however, many additional dimensions that

were far beyond anything that one could produce in fantasy in a usual state of mind. The consciousness of this spermatozoid was a whole autonomous microcosm, a universe of its own. There was a clear awareness of the biochemical processes in the nucleoplasm; in a nebulous atmosphere I could recognise the structure of the chromosomes, individual genes, and molecules of DNA. I could perceive their physio-chemical configuration as being simultaneously elements of ancestral memories, primordial phylogenetic forms, nuclear forms of historical events, myths, and archetypal images. Genetics, biochemistry, mythology and history seemed to be inextricably interwoven, and were just different aspects of the same phenomenon...

The excitement of this race was building up every second and the hectic pace seemed to increase to such a degree that it resembled the flight of a spaceship approaching the speed of light. Then came the culmination in the form of a triumphant implosion and ecstatic fusion with the egg.[8]

The same person reported experiencing the early events following conception as part of the same session. It reads like a scene from the film *Fantastic Voyage* which takes place in the interior of the body. Moyotuka Hayashi's brilliant film *The Beginning of Life* which R. D. Laing showed in London to accompany his talk on 'Life before birth' (November 1975) is more colourful than any psychedelic film set, and intensely moving as it brings to life some of the immense events of embryogenesis. This is how these events were experienced by the man with the sperm-dream.

In a condensed and accelerated way I experienced embryogenesis following conception. There was again the full conscious awareness of biochemical processes, cellular divisions, and tissue growth. There were numerous tasks to be met and critical periods to overcome. I was witnessing the differentiation of tissues and formation of new organs. I became the brachial arches, the pulsating foetal heart, columns of liver cells, and cells of intestinal mucous membrane. An enormous release of energy and light accompanied the embryonal development. I felt that this blinding glow had something to do with biochemical energy involved in the precipitous growth of cells and tissues.[8]

A twenty-six-year-old student, called Richard, who came into therapy for relief from suicidal depression, described an inter-uterine experience that fits more modern knowledge.

He felt immersed in foetal fluid and fixed to the placenta, by the umbilical cord. He was aware of nourishment streaming into his body through the navel area and experienced wonderful feelings of symbiotic unity with his mother. There was a continuity of circulation between them: life-giving liquid – blood – seemed to create a magical link between him and her. He heard two sets of heart sounds with different frequencies that were merging into one undulating acoustic pattern. This was accompanied by peculiar hollow and roaring noises that he identified after some hesitation as those produced by gas and liquid during the peristaltic movements of his mother's intestines adjacent to the uterus. He was fully aware of his body image and recognised that it was very different from his adult one: his head was disproportionately large as compared with the body and extremities. On the basis of cues that he was not able to identify and explain, he diagnosed himself as being a rather mature foetus just before delivery.[8]

Immersed in amniotic fluid, cushioned against external pressures and virtually weightless, the floating foetus rooted to the uterine wall is in a state of security and contentment it may never surpass. This is the period that Le Boyer has called the 'golden age' and that Stanislav Grof compares with paradise.

31

Francis Mott suggests that some of the earliest libidinal feelings are generated over the entire foetal skin surfaces by the movements of the lanugo hairs in the amniotic fluid.

These hairs normally appear during the fourth month of foetal life and most commonly disappear before birth. The foetal movements commence usually during the fifth month so that there are generally three or four months during which the foetal body is moving in the waters of the amnion, its lanugo hairs waving minutely back and forth like weeds in a wind-driven pond.[9]

When the condition of serenity and tranquillity in the womb is recovered, it is experienced as a state of tension-free, melting, oceanic ecstasy. Groff relates this to the experiences of mystic unity and merging, to the peak experiences of later life. Freud similarly spoke of 'oceanic feelings' and Reich of 'cosmic streamings'. The uterus may be as near a person can get to the experience of heaven.

Since the growing baby is still embedded inside the mother, its body nourished by her like one of her own organs, this sense of good body-feeling has one essential pre-condition: that the mother who carries and contains it feels generally good in her body and feels good towards it. If the mother is stressed, tense or full of bad body-feelings, these can be communicated to the foetus, as can feelings of rejection, guilt or hostility about the growing baby. Based on memories of patients in therapy of this early life-period we can conclude that the foetus is sensitive not only to gross disturbances of its existence, such as mechanical pressures, loud sounds and intense vibrations, but distress if the mother is ill, exhausted or intoxicated. (We know the effects of nicotine cross the placental barrier and reduce the oxygen level in the foetal blood.)

Even more surprising are numerous independent claims that the foetus is aware of or shares its mother's affective states; subjects have reported in this connection foetal participation in the mother's anxiety attacks, emotional shocks, outbursts of aggression or hate, depressive moods and sexual arousal; or conversely in her feelings of relaxation, satisfaction, love and happiness. Another interesting aspect of this category of phenomena are accounts of the exchange of thoughts between mother and child in the womb that have the form of telepathic communication ... this multi-level communication with their mother made them keenly aware of being wanted and loved, or unwanted and resented.[6]

The foetal skin affect, described by Mott, is the basis for sensitivity in the adult to all impacts on him from the outside world, not only at the skin surface, but also in the special sense organs derived from the ectoderm, particularly the eyes and ears. The significance of eye and ear contact will be considered later. Le Boyer describes foetal sensitivity to light.[10] If the mother is naked in strong sunlight, the foetus perceives the light as a golden haze glowing through the abdominal wall. According to Smythe at University College, Auckland, flashing lights applied to the mother's abdominal wall produced fluctuations in the heart rate of the foetus.

Sounds are also impressed on the consciousness of the foetus. Since after birth it can be soothed by the sound of a heart beating, it seems clear that this sound is already imprinted from the time of its life in the womb. The sound of the mother's voice can well be imprinted in this time.

From at least twenty-five weeks the foetus will jump in synchrony with the tympanist's contribution to an orchestral performance ... Elias Canetti points out that all the drum rhythms in the world belong to one or other of two basic patterns – either the rapid tatoo of animal hooves, or the measured beat of the human heart. The animal hoof pattern is easy to understand from the ritual and sympathetic magic of hunting culture. Yet interestingly, the heart beat rhythm is more widespread in the world, even in groups like the Plains

Indians who hunted the great herds of bison. Is this rhythm deeply imprinted on human consciousness from foetal life?[6]

Experiments in Sweden, according to Janov, have shown that the foetus responds to mild noise by increasing its heart rate: 'Just because the foetus cannot conceptualise the stress does not mean that it isn't being hurt by it, or that the stress is not having lasting effects on later behaviour.'[11]

Another remarkable account of the foetal sensitivity to sound which can be independently verified is given by Grof's subject, Richard.

In this state he suddenly heard strange noises coming from the outside world. They had a very unusual echoing quality as if resounding in a large hall or coming through a layer of water. The resulting effect reminded him of the type of sound that music technicians achieve through electronic means in modern recordings. He finally concluded that the abdominal wall and foetal liquid were responsible for the distortion and that this was the form in which external sounds reach the foetus. He tried to identify what produced the sounds and where they were coming from. After some time, he could recognise human voices laughing and yelling and sounds that resembled carnival trumpets. Suddenly, the idea came to him that this must have been the fair held in his native village every year two days prior to his birthday.[8]

His mother was seen independently and was not told about Richard's account. She had indeed gone to the village carnival just before the birth and believed that the excitement and noise had helped to precipitate the birth two days later.

The consciousness of the foetus is probably nearer to dream consciousness than anything else. In fact there is evidence that the foetus dreams much more than the new-born baby, just as the baby dreams more than the adult. Premature babies spend

85 per cent of their sleeping time in the stage of dreaming, as judged by rapid eye movements, while a baby spends only half of its sleeping time in this way. The adult rate is 25 per cent. Howard Roffwarg and his colleagues at the Montefiore Hospital in New York have argued that the dream state may be nourishing the growing nervous system of the foetus. Dream time is a time, according to Gay Luce in her book on biological rhythms, when 'the baby may sometimes appear to be aware, for he kicks, making small twitching movements of his fingers and he may suck, smile and grimace . . . perhaps he has had prenatal practice in survival behaviour such as kicking and thumb-sucking during rapid eye movement states.'[12]

The womb is the Mother of dreams. In the myths of the Aborigines, when they want to refer to their origins, they speak of the dream time. Many people, sleeping as adults, resume the foetal position they last adopted in the womb. The foetus also responds to the mother's dream states, foetal activity states often synchronising with the mother's dreaming cycle, according to research by Sterman.[12]

> In the womb the embryo passes through the image states of tens of thousands of antecedent years of its development. In this state it is not unreasonable to suppose that the developing foetus may be at best somewhat subject to the images of the mother, who may be trying desperately to get rid of it. Her communications to the sensitive image of the foetus must surely be somehow different from those of the mother who is welcoming the new life with its developing image enshrined in her heart.[13]

During the first half of foetal life, the container (the amnion) is growing faster than the contents; but in the last few months of foetal life the situation changes drastically as the foetus grows out and expands to make contact with the membranes that enclose it. The uterine ocean has shores. This is how Frederick Le Boyer conceptualises the discovery by the foetus that it lives, during this time, in a shrinking universe.

The baby begins to feel closed in; slowly the universe is contracting.

What was once unbounded space becomes more confining each day. Gone is the limitless ocean of earlier – and happier – days; that absolute freedom is no more.

And one day the baby finds itself ... a prisoner.

And in such a prison.

The cell so small that the prisoner's body touches the walls – all of them at once. Walls that draw nearer all the time. To the point when one day the infant's back and the mother's uterus seemed to be fused together.[10]

The baby is enclosed for the first time in an embrace of flesh. There is no reason to assume that this earthy grip is unpleasant after the wide spaces of water. Much will depend on the tone of the uterus and the body sensations of the mother. Just as in early infancy, the quality of the holding will determine whether the infant delights in being closely hugged, enclosed and enfolded in its parents' arms, or whether it struggles in distress.

During the ninth month, the enfolding arms of the uterus are rehearsing the movements of contraction. Janov suggests that the contractions have the function of stimulating the baby's skin, which in turn stimulates the bodily systems it will need after birth, in the same way that animals stimulate the skin by licking their young.

'Once the infant has recovered from its initial fright', Le Boyer writes, 'it comes to like them. To wait for the contractions, to hope for them.'

'When they come – embracing the infant, hugging it – it surrenders to them; arches its back, quivers with pleasure at this sensual game.'[10]

Recent research suggests that the foetus chooses its position in the womb and the time of its delivery.

The realisation that the foetus himself determines the way he will lie in pregnancy and present in labour by making the best he can of the space and shape available to him, puts the practice of version in a new perspective and nowadays fewer obstetricians assume they know better than the foetus how he will be most comfortable. Of course, in selecting a position of comfort in late pregnancy, the foetus may have chosen a position which is difficult or impossible for vaginal delivery. In this regard he may be accused of lack of foresight, but this is a trait not unknown in adults.[6]

The developed body of the baby lies in its amniotic fluid. It is pulsating with life and the only culture it knows is the uterine ocean. It is ready to enter the gravitational world of walkable earth and breathable sky, though it will be twenty years yet before the slow swelling of the tissues and filling-out of form called physiological growth is completed. Embodied now, the child prepares for the 6-inch journey into the world beyond the womb.

CHAPTER 4

TRANSITIONS TO ESTABLISHMENT

First impressions of the world

Birth is a formative drama which can potentiate some of our deepest personality patterns. Whether birth is also a trauma or not will largely depend on the conditions prevailing at the time, and the attitudes of the participants. During a normal birth the baby comes head-first into the world; it is its earliest grounding. Any understanding of later character dynamics rests on this first engagement with the outside world.

When the foetus is ready it induces labour. This seems to be primed also by a biological clock, linked to the age of the placenta, which ensures that, somewhere around forty weeks after ovulation, contractions proper will begin in the uterus. Thus the first stage of labour begins. Lamaze has compared the uterine contractions to the tides; the waxing of contraction is the rising tide, the apogee is slack water and the waning of contraction is like the ebbing of the tide – again, another pulsation.

Grantley Dick Read,[1] one of the earliest modern pioneers of natural childbirth, has argued strongly that it would be surprising if childbirth was the one natural function which had an organic connection with pain. There is no reason to assume, as Rank suggested,[2] that birth for the baby is necessarily a traumatic experience. 'Only traumatic birth is traumatic', Janov[3] reminds us. As a birth that is painful for the mother is likely to be stressful for the baby, it is worth recalling the dynamics of pain in the first stages of labour.

The uterus has three layers of muscles: an outer layer of longitudinal muscles; a middle layer of muscle fibres running in many directions; and an inner layer of circular muscles. The function of these three layers is as follows. The longitudinal muscles pull open the mouth of the womb, dilating the cervix and opening the birth canal for the baby to begin its descent. The middle-layer fibres are matted closely together. These, the most important fibres, are entwined in 'figure-of-eight' formations and rolls around the large blood vessels. The fibres constrict the blood vessels when they contract and open the blood vessels to oxygenate the womb when they relax. The inner circular layer of muscles closes the mouth of the womb. The longitudinal muscles are governed by the sympathetic nervous system. What follows is a function of the way these systems adapt, or maladapt, to each other.

A mother who is relaxed and not suffering from conscious or unconscious stress will be under the predominant influence of the parasympathetic system. The longitudinal muscles will dilate the cervix. The 'figure of eight' muscles will open the blood vessels to carry away the chemical products of exertion and bring in fresh oxygen. The circular muscles will relax. This is how the system is designed to function. Such contractions should not be painful, except possibly during the last half hour or so when the cervix is at maximum stretch before the second stage begins.

Then, as Sheila Kitzinger writes:

> As each contraction comes, it feels like a wave gathering in the distance. She automatically adjusts her breathing rhythm to meet it and as it comes towards her she 'swims' above it with careful deliberate strokes, right up to the crest; then she begins to feel it fade away and her breathing becomes softer, and she rests. At the end of each contraction she takes a few deep breaths in and out.[4]

The baby should experience these contractions as a closer and closer embracing, a firmer and firmer massage, but in no sense

39

a crushing pressure. Ashley Montague writes:

> During this period the contractions of the uterus
> provide massive stimulations of the foetal skin ... these
> stimulations are greatly intensified during the process
> of labour in order to prepare the sustaining systems for
> post-natal functioning in ways somewhat different from
> those which were necessary in the aquatic environment
> in which the foetus has thus far spent his life.[5]

Alternatively, a mother who is tense, stressed, or in fear of
pain, will be governed by the sympathetic nervous system,
which is dominant in stages of tension and anxiety. This
means that the cervix will contract, blocking the exit from the
womb. The 'figure of eight' muscles will contract,
constricting the blood vessels and lowering the blood flow and
the vital oxygen supply to the walls of the womb.

The constriction of the blood vessels also affects the nerve
endings. 'Pain is registered in the uterus,' Norman Casserley
points out, 'when nerve endings are not bathed sufficiently in
blood. A tense uterus squeezes out the blood and pain results.'[6]
A further consequence of the sympathetic action is that the
longitudinal muscles receive fewer impulses from the parasympathetic system. They will go on contracting nevertheless,
because they are primarily governed by the hormone oxytocin
which stimulates them to contract.

We now have a situation where the womb is trying to do
two mutually antagonistic things at the same time: it is both
trying to open, under the influence of the biological clock
acting through the hormone, which prepares the way for the
baby to be born; and it is at the same time trying to stay shut,
under the influence of the sympathetic nerves brought into
play by fear. It is like trying to bend your arm and straighten it
at the same time; the arm goes into spasm and becomes
painful. This is exactly what happens to the uterus in a
mother unable to relax and conditioned to expect pain.

What are the effects on the baby? It is now in an intolerable
situation where what could have been a firm massage begins

to feel like a crushing to death. Grof describes it as the experience of 'no exit', or hell. A subject of his in therapy recalled the state in these words.

> I was totally submerged in a situation from which there was no escape except through death. I felt I would do anything to escape, but was there any way of escaping? ... I felt trapped in a maze from where there was no egress. I was stuck and that was my fate, to be someplace that was not the creation of living but being caught on the wheel of suffering ... It was as though I was a prisoner in a concentration camp and the harder I tried to get out the more I would be beaten, the more I struggled to free myself, the tighter the bonds would become.[7]

People who establish contact with bad experiences during this stage of labour associate them with feelings of intolerable dread, total alienation, helplessness and hopelessness. Grof distinguishes these feelings with difficulties found in the second stage of labour by the unique emphasis on 'the role of the victim and the fact that the situation is unbearable, inescapable and eternal – there is no way out either in space or time'.[7]

There seems to be no exit. But even in a tense mother the relentless tides of the uterine contractions will eventually win out over the reluctant constrictor muscles that grip the cervix if she is unable to relax. Easily, or with difficulty, the cervix finally stands open and the way is clear for the baby to descend. The second stage of labour is about to begin.

From now on every uterine contraction exerts a pressure on the baby to which it can only yield as, centimetre by centimetre, it begins to move down the birth canal. The mother can participate more actively now. Whereas relaxation was urged on her during the first stage, active effort is called from her now. By holding her breath to anchor the diaphragm in 'bearing down', she can assist and ease the process of delivering the baby. But again there is a troublesome error she may fall into. The muscles of the diaphragm and the muscles of the pelvic floor are antagonistic to each other; whereas contraction of the abdominal muscles in 'bearing down' assists delivery, the pelvic floor is required to relax. Many people, particularly those with the character of being 'pushers and squeezers', involuntarily squeeze the pelvic muscles together and thus obstruct the delivery. Pierre Vellay explains the process as follows.

> A woman who pushes in this way during labour creates an obstacle to the passage of her baby through the vagina. This effort not only fails to meet the needs of the moment, but is contrary to them. You must not push like this. Of course the baby is born nevertheless. He manages to cross this obstacle, simply because the three forces together – the contraction of the uterus, the work of the abdominal muscles, and the pressure of the diaphragm – make up a force greater than the constriction of the vaginal cavity by the muscles of the pelvic floor. But the obstacle is crossed by force, which means that the woman has to produce much stronger and especially much more prolonged efforts.[8]

Sheila Kitzinger explains that the action of the abdominal muscles is actually not only unnecessary but undesirable.

> The action by which the baby is pressed down the birth-canal should be piston-like, with all pressure being exerted from above on to the fundus of the uterus, and the pelvic floor muscles completely relaxed. If you hold a cardboard cylinder in your hand and press a marble through it from the top (with the finger of the other hand performing the role of the diaphragm) the journey will be made rather more difficult if you grip the cylinder more firmly than if you release the pressure. If the abdominal wall is drawn taut and pressed on the contracting uterus, pressure is necessarily exerted on the sides of the uterus, and in this way the

pressure from above is prevented from having its full effect.[4]

Constance Benyon's research into the second stage of labour showed that the easiest births took place when the mother economised her muscular efforts and was not encouraged to push in any way, except when the urge to do so was an involuntary one. Her work began with a study of cardiac cases who were not allowed to strain during labour and who had their babies more easily as a result. She writes:

> Furthermore in nearly all cases, a hardening, a reflex tension, develops in the perineum, and this itself presents difficulties. It is very unfortunate because, during delivery, the head of the baby leaves the uterus, presses behind on the tissues of the perineum, and as it progresses pushes all these tissues in front of itself. These tissues gradually become quite considerably stretched, but only under one condition. For a tissue to become stretched, it must remain elastic. Now, where women push wrongly, these tissues lose their elasticity, and create an obstacle to the good progress of the head. You can understand why women are torn. These muscles and tissues cannot stretch, and a moment arrives when they give way.[9]

One consequence of this is that some doctors use episiotomy (incision of the perineum) as a standard measure, considered preferable to 'tearing'. But both are avoidable if the mother is helped to relax and the birth is unhurried. Dr Fred W. Petersen in his book *Experiences in Obstetrics* writes as follows:

> I have never been able to see any logic in episiotomies, and I certainly see no use for them before delivery. Why, under any circumstances, cut at a point where blood vessels, nerves and muscles must be severed? Many a woman with an episiotomy has complained years afterwards of numbness below the line of cutting, as a result of important nerve-severing ... It was only after

43

years of painful experiences I discovered that if I slow up the delivery giving the parts ample time for stretching, guarding well the perineum to the last, there need be no laceration.[10]

We are describing the results of a tense and strained second stage. How are these experienced by the baby? Stanislav Grof compares it to a death–rebirth struggle, with an atmosphere of a titanic fight closer to the concept of purgatory than to that of hell. He sees the struggle as occupying a border zone between agony and ecstasy. It is a volcanic experience by comparison with the oceanic stages within the womb. The physical manifestations he describes include:

Enormous pressure on the head and body, choking, suffocation, and strangulation; torturing pains in various parts of the organism; serious cardiac distress, alternating chills and hot flushes; profuse sweating; nausea and projectile vomiting; increased bowel movements; urge to urinate, accompanied by problems of sphincter control; and generalised muscular tension discharged in various tremors, twitches, shaking, jerks, and complex twisting movements.[7]

A very full account of subjective experiences from reliving of birth has been given by Frank Lake in a paper in *Energy and Character*.[11] These traumatic experiences need not occur if the forces that assist the baby's descent act in harmony with each other.

One further force can be used, and it is surprising that it is not taken more advantage of – the force of gravity. Barbara Yunker, in an article on delivery procedures, describes the gravitational position for delivery as follows.

The natural position for a human birth is for the mother to crouch – or, after civilisation brought in midwifery, to sit on a birth stool with her back supported. Now the customary position which started when physicians began tending the births of upper class women in the 1700s is to put the woman in labour flat on her back, legs elevated.

Unfortunately, in this position, gravity is working against the mother instead of for her. The weight of the womb presses on the main vein from the lower body. This lowers the mother's blood pressure which can slow the infant's heart. The main artery bringing oxygen to the baby is also compressed. If the mother is on her side, or sitting, or walking, the blood circulates freely.[12]

Norman Casserley, a natural childbirth midwife, who delivers thousands of babies by more natural methods, regularly delivers them with the mother lying back in a chair or in a semi-reclining position. 'Strapped on one's back with one's legs in stirrups is the worst possible position for giving birth,' Casserley says. 'The main veins and arteries are along the spine, and in this position the weight of the baby, the uterus, and the amniotic fluid is on the back. Blood clots are frequent in this position.'[6] In contrast, a mother who can participate harmoniously in the second stage of the birth of her child does not undergo a titanic struggle, though she is totally committed to assist in the descent of the baby.

A patient in bio-energetic therapy, a thirty-five-year-old married woman who was the mother of four children, developed aching joints and pain in other parts of her body, especially in her shoulder girdle. Zelig Selinger, her therapist, described how her states of fear and panic increased. This is what happened next.

One month ago with some embarrassment she confessed to a feeling she had had for two months. The feeling was almost a vision; she was about to enter a dark tube which was very frightening. 'It sounds crazy but this is what made me so sick.' On further questioning she began to 'see' that the tube had a small opening at the other end and that there was light at the opening.

The comments brought to mind Nandor Fodor's articles (*Psychiatric Quarterly*, 1946) and his book, *Search for the Beloved*, a clinical investigation of the trauma of birth and pre-natal conditioning [Hermitage Press, New York, 1949]. It also recalled my experiences with hypno-analysis during which, on regressing, some patients spontaneously felt themselves in dark caves with water and openings with light shining through, re-experiencing what the patients and I believe to have been a birth trauma. The re-living experiences were of great benefit to the patients.

These thoughts and memories led me to ask the patient to lie down on her back on the bed with her knees raised. I sat at the edge of the bed holding her hand between my hands and applying gentle pressure to it on both sides. Her vertex, where the fontanelle used to be, was very painful; a condition she never experienced when I worked on her before. I encouraged her to enter the tube. She felt herself go slowly into it and move towards the opening. She was frightened and felt great pain in her head. I continued to encourage her as I applied greater pressure on the head. After two or three minutes, she began to feel a great force at her legs pushing her body towards the opening. She became terrified. As I rotated her head I felt the same force in the patient as she continued pushing towards me, her head coming off the bed and down towards the floor. As I continued to support her head, her body movements reminded me of the deliveries I had performed.

Suddenly she relaxed completely, slowly propped herself on her elbows and then sat up smiling and looked very pleased. She went over her experience step by step being especially impressed by the force she felt in her body as she pushed herself out of the tube and into the light. The pain and pressure in the vertex was no longer felt. She left the office in good spirits, something she had not done in a long time.[13]

Paul and Jean Ritter, in an important article on birth, have stressed the pleasure associated with healthy birth, and have summarised the following characteristic resemblances between birth and orgasm.

1 The involuntary nature of the movements, i.e. the contractions and convulsions involving the whole organism.
2 The mounting tension and charge, as seen by the nature of things only in the mother.
3 The marked and remarkable intermediary release and pleasure experienced between contractions, corresponding to the minor peaks in love-making.
4 The ecstasy felt after the acme of crowning.
5 The same extreme anxiety and fear of death, bursting and splitting as in extreme copulative orgasm anxiety of those incapable of bearing the full pleasure.
6 The full radiant, pulsating, satisfied faces of mother and child after a healthy birth ('transfiguration', Dick Read calls it) so reminiscent of the lovers' faces after an uninhibited embrace; or the flat depressed highly neurotic anti-climax of the unhealthy birth, which corresponds to the aftermath of inhibited intercourse.[14]

One of the features of natural childbirth is that it can often induce an orgasm in the mother as she is giving birth. Norman Casserley claims: 'A baby passing through the birth canal touches and stimulates the same areas that are stimulated in sexual intercourse.'[6] Eva Reich, a paediatrician and Wilhelm Reich's daughter, even suggests stimulation of the genitals to help the birth.[15]

But it is more than this. We are dealing, as the Ritters showed in their classic paper, with the superimposition and climaxing of two energy systems. Wilhelm Reich reminded us long ago that the foetus was another energy system inside the mother. The Ritters again describe the process as follows:

The 'I want to get out' convulsions of the foetus are one force and the 'I want to get you out' convulsions of the mother are the other. The former acts within the uterus in the first instance and can be deduced or noted as positive action by the foetus throughout parturition, particularly at the crowning of the head. The 'I want to get you out' force is the involuntary pressure of the contractions of uterine muscles in conjunction with the auxiliary forces. The meeting point is the perineum. Diagrammatically the two forces represent two spiral arms superimposing and fusing at this point. The urge to get out and the efforts to push the child out reach a climax. Tension, at its highest, is followed rapidly after the crowning, with a tremendous relaxation *in both systems*, first fused, and then as two separate organisms.[14]

That birth can be an orgastic experience for the baby as well as the mother, is also confirmed by subjective recall in pre-verbal therapy. Many people who have relived their birth describe feelings of powerful currents of energy streaming through their whole body. One of Grof's patients described his re-experiencing of delivery in these words.

It became very clear to me that there was no difference between sex and the process of birth, and that the slippery movements of sex were identical with the slippery movements of birth. I learned easily that every time a woman squeezed me I simply had to give way and slide wherever she pushed me. If I did not struggle and did not fight, the squeezing turned out to be intensely pleasurable. Sometimes I wondered if there would be an end and no exit and if I would suffocate, but each time I was pushed and my body was contorted out of shape, I let go and slid easily into wherever I was being sent. My body was covered with the same slime as it was earlier in the session, but it no longer was a bit disgusting. It was the divine lubricant which made it so easy to give way and be pushed and guided. Over and over again I had the experience that 'this is all there is to it', and 'it is so incredibly simple' that all the years of struggle, of pain, of trying to understand, of trying to think it out were all absurd and that all the time it had been here right in front of me; that it was so very simple. You simply let go and life squeezes you and pushes you and gentles you and guides you through its journey.[7]

The mother who can participate fully in the convulsive climax of the orgasm reflex will be better prepared for the energetic thrust of the expulsive reflex. She *gives* birth. The baby is not taken from her. The baby, like the orgasm, is allowed to *come*.

Michael Silvert, a colleague of Reich's, who was particularly concerned with the conditions of healthy birth, wrote as follows about a satisfactory delivery.

Steady encouragement of the mother to yield to her contractions leads to gratifying progress of the baby through the birth passage. Especially striking is the response of the foetus, in terms of foetal heart-rate and foetal movement, to the smooth wave-like contractions as contrasted to the contractions where the wave-like quality is not achieved ... The mother able to yield to the birth process holds lightly to a wall breast-high for support, her elbow bent and relaxed. Her head falls back and her chest goes down softly when she breathes, her pelvis comes forward in a movement suggestive of sexual surrender, knees bent and soft sighs come from her partially open mouth. Colour is pink, eyes are bright, and the thoughts are equally expressive: 'Why, this is just like sex. I actually enjoy it. Why don't people know about this, it's wonderful. I'm so happy.'[16]

If the climactic moment of crowning is the final act in the process of delivery, it is also the earliest moment in the process of arrival. The baby opens its eyes on the world for the first time, as it lands.

I have described, at length, the process of birth, not only to help understand some of the forces involved and possible subsequent traumas, but also to advocate more natural births and thus hopefully reduce the incidence of birth traumas.

So we come to the arrival: the establishment of the newborn.

A child at birth makes a transition between the two worlds, the amniotic and the terrestrial, the world of near-weight-lessness and fluidity and the world of gravity and solidity. The last time it made a landing was as a microscopic zygote, barely a week old, bedding down in the uterine wall. That first landing was an implantation, a rooting down. The landing it makes now involves a radical uprooting. The baby's root system, the placenta, which has been the only source of nourishment throughout its existence after that first week, is dying. The change of existence is almost total, as dramatic as the shift from the ocean to the land in evolution – and that took millions of years to accomplish. The baby transits this in less than quarter of an hour. This is how Theodor Schwenk describes it.

> The child before birth is in a protective envelope of water, prior to his final entry into the sphere of earthly activity. As though lying within a sphere, he moulds his as yet liquid form, which gradually becomes more condensed. On being born he leaves the spherical space of water and enters into a relationship with the directional forces of the earth. The more he yields to these forces the more his body becomes solidified, which is essential to standing up and learning to walk.[17]

The parallels between life in the womb and life in a space module have been drawn by many people, but are captured particularly well in the poem 'Cosmonaut' by Geoff Roberts.

Timeless, weightless
I freely float in orbit
snugly encapsulated
in air-conditioned darkness,
safely insulated
but with my delicate precision instruments
waiting to be used
all five of them
fastened to the intercom, warmed, fed,
listening to the pumping
of the mechanism,
freely floating in orbit, head
down, waiting for the boost
and leaving to someone else
all consideration
of the problems of re-entry
at the nine-months end.

Here too is how a child of eleven expressed her perception of the emergence from the world of the waters.

The baby slips out of the Mother like an otter sliding into the water. When the baby is out of the Mother it is as damp as a piece of sea-weed. Its hands are curled like water-filled sea shells. Its ribs make it look as though it has a spindly bird's cage inside it. Its eyes are like unopened oyster shells. Its cord is as curling as a tree creeper, with a twirling of milky and red veins. His hair is as sleek as a water-rat's. He opens his mouth and lets out his very first sound. He looks very new and polished.[18]

At least four separate transitions are involved in this process and each transition may be experienced as a pleasurable expansion, or as a catastrophic shock, according to how the baby's arrival is handled.

The first transition is the *sensory transition*. The child comes out of dimness and enters a world of blinding light. It leaves a world in which, if there was not silence – and we have seen that there was not – all sounds are at least diluted by the cushioning effect of water. It enters a world of harsh and deafening sound. Frederick Le Boyer, in his prose poem *Birth Without Violence*, puts the importance of dimmed lights and hushed sounds in his first recommendations for humanising and sensitising the conditions in which the new-born arrives, if we are to avoid unnecessary shock to the sensory system: the eyes can feel burned by too much light, just as the ears can feel assaulted by too much noise.[19]

The amniotic fluid is at blood temperature. The average delivery room is probably no more than 70 °F. The temperature drop is of the order of 30 °F. The temperature regulating processes in the brain are triggered into action by the act of birth, but it takes many weeks before they become efficient. The danger of hypothermia is a real one for some babies.

The skin is the largest organ of the body and offers the largest area for sensory experience. Through the early experiences of skin contact, the infant will learn what kind of world it has entered; one that caresses it and warms it, or one that chills it. Janov has suggested that temperature sensitivity in later life may partially depend on these early experiences: 'It may well be that a difficult birth, plus the shock of temperature drop at birth, may permanently impair the proper functioning of temperature control mechanisms so that the person is thereafter too hot or too cold.'[3]

Le Boyer recommends two ways of reducing the shock of temperature drop in the newborn: placing the infant face down against the skin of the mother's abdomen immediately after birth; and the subsequent use of a warm bath as a pleasurable sensory experience. He writes about the latter, recommending:

> Let us place the infant, replace it rather, into water. For
> the baby has emerged from water, the maternal waters
> that have carried it, caressed and cradled it. Make it
> light as a bird. A bath has been prepared in a basin. At

the temperature of the body or thereabouts – ninety-eight or ninety-nine degrees. We place the child in it. Once again extremely slowly. As the baby sinks down, it becomes weightless, and is set free of the body that is overwhelming it – this body with all its burden of harsh new sensations.[19]

There is a lovely book called *Water Babies* by Erik Sindenbladh[20] that demonstrates how natural the watery environment is, even to babies out of the womb. This can also be connected with the evolutionary theories of Sir Alister Hardy, put forward in Elaine Morgan's book *The Descent of Woman*,[21] where she postulates that development during the twelve million years of Pleiocene drought took place by the sea-shore – in and out of a watery environment – and that the benefits of this evolution turned the resulting Pleistocene humanoid into our great-great-grandmother.

The advantages of putting the newborn baby immediately in contact with the mother's abdomen are many. Firstly, this can be done before the cord is cut. Secondly, it is the most reassuring place for the baby to be, belly to belly with the body that has enclosed it for all of its existence so far. More are mentioned later.

What better place could there be? Her belly has the infant's exact shape and dimensions. Swelling a moment before, hollow now, the belly seems to lie there waiting like a nest. And its warmth and suppleness as it rises and falls with the rhythm of her breathing, its softness, the glowing light of its skin, all work together to create the best possible resting place for the child.[19]

The second transition is the *circulatory transition* and the *birth of breathing*. For the past ten months the baby has been oxygenated with air breathed by the mother. For the rest of its life it will breathe its own air. Although its heart has been pumping blood around its body since twenty-five days after conception, very little if anything has gone into the lungs, whilst a large amount has gone into the placenta. All this must now change.

The changes that take place in the circulatory system in the first few seconds and minutes after birth are revolutionary. The vascular system has to be recanalised. The best way to understand is to look carefully at what is happening in the four chambers of the heart before and after birth.

Before birth, in the placental circulation, the heart receives and expels blood as follows.

Left ventricle. When this ventricle contracts it drives the blood through the aorta and round the body of the foetus; but a large proportion of the downward flow goes through the two umbilical arteries to the placenta, where it is re-oxygenated.

Right auricle. This chamber of the heart collects the returning blood from two sources: the body of the foetus; and the placenta. The freshly oxygenated blood returning from the placenta flows through the umbilical vein, passing to the heart either via the liver, or by a shunt connection back into the main body circulation, called the ductus venosus.

Right ventricle. This takes some of the outgoing blood and disposes of it as follows. A trickle flows through the pulmonary arteries to the lungs, but most of it flows through another shunt, the ductus arteriosus, to join the main aortal flow round the body.

Left auricle. Only a trickle enters from the lungs, by the pulmonary vein. Most of the supply enters from the right auricle through a membranous opening between the auricles, the foramen ovale. (If this remains open at all after birth it forms the 'hole in the heart' syndrome.)

After birth, reflex vasodilatory impulses open up the vascular flow to the lungs and at the same time reflex vasoconstrictor impulses close down the ductus arteriosus. The effect of this is to increase the pressure of blood flowing into the left auricle from the lungs. The umbilical arteries also constrict, reducing the pressure of blood entering the right ventricle from the placenta. These two effects lead the pressure in the left auricle to exceed that in the right auricle and this closes the membrane between the auricles, which after a few days solidifies as a permanent barrier between the two sides of the heart.

The infant's first cry expands the lungs and sets these reflex circulatory changes into motion. They are rapid, but not instantaneous. The cord continues to pulsate for many minutes after birth. The final stream of blood from the placenta runs back into the born body of the baby. If the cord is cut before it has stopped pulsating the infant will experience a double shock: a circulatory shock and a respiratory shock. The circulatory shock arises from blood still pulsing down the umbilical artery which is being tied off, creating what R. D. Laing referred to as a 'wash-back' effect, a back-pressure into the general body circulation putting unnecessary stress on the newly functioning heart. The cutting off of the last few pulses of placental flow down the umbilical vein deprives the baby of valuable oxygen and may cut down the number of circulating red cells. The respiratory shock arises from the need to take in all the oxygen at once through the newly expanding lungs. Frederick Le Boyer explains it this way.

> Two systems functioning simultaneously, one relieving the other: the old one, the umbilicus, continues to supply oxygen to the baby until the new one, the lungs, has fully taken its place.
>
> However, once the infant has been born and delivered from the Mother it remains bound to her by this umbilicus, which continues to beat for several long minutes: four, five, sometimes more.
>
> Oxygenated by the umbilicus, sheltered from anoxia, the baby can settle into breathing without danger and shock. At leisure, without rush.
>
> In addition, the blood has plenty of time to abandon

its old route (which leads to the placenta) and progressively to fill the pulmonary circulatory system.

During this time, in parallel fashion, an orifice closes in the heart, which seals off the old route for ever.

In short, for an average of four or five minutes, the newborn infant straddles two worlds. Drawing oxygen from two sources, it switches gradually from one to the other, without a brutal transition. One scarcely hears a cry.[19]

As we have seen, the best place for the baby to be in this transition period is on the mother's abdomen, or even at the breast.

Those who have seen a baby arriving by Le Boyer's methods, either in the flesh or on film, will have noted how, instead of crying with distress, involving an almost instantaneous full-blooded use of the lungs, giving the sensitive tissues no time to acclimatise themselves to the searing blasts of air, the baby's breathing comes into its own slowly, hesitantly. It gives little pants of pleasure; the waves of its breathing are eddies and ripples, rather than breakers.

If the experience has been traumatic, as it is for many infants, there is all the more reason for maximum attention to be made towards making the conditions for arrival and transition as smooth, unhurried and harmonious as possible. There is nothing to better the study of Le Boyer's remarkable book, with its emphasis on gradual and gentle qualities in touch and handling and a total respect for the extreme sensitivity of the newborn. Very similar work, with a great respect for the mother and her natural abilities to produce her child safely, occur in Michel Odent's hospital at Pithiviers. For these two pioneers and all those involved with this type of work, the arrival of each baby is a true nativity.

The third transition is the *gravitational transition*. Le Boyer calls this the fourth step in the path of birth, when the newborn baby is first brought in touch with *terra firma*. Again this is how he describes it.

Leaving the water the baby finds a new master, another tyrant: the weight of gravity, the new burden of its own body.

For nine months the baby has been an eternal voyager: its shifting world has never ceased to move. Sometimes gently, sometimes violently. Wasn't mother's body always in motion? And even when she was still or asleep, there was always the great rhythm of her breathing, of her diaphragm. The baby has lived in perpetual motion. Now a truly appalling change, everything stops. For the first time. Nothing moves. The world has frozen, died. It is the unknown.[19]

How this experience of contact with the ground is felt would depend on how we introduce the child to the ground. For some it is an experience of utter abandonment and desolation. The child feels threatened by the vastness of space with the frozenness of the ground. It experiences itself as falling to bits. This is the basis of the sense of agrophobia, the fear of open spaces and of being unbounded, de-wombed. It is the exact opposite to the claustrophobic experience, which is one of being over-confined and compressed, trapped in the womb. However, if the child is introduced to *terra firma* gradually, as Le Boyer has suggested, the experience can be a novel one. Here is something firm and unyielding which it learns to push against. Against its solidity, the child tests out the life rhythms of its own body and learns to distinguish them from the life rhythms of other people. People who are in some sense undergrounded, withdrawing from testing their strength against the solidity of the ground and pulling back their aggression, tend to have deficient ego boundaries or be unsure of where they begin and the other person stops. They are more easily invaded.

In the young infant his sense of gravity is related to the experience of falling. If he is held securely and rocked or raised or lowered, the movements of temporary weightlessness recapture the sensations of being rocked in the uterine fluids within the mother. Playing with gravity is then akin to flying.

The insecure child, on the other hand, is afraid of falling. Gravity is a threat, the ground is the place of abandonment or the hard surface he will hit if he is dropped. No child can fall inside the womb. But he can fall outside it. Fear of falling leads to an organismic contraction, to the freezing off of the streaming sensations and pleasurable currents in the body and to the imprinting of the primitive startle-reflex patterns that underlie all later neurotic tension patterns. Here is how Wilhelm Reich described falling anxiety in an infant of three weeks.

> At the end of the third week of life there was an acute
> falling anxiety. It occurred when the child was taken
> out of the bath and put on his back on the table. It was
> not immediately clear whether the motion of lying him
> down had been too fast, or whether the cooling of the
> skin had precipitated the falling anxiety. At any rate,
> the child began to cry violently, pulled back his arms as
> if to gain support, tried to bring his head forward,
> showed intense anxiety in his eyes, and could not be
> calmed down.[22]

Next day Reich noticed that the right shoulder blade and right arm were pulled back and were less mobile than the left arm. During his anxiety the child was tightening his muscles as though to keep a hold. Reich relates what is happening to the sudden withdrawal of bio-energy (orgone) from the periphery of the body towards the centre.

> The sensation of falling is the immediate inner
> perception of the immobilisation of body periphery, of
> the loss of equilibrium. It follows that the equilibrium
> of the body in the field of gravity is a function of the
> full orgonotic pulsation in the periphery of the
> orgonotic system.[22]

The full implications of falling anxiety will be developed in another context. For the present it is enough to establish that how we handle the infant in these first early hours and days establishes basic patterns in how he holds his body, his muscular organisation as he resists and opposes or surrenders to gravity.

The fourth transition is the *alimentary transition*. This is when the infant takes his first external nourishment, and his digestive system learns to function smoothly. This is a longer transition which may take some weeks to effect. Its achievement is usually referred as the 'establishment'. Whereas the umbilical connection ensured a steady supply of nourishment, the newborn baby has only a temporary connection, the coupling of mouth and nipple. It is significant to note that the umbilical cord is exactly long enough to allow the mother to suckle the baby before the cord is cut or the placenta detaches. Indeed the sucking action triggers a hormonal release that closes the blood supply to the uterus and brings on contractions – exactly what is needed to reduce the risk of haemorrhage.

The infant has to learn to coordinate the movements of drinking and breathing so as not to choke on taking milk into the lungs, or develop stomach-ache through taking air into the intestines. Its self-regulatory tendencies can function only in the presence of a mother who is sensitive enough to her own rhythms to adjust the flow of nourishment to the demand, learning to distinguish the cry of hunger from the cry of discomfort due, perhaps, to wind. Distress in this period is so common it is known as 'three-month colic'.

The New Zealand paediatrician, Bevan-Browne, has described how the suckling relationship is the first experience the baby undergoes, in which it has to seek actively the source of nourishment and attach itself to this source. The term 'rooting', which describes the side-to-side movements of the baby's head as it seeks out the nipple, emphasises that it is re-establishing, through the mouth, the rootedness which it could take for granted within the womb via the umbilicus.

We call this instinct or tendency a copulative tendency. This is to be observed in creatures as far back as the protozoan ... In the mammals and in man this copulative tendency is of supreme importance in the first months of life. We are seeking to point out that the infant has an urgent need to copulate with a person, to wit, the Mother, through the medium of the nipple and the mouth; and this need transcends the mere need for chemical sustenance. In other words suckling is a sensuous experience which includes:

1 Intense sensations derived from contact of lips, tongue and palate with the nipple.
2 Sensations from contact of the nose and cheek with the breast.
3 General sensations of softness and warmth.
4 Sensations of being enfolded, supported, embraced or held.
5 Bodily odours from the Mother.
6 Sensations of satisfaction in mouth, pharynx, oesophagus and stomach of receiving warm milk.
7 Sounds of appropriate quality made by the Mother.
8 Sensations in the hands of caressing, squeezing and patting the breast.
9 Sight impressions of the Mother's facial expression.[23]

Infants who are fortunate to experience breast feeding in this full and fulfilling sense will often show a total body response which is the prototype of orgasm in the adult. The sucking reflex develops into tremors of the whole body, arms and legs – an oral orgasm.

Biologists at the Peckham Health Centre recognised the subtleties of the learning process of relating not only to the emotional mood of the mother, but to the intake of external nourishment.

Once born the child must feed through its own alimentary canal, all the organs of which are formed

and ready for use by the time of birth. But it cannot
instantly master the use of these organs, any more than
when born it can immediately use its legs to walk, or its
eyes to see. It is a learner from the moment of birth, just
as it had been a learner in the womb. The infant has
still to learn the process of assimilation of milk through
its alimentary apparatus. So it is that one of the first
signs that the biologist looks for in the life of the new
born is its establishment, meaning by this that it has
mastered the process of digestion of its Mother's milk.

Establishment is recognised by the general aspect of
the infant which loses what is sometimes an anxious
and always a pre-occupied mien and acquires a serenity.
Its body fills out; its skin now fits its figure accurately;
its eyes open widely when awake and like a satisfied
puppy it sleeps deeply and peacefully in the intervals.[24]

A satisfied newborn baby alternates between periods of
suckling and periods of sleeping, but it experiences also that
neither process is timeless. The coupling to the breast is an
active receptive process – able to lay the foundation for contact
and the ending of contact in later life. Periods of immersion in
the flow of milk and the contact with the breast alternate with
wakeful periods of general contact and handling with the
mother, which are just as basic for the development of a well-
rooted sense of self. Eye-contact with the mother is often said
not to develop until at least four weeks after birth, but the
work of Le Boyer and others suggests that it can be present
much earlier. This is how Miriam Dror described the eyes of
her daughter Alissa:

I felt a wonderful slippery body full of life coming out,
and there she was on top of me lifting herself up on her
little hands and looking me straight in the eyes like I
have never been looked at before. And it is this look that
I have yet to capture in words. She hadn't even taken a
breath of air from the world yet, still connected to my
body and breathing through the cord, and yet ... with a

wisdom far beyond comprehension. The gaze steady, and steadying made me stop short. I'm sure that my heart skipped a beat and that the two of us stood in a space outside time for that brief interchange.[25]

So we come to the *pains of transition,* for the transitions mentioned so far are basic to the child's emergent sense of itself outside the womb. They may be experiences which nourish and fulfil the born body of the baby, or they may be experiences that stress it and crease it into knots of tension and howls of hurt and pain.

A patient of Francis Mott had a nightmare in which she had four specific fears: the terror of the lightning flash; the terror of the thunder's boom; the terror of rushing winds; and the terror of the water thrusting angry waves through a gap in the sand hills. Mott comments on the biological origin of these fears.

> The reason why she had remained so largely 'unborn' is that she had reacted so fearfully to the opening of her head orifices at birth. She had feared the light in her eyes, the sound in her ears, the breath in her lungs and the food in her mouth. It was these fears which had been reawakened by the thunderstorm. The lightning had re-evoked the fear of the light in the eye. The thunder had re-awakened the fear of the sound in the ear. The rushing winds had re-awakened the fear of the air rushing into the lungs. The thrusting waves had re-awakened the fear of the milk rushing into the mouth. My patient in short never opened herself to the free and fearless reception of the world and so she had remained a foetal individual.[25]

Mott has built an entire theory of human development – which he called 'bio-synthesis' – out of his insights into the nature of the transitions from the womb to the outside world. For if the basic rooting of a person in the world is turned into a shocking or shockful experience, so that the organs of contact are only hesitantly extended, the basis of security in the world, in one's own body or amongst the bodies of others, is undermined, weakened or destroyed. In my practice I have built on this theory and, as the concepts are central to my therapeutic work, I have adopted the name, as previously mentioned.

Before the birth of language, before any word is uttered, the basic sense of identity, or lack of it, is already formed. It flows from the matrix of the umbilical pulsations which stop when the cord is severed and are replaced by the rhythms of breathing and suckling. It is stroked into being by the contact of skin on skin, which replaces the movement of the womb fluid over the lanugo hairs, and the rhythmic sounds of the voice caressing the ear, familiar from the inter-uterine period. It is born out of the spontaneous movements of the body, which, contained for nine months in the cushioning fluids of the womb, now stretch out and experience the immeasurable finality and solidity of the earth. It is shaped by the tensions and relaxations of muscles responding to gravity.

The newborn child has arrived on the earth and is handled by its parents. The complex social relationships of its particular part of the world lie all around, but it is not aware of them yet. Naked of culture, it waits for the process of conditioning which will lead to character formation.

CHAPTER 5

HEAD, HEART AND *HARA*
The dynamic morphology of the body

Following the account in the last two chapters of embryonic and early post-natal development, we can begin to look at how the embryological history is expressed in the form of the adult body. In this chapter the emphasis is therefore on the understanding of some of the aspects of the design of the body and the relationship between the embryological layers and the regional development of the body. We move from formative processes to structures; from the history of life in the womb to the morphology of the body.

The three embryonic realms become differentiated into three primary regions of the body. All the main ectodermal organs, except the skin, are concentrated inside the head: the eyes, the ears, the nose, the tongue, the brain. The organising centre for the major muscles of the body and for the bony structure of the skeleton is the spine, with its extensions into the arms and legs and head – this latter's external structure can also be used as a fifth limb, as in the yoga head-stand or in the descent down the birth canal. The spine and these limbs are the main executive organs of the mesoderm. The internal organs of the trunk, the lungs and the abdominal organs, can be thought of as the main reservoir of energy from the endoderm.

We can look at the morphology of the body in terms of the way these three regions of the head, spine and gut are linked together.[1] The three major junctions in the body link the three regions. The head is joined to the spine at the base of the neck.

If the neck is tensed the flow of connection between the ectoderm and the mesoderm is interrupted. Thinking and action become dissociated. If more energy is trapped above the neck block than below, we have a tendency to be over-identified with thinking at the expense of movement. *In extremis*, this creates a compulsive or obsessional pattern of behaviour. The obsessional person spends an inordinate amount of time planning activities but the free energy for moving himself into activity is tied up in the head. The manner of thinking becomes thought-blocking. The loosening of neck tension typically allows activity to flow down the spine as a flow of expressive movement. Many headaches are created by neck tension, and may be relieved as the energy redistributes following the flow into expressive movement.

If the energy is trapped below the neck block, there may be a pattern of over-activity with a lack of forethought; a typically impulsive pattern of movement. The body may be over-charged and the head under-charged. The person is in flight from thought. The loosening of neck tension allows energy to flow up the body to the face, the eyes, the voice and the brain, bringing about more possibilities of reflection and communication.

The junction between the head and the gut is in the throat. Here the ectodermal region of the head joins the endodermal region of the gut. Thinking and feeling are integrated through the expressive function of the voice. If the voice is mechanical, language remains explanatory. Explanation means to flatten out. Head-talk is cut off from feeling. Exploration means to flow out: exploratory language integrates thinking and feeling.

When a child learns to swallow feelings, the throat block acts to keep feelings down. The emotional energy gets trapped in the trunk and has no outlet to the face. Such a person feels the pressure of strong emotions but feels he will lose face if he shows them. The face remains impassive – feelingless in contrast to the emotional pressure within. The opposite pattern is where much emotion is expressed through the face but little contact is kept with the centre of the body. It is as though the emotion is vomited out to relieve the internal pressure.

A woman I worked with, who showed this pattern, had the tendency to scream and cry out in response to stress. Her face went red and all the energy was pumped up into her throat and face. I put my hand on her belly which felt like a collapsed plastic bag, limp and lifeless. What she needed to do was to loosen the emotional pressure that was pulled up into and above the throat and to let her expressive energy become distributed through the whole body. As the pressure in her throat and face relaxed, her belly began to ripen and fill as though she was becoming pregnant with new life.

The pattern of swallowing emotions and keeping them out of the face is typically masochistic. The pattern of pumping energy up into the voice and face is typically hysterical. But a person in a hysterical state may choose to scream, rather than express the feelings through language with its higher level of ego perception. So the work of dissolving the throat block may in one case involve helping a person who swallows their feelings allow those feelings to rise up cathartically; and, in the case of the person who is over-cathartic, involve helping the integrative functions of language to come to the fore.

The third primary junction in the body is that between the spine and the gut, between the mesodermal axis in the backbone and the endodermal energy of the trunk. The bridge is made by the diaphragm, which is the principal pump in the body for breathing. When the diaphragm is free it is the main regulator for the breathing and also gives an effective massage to the internal organs. This will be explained in more detail in the next chapter on breathing. However the diaphragm is anchored to the spine at the upper lumbar vertebrae. A tense diaphragm acts like a guy-rope on the spine and causes it to tighten. This splits the unity of breathing and movement. When we watch a happy baby lying on its back kicking, we see the integration of movement and breathing; for the baby, kicking is breathing and breathing is kicking.

Once again there are two typical patterns of disruption. In one of them a person moves mechanically with little emotion and little obvious change of breathing. In the opposite pattern a person increases his breathing rate, typically in an anxiety state, but finds no way to translate the energy mobilised by the breathing into movement. The breathing is over-active and the muscular system under-active. This condition often occurs with hyperventilation, which is discussed in Chapter 6.

The three bridges are clearly the nape and the throat – that is at the back and front of the neck – and the diaphragm. But the diaphragm can be thought of as the bottom of the neck, for it originates there embryologically and grows downwards during foetal development. The main phrenic nerve to the diaphragm goes through the spinal column by the fourth cervical vertebra in the neck. Softening the neck and mobilising the tissues in this area is frequently followed by a relaxation of the diaphragm.

The two tensions in the neck combine to form a ring of tension dividing the head from the body. The diaphragm in Japanese is called *o-kaku-maku*, which means the horizontal separating membrane. When this membrane is chronically tensed it cuts the trunk into two compartments which show little connection. The heart is boxed in between the tensions in the roof of the chest, at the neck, and the tensions in the floor of the chest, at the diaphragm.

This gives a new perspective to the work of therapy. Not only is it a process unifying the three embryonic realms and the three regions of the body which represent them, but it also encourages an integration between the head area of the body, the heart area of the body and the *hara* – the Japanese name for the abdominal region of the body.

Wilhelm Reich described seven rings of tension,[2] due to muscular armouring, which lie at right-angles to the main axis of the body and divide the body into segments. The face falls into two segments: the eye segment consisting of the eyes, the forehead and the large muscle of the scalp; and the mouth segment consisting of the muscles surrounding the lips, the chin, the jaw muscles and the expressive muscles of the cheeks. The third segment is the neck itself with all the intricate muscles of the throat and larynx, as well as the skeletal muscles of the neck – the scalena, the levatores scapuli and the sterno-cleido mastoid muscles. The fourth segment, the thoracic, contains the heart, the lungs and the arms. The fifth segment is the diaphragm itself. The sixth segment is the abdominal area of the intestines and the lower back, while the seventh segment contains the pelvis, the sexual organs and the legs.

Not only can the trunk be divided into segments, but the limbs can be too. The division occurs naturally at the main joints which divide each limb into three segments; we can think of these as the head, heart and belly of each limb. The foot and the hand, the ends of each limb, correspond to the 'head'; the forearm and the lower leg correspond to the 'heart'; and the upper arm and thigh to the 'belly'. We can also think of the wrist as the 'neck' of the arm and the ankle as the 'neck' of the foot. Frequently when the throat is under-charged with a restriction of energy to the head, the wrists and ankles will be found to be constricted too, cutting the blood supply and energetic circulation to the hands and feet. Loosening the ankles and wrists can re-stimulate the relaxation and expansion in the neck.

Reich's formulation of seven segments bears a close relationship to the Eastern system of seven chakras, which will be mentioned again later. The chakras also divide the body into segments (each under the influence of a chakra) and are also centred on the spine. They are numbered from the bottom of the spine upwards and each seems to associate with a specific nerve centre or plexus. The first chakra is the root chakra, associated with the sacrum and the coccyx, with the centre at the perineum. Anatomically it regulates the energy of the sacral plexus in the pelvis and the adrenal glands.

The second chakra is related to the *hara* and the lumbar plexus, including the spleen. The third chakra is related to the solar plexus, just below the diaphragm and to the pancreatic glands. The fourth chakra is the heart chakra, also associated with the thymus gland and the cardiac plexus. The fifth chakra is the throat chakra, connected to the pharyngeal plexus and the thyroid gland.

So all these five chakras correspond very closely with Reich's lower five segments. Above the throat there is a slight difference. Reich's oral segment is seen in the Indian system as a subdivision of the throat area. The sixth chakra is between the eyes and is related to the pineal gland. It corresponds to the lower part of Reich's ocular segment. The seventh chakra is at the crown of the head in the area of the fontanelle. It is also part of Reich's ocular segment in the centre of the scalp.

If anyone believes that Reich or the originators of the Indian chakra system were arbitrarily fascinated with the mystical number seven, it is important to recognise that the anatomy of the spine naturally generates seven nodes corresponding to the chakras. The spine can be thought of as a pulsating sine wave, a double S shape, with two concave surfaces at the nape and lower back, three convex surfaces at the occiput, scapulae and buttocks, and two end-points at the crown of the head and the coccyx (see Figure 5.2, later in this chapter).

In acupuncture, the energy of the superficial meridian system is believed to flow in a four-fold circulation which runs three times round the body, generating twelve meridians. If we take as an arbitrary starting point the first point of the lung meridian in the chest, the energy flows from the chest to the little fingers, from there back up the arm and up into the face, from there descending the body to a point in the toes and from there re-ascending the legs to a point in the chest. We can schematically represent this flow as moving from 'heart' to 'hand' to 'head' to 'heel' to 'heart', and see that it describes the conduction of energy from the trunk (centre) to the hands (upper ground) to the face and then down to the feet (lower ground) and back. The flow of energy shows a centrifugal movement (heart to hands) followed by a corticopetal movement (hands to head) followed by a corticofugal movement (head to heels) and finally by a centripetal movement (heels to heart). This four-fold movement neatly combines the principles of centring, grounding and facing with the three regions of chest and arms, face and head and belly and legs. The practical importance of these relationships will be developed more deeply in later chapters.

We can now look on character as an expression of how a person organises the charge, centred in the gut and concentrated in the abdomen. This will be indicated by the level of tonus in the muscle sheets and the amount of grounding present in the limbs and spine and also by the degree of focus present in his perceptual system. We are dealing with preferred styles of behaviour which can be utilised in the protection against various forms of threat. These behavioural styles, which form the basis of character differentiation, are part genetic (reflecting the embryological endowment as seen in the work of Sheldon[3]) and partly a response to environmental stress, from the time in the womb and throughout childhood.

The human being has three principal nervous systems, each of which gives a particular sensory input. Whilst the nervous system has its origin in the ectoderm, each of these three systems seems to have a functional relationship with the three embryonic layers and their interaction can be used as a basis for character discrimination. The *cortical sensory system* functions with the twin principles of *facilitation* and *inhibition*. The person who is low on inhibition will have a low threshold to incoming stimuli, which will be difficult to inhibit. He or she will be easily flooded with information (sight, sound, other people's feelings, psychic influences, etc.). This will lead to a tendency to be under-focused. The over-inhibiting tendency, on the other hand, will tend to screen out any 'unwanted' impressions and will develop into a more over-focused, even obsessional, approach to life.

The *sub-cortical* or *extra-pyramidal system* regulates posture. When muscle tone is hypertense, the body is braced for action and rigidly defended against collapse. We can call such a muscular attitude 'over-grounded' as more energy is used than is necessary to maintain the upright posture. Such a person may have workaholic tendencies and will be identified with action and the material world. Alternatively, when the muscle tone is over-slack or hypotonic, the body will feel sluggish and will show a tendency to weaken or collapse. Lack of trust in the ground may lead to an overdeveloped imaginative life, coupled with a weakened sense of external reality.

The third nervous system of the body is the *vegetative*, which regulates the flow of the emotional life. It has two great branches: the *sympathetic*, preparing us for fight or flight in response to a fright or emergency; and the *parasympathetic*, with its more tranquillising and restful influence in the direction of well-being and restoration. A person under the dominant influence of the sympathetic system will show a tendency to over-charge. This person will actually seem to be a 'discharger', trying to syphon off this over-charge into easily-triggered emotionality. The person under the opposing influence of the parasympathetic will have a reluctance to build up a charge and, when faced with a crisis, will tend to be a 'relaxer', with a propensity to emotional passivity or withdrawal from conflict. In extreme forms this under-charge may show up as a depression.

Combining these three functions – focusing, grounding and charge, each with two possible extreme states – we can look on character as a bipolar tendency. We have a $2 \times 2 \times 2$ schema which allows us to look at character dynamics in operational terms, so that therapy can be seen as a way of helping a person to move towards a better balance by developing the qualities of the excluded polar function. From this we can express the eight character tendencies in a diagrammatic form (see Figure 5.1). The six faces of the cube define the six polar states: under-focused, -grounded and -charged; and over-focused, -grounded and -charged. The eight corners define the eight character tendencies: phallic-narcissistic, passive-feminine, psychopathic, hysterical, de-

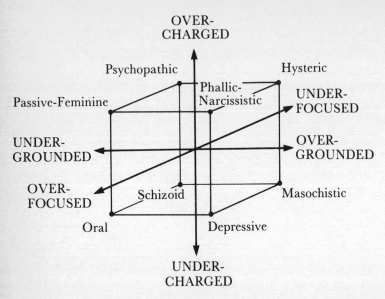

Figure 5.1   Diagram showing the six polar states as faces of a cube

pressive, masochistic, schizoid and oral. These concepts are developed further than Reich went originally and are more fully expounded in *Maps of Character*, which I wrote together with David Smith.[4] A deeply-founded characterology, based on embryological principles, is developed also in great detail by Stanley Keleman in his masterly book *Emotional Anatomy*.[5]

An alternative way of looking at the principal character structures and their problems is to look at them as disturbances in the primary functioning of the seven chakras. These energy centres in the body are recognised in yoga, acupuncture and throughout many different and well-established disciplines. That they and the concept of energy within the body are not recognised in modern Western medicine is rather to its detriment than anything else. The location of the chakras and their anatomical and neurological associations has already been mentioned, so I now want to look over the chakra system again, but this time describing their relationship with character patterns. Too much has been written about them to recommend anything else specific, though a pamphlet by John Pierrakos, *The Energy Field in Man and Nature*, originally published in *Energy and Character*, gives a good introduction.[6]

The root centre

The primary function is *grounding*, in the sense of commitment to the body and a will to survive. The root chakra is related to the sense of having a good spine which can stand up in the world. There is a sense of independence and personal power in a person with a well-developed root chakra.

Dysfunction will show as tendencies to be over-grounded and afraid of dependence, or under-grounded and afraid of independence. This will give a polarity between rigidity and helplessness, between control and collapse.

The *hara* centre

The primary function is one of charge. This centre is closely related to the navel and to the sense contact (via the connection with the umbilical cord). In infancy it is the *centre* of well-being, sustained by good experiences at the breast ('well-fed'). In adolescence and after, it relates to the sexual centre.

Dysfunction will show as over-charge and under-charge, where over-charge is related to problems of hyper-sexuality and casual contact and a difficulty in achieving a satisfactory relationship, and under-charge is related to hypo-sexuality, to problems of impotence, frigidity and sexual anaesthesia through an inability to go out and make satisfactory contact.

The solar plexus centre

This chakra is connected to the child's struggles over power and mastery, its handling of conflicts and ability to cooperate. There is a strong vegetative charge which can involve the person in identification with anger or anxiety.

In anger there would be a tendency to invade others; in situations of anxiety, one would be too easily invaded by others. This centre is therefore concerned with *boundaries*. The basic conflicts will express themselves as identification with power against others and domination, or the surrendering of power to others (submission), rather than the blending of one's power with others in acts of cooperation.

The heart centre

The core function is compassion. The ability to love in a deep way and to form strong human relationships is central to humanity. So the heart chakra is the chakra of *bonding*.

This bonding can be disturbed in two ways. The person may get over-bonded, developing addictive patterns in relationships and fusing with the loved one in a way that blocks the individuality of both. Alternatively it may lead to under-bonding, expressed either as superficial or transitory relationships, perhaps with a degree of indifference, or as a withdrawal from the relationship altogether.

The throat chakra

The core function here is that of communication or *sounding*. It is related to how well we can express the heart through the voice and speak clearly about our perceptions and feelings. How well we can be expressive in general and to be creative in our language and voice is indicative of the health of this centre.

Its disturbances show as two distortions in language: introjection, which is believing other people's views and swallowing their judgments without any form of discrimination or listening to one's own feelings; and projection, which is believing that other people have attributes that one is unwilling to ascribe to oneself. Guilt and blame are strongly implicated when this centre is blocked.

The brow centre

Sometimes called the 'third eye', this centre is concerned with vision and contemplation – looking out and seeing in. It carries the ability to *face* oneself and others clearly. It is related to the power to imagine, as well as to see deeply into the essence of a situation.

Dysfunctions show as obsession, the narrowing of vision to a single fixed beam, and the loss of imaginative insight. It is connected to a situation when people feel possessed, which is the feeling of being invaded by images or the intentions of others; a situation where the person is too telepathically open. This is quite common in schizophrenics.

The crown centre

This centre is from where we communicate with the cosmos. It is concerned with having an opennesss to something greater than the self, whether in a religious or naturalistic sense.

When disturbed it can lead either to a messianic inflation, with the sense that one is all-powerful, or to a nihilistic deflation, with an existential depression and a fear of death – ultimate meaninglessness.

The function of the chakra is related to the contact between *space*, inner and outer space. The disorders are related to spacing out and fear of extinction in a void.

Summary

These functions can be summarised as follows and further explanation will be found in the following chapters:

Root	Grounding	Chapter 7
Hara	Centring	Chapter 6
Solar plexus	Bounding	Chapter 9
Heart	Bonding	Chapter 10
Throat	Sounding	Chapter 8
Brow	Facing	Chapter 8
Crown	Spacing	Chapters 10, 11

It was seen before that there exists an interesting comparison between the location of these centres and the 'rings' or 'segments' of armouring that Reich describes in

Character Analysis. This is shown in Figure 5.2. Here again, as with the nervous systems earlier, we can see the relationship between the energy and character structures as being analogous.

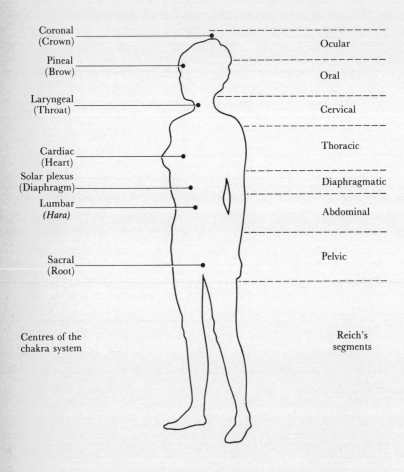

Figure 5.2   A comparison between Reich's seven armour-segments and the Eastern concept of seven energy centres (chakras). The chakra is shown in its *forward* projection from the spine.

CHAPTER 6

WAVES OF BREATH
Rhythms of respiration and feeling

I have mentioned the importance of breathing not only as a pump of life energy and as a mechanism for mobilisation but also, as involved with the diaphragm, a link between the mesoderm and the endoderm.

I use breathing as an essential indicator of what is happening to the client and as their expression of their emotional state. Re-balancing the emotional energy is so intrinsically linked with the re-balancing of the breathing that I consider working with one inseparable from working with the other.

The relaxed pulsation of breathing builds a sense of centre. We call a person 'centred' when he is connected to the rhythm of his breath. Strictly speaking the gravitational centre of the body is at the *hara*, 2 inches below the navel. When a person floats in water his weight is distributed either side of this point. Anxiety breaks the rhythm of the breath, creates a contraction and the person sinks; his connection to the centre has been lost.

Breathing has a rhythm like the sea. We can see the waves rising and falling in the abdomen and chest; we can hear the sound of in-breath and out-breath if we tune our ears. We can float our hands on the surface of the body and feel the inflation and deflation of the trunk.[1] In inspiration, the trunk expands and there is a lengthening impulse up the spine. In expiration the person gets smaller and shorter. Breathing out is a giving-up and letting-go. Breathing in is a filling and containing; a preparation for action.

The emotional centre of a person is felt at the heart; the energetic centre is felt in the *hara*. If the diaphragm is relaxed, these two centres are connected and feel unified: if the diaphragm is tensed, the connection is broken. It is then possible to feel connected to one's heart, but also to feel the heart unsupported by the energy of the lower half of the body. Alternatively one might feel power and vitality in the *hara* centre and be contracted or empty and cold in the heart. We could call these two centres the 'love' centre and the 'power' centre. When they are divided we have powerless love or power without love. When the connection of the diaphragm is open we have a person who is centred in the power of love.

So breathing can be both an expression of spontaneity or a reflection of the conditioning of the character.[2] The way a person breathes conveys a sense of rhythm and inner well-being or it communicates stress, discomfort, pressure or lack of ease.

The heart centre is related to thoracic breathing, the *hara* centre to abdominal breathing. In thoracic breathing the chest is pumped up and held in the inflated position. Feelings are held back, creating a sense of over-containment. There is a fear to breathe out fully; letting go would feel like dying (expirate = expire), like dissolving the boundary and falling into more self-expression. Paradoxically, this sense of thoracic pressure actually creates a risk of dying, since the over-inflated inspiratory breathing pattern is frequently associated with Type A (rigid) personalities who are prone to high blood pressure and heart-attacks. The heart feels caged. Such a person, when he does get emotional, tends to push the emotions. This pressure of pushing, together with the rigidity of the chest container, increases the risk of straining the heart.

Edouardo was a man who, as a child, had been frequently beaten by his mother. He had tried very hard to earn her love by performing well in a number of ways. Always she found fault with him and beat him with an electric flex. When he grew up he trained in karate and achieved the level of black belt. Karate allowed him a physical outlet for aggression, but he was very over-contained in expressing the rage that he felt from his childhood. The repressed rage had to be held in and Edouardo felt periodic chest pains. He had to be helped to soften the chest and relax his breathing in order to depressurise the chest. In general, in order to help someone breathe out, I help them to move out. Ways of doing this will be described later.

The tendency to over-contain in the abdomen is found frequently in people who have learned to swallow and hold down their feelings (the 'masochistic' characters). They create a strong pressure in the abdomen to prevent their bad feelings bursting out.

The opposite of this masochistic pattern is found in people with active hysterical patterns, who tend to be under-contained. They are identified with breathing out. The out-breath carries with it a scream, a cry, or some other strong emotional expression. What can be seen on looking closer is the lack of contact with the in-breath. People in a hysterical process easily lose their sense of centre. The belly is agitated and tends to be held in deflation. So helping such a person to contact the in-breath in the abdomen in order to build a sense of centre and containment is a crucial part of the necessary therapeutic work.

In over-needy dependent people (the oral character structures) there is a reluctance to take in air, just as there is an inhibition of sucking and of reaching. The person looks and feels empty and weak, and this undernourished feeling goes with a low inspiration in the belly and the chest. This maintains a low metabolic state that sustains the sense of deficiency.

When Reich began to work on helping patients pay attention to their breathing, he saw many people who showed the inspiratory tendency. He focused principally on the importance of breathing out and of emotional release. I have sometimes seen poorly trained Reichian therapists seeking to encourage this kind of response in people who needed exactly the opposite kind of help. My experience, after two decades of working with several thousand people, is that at least half of the people I meet need to learn how to deepen their inspiration; the other half are helped by work on deepening the expiration.

One of the least well-understood processes in those working with breathing is the origin and dynamic of hyperventilation.[3] The signs of hyperventilation are readily detectable: the patient has speeded up his breathing or is prolonging or pushing the out-breath; he will tend to be under-active and under-expressive of feeling; after a while his fingers will start to cramp in a characteristic spasm and the whole body will begin to tighten. The symptoms of hyperventilation are, in the early stages, a mild tingling, which may feel pleasant but which later becomes unpleasant, followed by sensations of tightness, pain and numbness, first in the fingers then perhaps in the lips and tongue, with a resultant difficulty in speaking. There is often a sense of dizziness or unreality, panic or confusion, with usually a feeling of pressure or tightness in the abdomen.

The cause of hyperventilation is loss of carbon dioxide. The over-speedy breathing or the forced exhalation blows off too much carbon dioxide. The carbon dioxide level in the blood falls, with a shift in the blood pH towards the alkaline. This alkaline shift potentiates a calcium shift in muscles and nerves, the calcium shift creates a rapid firing of nerve signals to the muscles to contract, and thus the muscles begin to move towards a state of tetany, beginning with the most peripheral regions (fingers, toes, lips and nose). Many people enter such a state of hyperventilation spontaneously in a situation of strong anxiety.

A doctor writing in the *Observer* newspaper expressed the view that some 40 per cent of all complaints that people brought to him in general practice were side effects of unrecognised hyperventilation. A psychotherapist working with a patient in an anxiety state may be seriously handicapped if he does not recognise a dysfunctional breathing pattern and find ways to remedy it. Similarly a purely physiological approach to correcting hyperventilation is weakened if the psychic aspects of anxiety states are ignored.

In the last decade or more a number of therapies have used hyperventilation deliberately as a therapeutic tool, in the belief that they are 'creating more feeling' or 'breathing through the resistance' if they push a person into carbon dioxide deficiency. Rebirthing therapy has specifically advocated this as a method and has consistently ignored the fact that the hyperventilation symptoms are the body's distress signals in response to a deficiency. The resulting overload on the psychic system, as disorientation or confusion, or on the somatic system, as increased tension or spasm, can occasionally be lethal. A man with some pre-psychotic tendencies left a rebirthing session and murdered his landlady the same evening. Of course there was no connection, the defenders of rebirthing will say. A second man died of a heart attack during hyperventilation in a rebirthing session in Germany. Of course, he was due to have one anyway or brought it on himself, will be the defence. A man in London who was pushed into hyperventilation by an untrained therapist using bio-energetic stress positions had a latent claustrophobia activated, which troubled him for some months. He decided to commit suicide unless his claustrophobia improved before six months was up. Fortunately it did. I met him some time later. He proved to be a natural hyperventilator who needed help deepening his inspiration.

Another therapist who works with hyperventilation is Stanislav Grof, who is interested in the altered states of consciousness that can be induced through it.[4] This is in lieu of LSD, which is no longer legal to use. I have great respect for Grof's theoretical model of the unconscious and of pre-birth states, but less respect for the methods he used to obtain his material, since hyperventilation throws all the major systems of the body into dysfunction.

Followers of Grof and the rebirthers defend hyperventilation by arguing that, if a person continues with his exaggerated breathing, he will 'break through the blocks' and the symptoms will disappear. The physiology of this belief has never been explained to me. There are two possibilities. One is that, by pushing the body into even more hyperventilation, the brain goes into emergency cut-off (technically called a depolarisation block). It is the equivalent of jamming. But to rely on this emergency system to release the patient of the effects of the abuse of his body seems grandiose and illegitimate. The second possibility is that the patient begins spontaneously to breathe *in* more deeply and this brings the oxygen and carbon dioxide in the breath back into balance and corrects the carbon dioxide shortage. This is actually a change *out of* hyperventilation (which is dysfunctional) into deep balanced breathing, which is an improvement in most people's functioning.

So we come to the treatment of hyperventilation. Since hyperventilation symptoms are created by a loss of carbon dioxide, they can be removed by slowing the rate of carbon dioxide loss until the alkaline blood comes back into balance and the calcium shift has been reversed. There are several ways of putting carbon dioxide back into the blood. One way is to use the principle of rebreathing; the patient breathes into a bag or with a handkerchief over the face. This traps the carbon dioxide so that it is breathed back with the next in-breath.

A second way, which only works in the early stages, is to encourage movement. Hyperventilators typically over-breathe and under-move. If the patient becomes active, the activity generates lactic acid which counteracts the alkalinity of the blood. Contact and reassurance also help because they reduce the tendency to blow off air in a panic and stimulate taking-in and receiving which helps the in-breath.

The most helpful way is to support the person in developing his in-breath and to explain the dynamics of the process. These give the patient the possibility of managing his own anxiety attacks with some hope of success. In the first of these,

the therapist can work with his hands to support the lumbar
or cervical curves of the spine with the patient lying on his
back, giving a mild lifting impulse as the patient breathes in
and relaxing his hand as the patient breathes out. The
therapist can lift the patient's arms, slowly, in the rhythm of
the in-breath, lowering them on the out-breath. This work
with the arms stimulates the expansion of the chest. The
patient can be asked, while lying on his back with the knees
bent, to press gently down into the floor with the in-breath
and to relax the pressure with the out-breath. This will
emphasise the containment function of the breathing. This
can also be helped by a similar pressure from the therapist's
hands to the patient's shoulders, giving gentle resistance to
them during the in-breath, and relaxing this during the
out-breath.

This in-breath work is basic, not only to counteract hyperventilation, but in all cases where there is low charge, weak
boundaries or an over-readiness to fall into emotional release.
Will Davies, an American therapist using similar principles,
calls it 'working with the in-stroke'.[5]

The centrality of breathing to the regulation of the energy-
economy of the patient can better be understood when
looking at specific emotional states. I have said already that
what is common to all neuroses is a loss of part of the full
range of human responses. Reich also found that all neurotics
have a disturbance in their sexual life. The central mechanism
that is common to all forms of armouring is a breathing
disturbance. When we deal with the centre of the body, we
deal with the breathing and emotional rhythms. The balance
between in-breath and out-breath is also the balance between
emotional containment and emotional release.

When Wilhelm Reich first discovered the basic role of
inhibited breathing in every neurotic character, he described
this discovery as a 'breakthrough into the vegetative realm'. It
led him to investigate the hidden, inner realms of the body,
the pulse of life through the arteries, the beating of the heart,
the flow of secretion from glands and the peristaltic pulsation

in the gut. Wherever there were chronic patterns of disturbed breathing, he found disturbances in these internal rhythms; blocks to the smooth, harmonious pulsation of the internal organ system.

An animal, living through a temporary emergency, experiences acute states of stress, during which these basic metabolic rhythms are altered or interrupted. They can only return to the smooth rhythms which characterise the body when it is in a state of relaxation and well-being, as soon as the challenge or threat has passed. Human beings, from the earliest times of life onwards, are very often exposed to long-term emergencies; the difficult conditions of a depriving, or over-protective, or directly frustrating upbringing. A baby who is left to cry unnecessarily for long hours, an infant who learns tension and guilt over toilet functions, a child who is smacked or shamed for being sexually alive, does not experience a temporary emergency, where all is restored to harmony shortly after, but nigh on two decades of conditioning in how to suppress or distort its natural feelings. These conditions lead to *chronic* stress.

Awareness of the relation between muscular tension and stress is not new. Many forms of relaxation therapy have been developed, which differ in important ways from the vegeto-therapy developed by Reich, as a means of releasing pent-up vegetative energy and restoring the natural rhythms of the body.

In the course of a therapeutic treatment, as blocked emotions are released and tense muscles give up their defensive function, spontaneous movements in both the skeletal and the smooth muscle systems take place. The relationship between the tensions of the main skeletal muscle sheets and the smooth muscles of the internal organ systems is a very complex one. Gerda Boyesen studied the intricate workings of the visceral armour in great depth. She developed a technique of listening to the changing rhythms of the intestinal peristalsis on a stethoscope so she could monitor the internal responses to her bio-dynamic massage.[6]

In 1933 Reich discovered that, at a certain point in the therapeutic work, the spontaneous muscle tremorings that were released when muscles gave up their bound-up energy charge began to unite themselves into a total involuntary rhythmic pulsation of the body. Because of its resemblance to orgastic movements, he called this the 'orgasm reflex'. I would like to explore the significance of this further. The orgasm reflex, as a spontaneous body reflex occurring in response to deep relaxation, was Reich's discovery. Why had it not been noted before? I think the reason is that the combination of deep relaxation with a high energy charge is an unusual one. Normally in a state of high charge one is impelled into some activity where the tension of concentration and the use of voluntary muscles is at a premium. The time when people most usually lie down and relax is when they are tired and need to recharge because their energy level has become low. The therapy situation, on the other hand, presents a situation where strong charge and high excitation (from emotional release) occur simultaneously with muscular relaxation, which is the method of achieving that release. It is at such times that the orgasm reflex can occur, provided that the principal blocks that restrict the free development of the reflex have already been dissolved. As mentioned, a similar reflex pulsation of the body is sometimes noticed in the sucking infant. It is known as the oral orgasm.

There is evidence that here we are dealing with a very basic and ancestral rhythm of the body, a life-reflex which is found earlier than birth. The developing foetus shows the capacity for coordinated rhythmic movements before the sensory nerves have developed. Once the early sensory connections in the developing nervous system have been formed, excitations of the skin periphery can induce a basic foetal convulsion pattern. As early as eight or nine weeks old, the growing foetus responds to gentle excitation in a manner that has been well described by Thorpe.

In response to light tactile sensations (usually circum-
scribed to the facial region) the responses are
neither simple or local. As neuro-muscular connections
develop, they extend chiefly caudally, involving more
and more of the trunk in a reflex of the same character
as that first appearing.[7]

Thorpe termed this response an 'expanded reflex'.

The coordinating responsive movements of the foetus
appear most prominently in the young infant in the sucking
reflex. The baby's pleasure is not confined to the mouth, but
spreads in reflex waves throughout the whole body.

Reich compared the reflex movements of the mature body
in sexual orgasm to the peristaltic movements of an intestine,
or the pulsating movements of a jellyfish, a comparison
which earned him some derision from his psychiatrically
conditioned colleagues. He described these movements thus:

The expressive movements in the orgasm reflex are
functionally identical with those of a living and
swimming jelly-fish. In either case the ends of the body,
that is of the torso, move towards each other, as if they
tended to touch each other. When they are close we
have contraction, when they are as far apart as possible
we have expansion, or relaxation of the energetic
system. It is a very primitive form of biological
pulsation. If this pulsation is accelerated so that it
assumes colonic form, we have the expressive
movements of the orgastic convulsion before us.[8]

It is as though, in the orgasm reflex, the entire body functions
like the intestine, and the skeletal muscles take on the
involuntary wave-like movements that one normally associ-
ates with the smooth vagal muscles.

So in Gerda Boyesen's psycho-peristaltic therapy it is
recognised that there are two avenues for energy to be
discharged involuntarily: one direction leads to emotional
abreaction, in the form of a release of rage, grief, anxiety or

whatever; the other leads to what she calls 'harmonisation', which is the re-distribution of energy, relaxing internally and spreading to other areas of the body without giving rise to strong expressions of emotion.

Frequently a rapid transformation from one form to the other can be seen in therapeutic work. Often a discharge of held-back feeling will be followed by a quieter period of harmonisation when the body will experience strong sensations of melting and streaming as currents of energy that were previously dammed up in the tensions that blocked the feeling are set free. These streaming sensations can be felt by anyone who is not held tense by chronic contractions and who relaxes and centres the attention on immediate sensations. They are the currents of the excitement of being alive which flow within us like a silent river, and which we are not normally aware of in the urgency of our efforts to deal with the problems or difficulties that beset us. They make for a warm radiating skin, good muscle tonus and a healthy tissue charge. The biology of these streamings is discussed in Chapter IV of my book, *Wilhelm Reich: The Evolution of his Work* (see Appendix 3) and in the writings of the Boyesens, and will not be dealt with any further here.

The streamings are related to what Francis Mott has called 'the foetal skin effect' and 'the umbilical effect'.[9] They are basic to a sense of being alive, but they are also trans-individual. Just as the ego has to surrender its ascendency for orgasm to occur, so it must also loosen the tightness of its grip on external reality for the streamings to be sensed. They can be felt at times when we are overcome by awe in the face of some natural phenomena or when we are moved deeply by a piece of music, but they are unlikely to be sensed when we are grappling with an emergency.

Reich has described the process of pleasure-anxiety. For some people there is a very low toleration for the sense of self-transcendence that accompanies the quivering of life as it creeps and flows back into tissues where the sense of it was formerly withheld or walled-off. There are three primary ways of avoiding full contact with the streamings and of reaching a condition that I shall call 'the open centre'. The first of these is the straightforward use of freezing or blocking mechanisms to inhibit the flow of life so that one deadens in one way or the other. These are the standard routines of *armouring*, many of which have already been described. The second way is to convert the pulsation into explosion, to run from pleasure into pain; this is basically a pattern of freaking-out and will be looked at more closely below. The third way is to mystify the streamings, to form a closed-centre, withdrawing from outer contact in order to preserve inner contact. This leads to a reaction pattern of freaking-in.

Freaking-out is a hysterical attack which converts the pulsatory rhythms of life into an explosive struggle; its prototypic form is found in the birth struggle. At one and the same time the hysteric is full of bad body feelings, centred in body sensations that cause pain and discomfort and intolerable distress, yet he is also in flight from that centre. The hysterical pattern is an uncontained one that scatters energy. It is characterised by the acting-out of anger in outbreaks of rage or of panic or in convulsions of anxiety. He tends to void feelings in order to discharge the pent-up centre, but avoids contact with the sense of inner fullness and is intolerant of the contained sense of quiet excitement and gentle streaming. I looked at the hysterical energy process in some detail in order to understand both how it differs from normal emotional expression and from the pulsatory flow of the coordinated life-reflex. These relationships were explained in the early sections of 'Between coma and convulsion'.[10]

In the turn-about from freaking-out to *freaking-in*, instead of staying open at the cost of losing their centre, a person stays centred at the cost of keeping open. One of the reasons why Reich did not encourage people to start haphazard 'breathing therapies' is because he recognised the power that charged breathing has to alter the consciousness. He was aware of the possible dangers from releasing inhibited breathing too rapidly, so as to flood the organism with more sensations than it could handle, without closing off in some way and thus possibly precipitating psychotic reactions. This is why Nic Waal, in a letter she wrote to me in 1952, stressed the need to work with vegeto-therapy cautiously and to build-up the ego beforehand.

So how can incautious vegeto-therapy trigger latent psychoses? It does so by strengthening the life impulses from the id without strengthening the containing functions of the ego. The world of uncontained de-personalised streamings is the world of a schizophrenic who is deeply alive and sensitive underneath his contactlessness. He or she senses the tremor of life, but does not recognise it as coming from their own body. In extreme forms the streamings may be experienced as persecutory electric currents emitted by some cosmic 'influencing machine'. The streamings can be mystified into 'Christ sensations' with the conviction that one has been specially chosen or is in touch with some special force.

What is actually happening is a process of regression to the last time one was in touch with such strong energy currents and into a state of pre-personal foetalisation; and the foetus lives a life of encapsulation. Its life is the life of the closed centre. It is a form of experience I sum up under the word 'cosmosis'. To be in touch at some level with a deep sense of vitality, yet to be unable to connect that adequately with the world of the outside and of the ordinary is to be in some way split.

The feeling of unity and cosmic togetherness is a sense of being all one and not alone any more. But if the awareness of pulsatory currents increases the depth of contact with the internal world, without work being done concurrently on the external contact functions – with the ground and with other people – then it is possible for streaming and splitting to coincide and even reinforce each other.

The role of breathing in centring a person's energy is well understood in many meditational systems, but most of these cultivate a closed centre. By techniques of deepened or slowed-down breathing, whirlpools of emotion can be stilled and thought processes brought under control. A meditation system used this way is really a subtle form of repression. Often techniques of defocusing the eyes, or focusing them internally on an object in order to induce a semi-trance, may be used. In trance the normal sensory inputs are reduced and extra-sensory channels may be opened. As a person withdraws into his centre from the world where his senses and his muscles are engaged, he may obtain heightened contact with his own internal sensations and with the realm of psychic experience. We can understand how this is so from having already taken a close look at the biology of sensory awareness.

On the other hand, it is possible to meditate with an open centre, simply by staying in touch with the internal movements of the body and the sensations of breathing, without any attempt to interfere with them and yet not withdrawing from the everyday world.

I worked with a girl called Gillian, who had been troubled by panic sensations, the fear that she would vomit and anxiety currents in the abdomen. When she lay down and breathed more deeply the anxiety began to reverse its direction and flowed through her in waves of pleasure. She had learnt, by reducing her breathing and stilling her expressive movements, to keep her anxiety from reaching too strong a level. She had also accustomed herself to a much lower level of bodily pleasure in consequence. When the sense of her own life streaming through her became too strong, Gillian experienced pleasure anxiety; that is she contracted against the expansion as though she was being taken over by some outside force. Her hands seized up in a specific contraction which occurs when the body over-breathes. At the same time she felt a numbness in her mouth and parts of her face. She found some difficulty in speaking.

The tendency for the body to react with contraction against deeper-than-usual breathing is a physiological contraction related, as I have shown, to a reduction in the carbon dioxide level in the blood. I described how it can be avoided if the person who is breathing more deeply is also using their muscles more vigorously. However Gillian's tendency was to internalise; to have her sensations and feel her feelings, but to keep them to herself. She did not share them with others present, nor moved them into a dance of joy or a squirming with pleasure. She did not allow them to develop through rhythmic movements into an orgasm reflex. Instead she lay with them, swam in them, floated in them and experienced the fear of drowning in them.

She needed help in integrating these internal energy currents that were fighting for space inside her body. She was helped by my getting her to open her eyes and talk about what she was feeling and to give in to the urge to reach out and hold on to someone who was near. She had a strong need to clutch for contact, but was inhibiting this. When she allowed her hands to flex deliberately in a holding-on contraction, the involuntary flexure caused by the over-breathing began to subside. In using her hands and arms to make contact with the world outside her own internalising, she opened her centre; the pleasure could begin the flow down her limbs as well as circulate in her trunk and start to discharge through her hands.

In his book *Character Analysis*, Wilhelm Reich clearly distinguished between a tertiary, secondary and primary layer in people's emotional drives.[8] The tertiary layer was the level of character defences, substitute contacts and the conformist social veneer well-adapted to the character pattern. The secondary layer was the repressed unconscious within its forbidden drives, frequently destructive or confused. The primary layer was made up of spontaneous impulses to reach out and make contact. Reich claimed that, if the destructive impulses of the secondary layer could be released from repression and dissolved, the healthy expression of the primary drives in each person would manifest themselves spontaneously. He observed this in therapy when he worked with the fundamental expressive language of the body at deep levels of plasma relaxation.

Experiences with people in groups and of people who have gone through therapeutic systems that emphasise emotional characteristics do not, however, necessarily confirm Reich's findings. Thus nowhere in the literature on primal therapy, for example, do we find a clear description of the qualities of vegetative aliveness and contact warmth that Reich described for people responding from their primary feelings.

It is possible, in some cathartic therapies, to go on for a very long time with the discharge of bad feelings, without necessarily contacting the good ones. I have known people who did this so violently that it led to intestinal inflammation, ulcer formation and other malfunctions. It is possible, in other words, to get stuck in the second layer.

When energy flows out from the central reservoirs of the body, it can move either into the motor system, seeking physical expression in movement, or into the channels of communication – touch, eye-contact and speech. What is crucial and often forgotten is the distinction between expression and communication, which are different functions. Emotional expression can take place in a room on one's own. People who do 'self-primalling' (primal therapy sessions on their own) may cry, scream, kick and enter into any number of involuntary body movements. These are expressive of what they are feeling, but they are not communications. Communications are what you share; the presence of another person able to respond in some way is essential for communication. Communication is a situation of reciprocity, interaction and mutual responsiveness.

The basic striving of the child is not to express rage, terror or impossible demands. Indeed, in childhood, expression without communication can lead to increasing despair, dissatisfaction, self-loathing and feelings of personal ineffectiveness. The same thing happens in many of the cathartic therapies. In order not to get into this trap, I believe it important to rethink the developmental situation. As Alexander Lowen and Stanley Keleman have observed, it is in the familial interactions of early childhood that a person grounds himself both in his body and in the social world.[11],[12] This is now developed in the next chapter.

CHAPTER 7

GROUNDING AS COMMUNICATION

Steps to transfiguration

The newborn child discovers many groundings. It lies across the mother's abdomen and is grounded on the outside of her body, sensing the same rhythms and heartbeats it has previously experienced inside. It holds and is held; encloses part of her in a hand, or the curl of its body, and is enclosed by the contact with her. When it sucks at the breast, it could be said to be grounding its mouth. When it looks at her face, it can be said to be grounding its eyes. In the flow of developing language, it begins to ground its ideas. In all the progressive movements from lying prone, to holding its head up, through crawling and squatting, to standing, it learns good or poor contact with the physical ground. All this takes place in an emotional environment which forms the background for the child's organisation of its activity.

Grounding is concerned with what happens when energy flows out towards the surface of the body and the quality of contact it finds there. Because these various forms of grounding have gone wrong for so many people, therapeutic work involves experiences of re-contacting the ground. The discovery involved is both how one has learned to communicate and the possibility of new ways of communicating. In doing therapy we want to establish a series of experiences in which the person comes to feel his own inner thrust in the social situation; how he has constructed himself in the past and what new grounding may be possible.

93

GROUNDING AS COMMUNICATION

All the work on providing grounding for the body through postural work, stress positions and cathartic release of blocked emotions have their place, but they are only the outer ground. We need to deepen and enrich this process by paying attention to how a person builds his life-space or organises his life-time;[1] what sense he has of his ability to form himself by participating more fully in his own process. We need to help him find his inner ground. This is the source from which his own healing energy wells up with the power to integrate him anew in spite of whatever he learned about how not to feel alive. By recapitulating and re-enacting various stages of the developmental process, a person can come to reclaim the patterns of self-feeling and interaction by which he meets the world. With proper guidance he can then try new kinds of grounding that are more enlivening and satisfying; literally to take the steps that will transform his living experience.

Lowen has systematically developed a number of dynamic positions that facilitate the flow of energy down the body and into the feet.[2] He has deeply enriched our approach to standing and to ways of holding one's ground. To understand the concept of grounding in its totality, however, we need to return for a moment to fundamentals, for grounding involves much more than standing, as I am sure Lowen would agree.

The foetus in the womb not only experiences umbilical affect and foetal skin affect, as Mott has described;[3] it also experiences kinaesthetic affect – the flow of feeling that comes from using its muscles in smooth coordinated movements. At first these movements are primitive swimming movements. The baby, when born, can readily learn to swim long before it is ready to walk because the support given by water calls for less voluntary coordination than is required to stand erect on land. The earliest experiences of intra-uterine swimming, associated as they are with the oceanic feelings of containment and contentment, are most closely approximated in later life in special conditions of water or air which encourage floating and weightlessness: suspension in a warm pool; sky-diving or hang-gliding.

Let us begin by considering the two ends of the body. The feet stand on the ground, the head is furthest removed from it. In bio-energetics we are familiar with the idea that a person who is 'stuck in his head' is pulled away from the ground. The foundation point for Lowen's departure from Reich, in developing bio-energetics, is really his use of the concept of the ground.

These foetal convulsive movements have already been described. Paul Ritter described them as the 'I want to get out' reflex.[4] The birth reflex movements resemble, but are different from, those of the orgasm reflex. Let us look at some of the principal differences.

Birth reflex	Orgasm reflex
The ends of the body push away from each other at the peak of the thrust.	The ends of the body pull together at the peak of the thrust.
The reflex is triggered by pressure at both ends of the body (soles of feet, top of head).	The reflex is triggered by charge at the centre of the body (genital focus).
The movements lead the organism from (floating) unconsciousness towards (landing) consciousness.	The movements lead the organism from groundedness (standing, reality, everyday life) with an alert consciousness, towards a more centred state (relaxing, melting, dimming of consciousness, oceanic feelings).
The urge is: I want to get out.	The urge is: I want to get in, or take in.

GROUNDING AS COMMUNICATION

| The extensor thrust is in contrast to the embryonic position of the previous nine months. | The embryonic curves towards which the ends of the body move in orgasm are in contrast to the extensor position of adult existence. |

Now for some of the similarities. Both reflexes involve the body in a more total way than most other experiences. Both are pleasurable, involuntary and involve powerful surges of energy focused in specific directions.

The birth-reflex is the basic organismic function which underlies all of a person's success or failure in grounding himself on the earth or in life. The first time that the organism focuses and harnesses its muscular patterns to ground itself decisively is in the experience of birth, when the baby propels itself by reflex extensions of the feet, head-first and against slowly yielding resistance, into the outside world.

This reflex can be recovered and re-experienced in adult life, fairly readily, by placing a person in a curled up position, lying down (usually on the side) and applying a firm pressure to the head and to the feet. A procedure like this was introduced and is regularly used by Frank Lake,[5] who pioneered birth-relax therapy in this country. He has the subject lie down with their feet against the wall and cups their head in his hands, one hand behind the head, one hand over the face. The subject is encouraged to relax and to breathe deeply. After a period of time, when the person lies quietly, small extensor movements of the legs begin, and eventually drive the person somewhat away from the wall. At this point Lake has three or more people move in to become a human wall and to re-flex the legs. They are taking over the function of the fundus of the womb. The course of the subsequent experience varies according to the birth-history of the individual going through it, but the organismic experience of tremendous propulsive effort moving towards a climax of crowning, can be recovered in many cases. Much will depend on the prior degree of holding or tension in the body. When I first witnessed these convulsive and propulsive body movements, the word that came to mind for them was 'sinuation'; the body insinuates itself through space, moves sinuously across the room. It is as though the whole muscular body sheath functions like a gut in peristalsis, expanding and contracting rhythmically and powerfully in aggressive locomotor movements. Later I discovered that D. W. Winnicott had used the word 'reptation' to describe the same phenomenon. He writes:

> In the ordinary birth the head of the infant is the
> forward point and does the work of dilating the
> maternal soft parts. There are several ways in which
> this is remembered. There may be retained as important
> a mode of progression which can be described by the
> word 'reptation'. This word appears in a book by
> Casteret, called *My Caves*. The author is describing the
> way he gets through holes in deep cave exploration.
> The point about reptation is that the arms are not of
> any use, nor the hands. In fact the reason why there is
> any forward movement is not clearly known to the
> author. I suppose that in the memory trace of a normal
> birth there would be no sense of helplessness. The
> infant would feel that the swimming movements of
> which we know a foetus is capable, and the movements
> that I have referred to under the word reptation,
> produce the forward movements.[6]

Some times the process of initiating this movement pattern triggers deeply repressed birth memories, and reactivates the primal struggle to live or struggle to die. At other times it acts as an integrating focus for the aggressive (forward moving) energies of the body. It gives the individual an experience of directedness and muscular focus that is both a source of deep pleasure and a source of insight into the muscular patterns and character patterns that usually block him from such satisfaction in his adult motor expressions. He is experiencing the basis of his groundedness.

He experiences this in the mounting excitement and the surge of inner directedness moving him in his interaction with the surround. As this process is repeated throughout time, the person can discover many things about his own assertion. He may find that he attempts to inhibit his thrusting forth by one bodily movement or another, or that his own involuntary inner surge is accompanied by feelings of panic, defeat, shame or guilt. The breath may be held or the jaw clamped shut. The power may not be translated into movement. Having had this realisation, the person can then be helped to experience the event in another way; to allow the breathing, say, or to permit the surge of one's own movement. The point, always, is not to get stuck in the pain of the past, but to experience it, understand it and move beyond it, to renew one's own pulsatory, sinuous and assertive movements.

The movement from lying to standing, in the post-natal period, is also led by the head, moving upwards, in opposition to the feet which press downwards. In therapeutic work with grounding it is possible to take a person through the various stages of erectness; from lying on the floor, to raising the head into the upright position (horizontal eye contact), to support on the arms, to a kneeling position on all fours, through to squatting (the embryonic position with support from the ground), through to standing.

There is a difference between the experience of lying down on one's back and lying down on one's front. Lying supine is a more open position, as the front is vulnerable and involuntary movements occur more easily. It is a more visionary position for, if the eyes are open, a person looks up into space. He may see the night sky or a blue sky with cloud patterns. He may see the dancing atmospheric light-spots that Reich describes. He may just see the ceiling, on to which a child will often project images and patterns, or be able to see the face of his or her mother looking down. If the eyes are closed, the position on one's back is favouring day-dreaming. Nightmares in children are, according to one old wives tale, associated with sleeping on the back. The supine position is the position of self-forgetting when the boundaries of the self get blurred and both body sensations and heightened perceptions can be maximised.

The position on one's side is the curled-up foetal shape which can bring comfort in the night as one gives up the need to relate to the world. People who over-breathe or who have a tendency to get hysterical can be calmed once they are put in this position. It withdraws a person from contact with the world and allows him to be nourished inwardly for a period. Gerda Boyesen refers to this as 'the position of polarisation'. The therapist can calm a patient by the placing of their hands on a couple of chakra points like the sacrum and the nape of the neck and by emphasising the client's breathing by a slight movement of the hands.

The position on one's front is the position of self-remembering. The child is in no danger of being engulfed by air or of drowning in water. It rests on a supporting surface and, at the same time, the vulnerable front is protected. If the surface is solid, like the floor, the sensation of yielding to gravity, so as to recover one's centre, is enhanced. The far-away visions of gazing into the sky or into the inner recesses of the mind are not encouraged. But in this position the child, raising its head on its forearms, first learns to direct its eyes on the near distance and bring part of the world into focus. Lying prone is the most fundamental state of groundedness; the ground-floor on which all the activities of crawling, crouching and then standing and walking will be built. The transition from the horizontal world to the vertical is one of the most momentous that we ever take.

If the emphasis of this work is not the final end-position, but on the experience of transition between positions, a whole range of buried feelings and new sensations become possible. Worlds of childhood are locked away in the muscular habit patterns we learned in adapting to gravity and contracting against our own rhythms.

In encouraging a person to move slowly, with awareness

and relaxation, from state to state, we discover a whole spontaneous yoga of the body. Tony Crisp, who works with these states of movement in his ashram in Devon, believes that the traditional asanas (body positions) of yoga are merely ritualised and systematised forms of spontaneous body expressions.[7] I learned from Stanley Keleman that making very slight postural adjustments to the body can produce profound alterations to internal rhythms, muscular tonus, self-image and body feelings. Provided that the postural adjustments are not carried out as bits of mechanical engineering on structure, but are contact-experiences, the helper uses his hands to sense out the buried life expression in the person he is helping.

Judy, in a group I took, was exploring the position of crawling. She got in touch with a lot of buried anger which came out in the form of growling and snarling in the animal position of being grounded on four limbs. As she felt the four points of contact with the ground, the aggressive energy surged up her back. It erected her neck (which had previously been hanging downwards under gravity) and the aggressive charge came through into her eyes. This was a woman who had had many difficulties with eye contact, whose character tendency was to withdraw from the ground and defocus with her eyes. The work of grounding distributes energy out towards all the contact points of the organism. She related afterwards that much of the anger was concerned with the memory of being made to stand too early by her mother, who did not like a child crawling round at her feet. A child who is robbed of a crucial stage of its groundedness (in this case the crawling position) is deprived of what it needs to focus aggressive energy for onward movement in later life. To reclaim one's crawling may be a necessary preliminary to the exploration of standing with more contact.

Positions of squatting may involve powerful emotions of guilt, disgust, power, contempt, aggression and self-assertion in relation to sitting. Excretion and locomotion both develop around the same time. A person who has contracted his

buttocks and anal sphincter because of conflicts in this area
has inhibited walking and contactless standing.

Rick was a man who had been through an English public
school education which had over-intellectualised him and left
him with a lot of withheld aggression and anal guilt. We
worked out some of his anger and he connected himself to
some of the feelings of mixed helplessness and power in the
squatting position. Then I took his hands and moved him
very slowly from the squatting position towards uprightness.
On the way up I was looking for qualities of response.
Usually where I detect a quality of resonating energy, an extra
tremor or tension in the flow of movement, I wait in this
position to see what arises. With Rick, what was triggered
halfway between squatting and standing was deep grief
connected with the death of his father at the age of three. The
slow standing with support brought back the organismic
memory of getting support from his father when learning to
stand, the loss of that support on his father's death and the
subsequent need to take on too early the tensions he associated
with being a man. In place of mature standing, he had
developed an over-active under-standing.

In re-experiencing the flow-of-movement expression, as the
body gathers itself against gravity and organises itself with the
minimum degree of tension that is functional in order to be
upright, it is as though we are recovering ancient evolutionary
rhythms. Fishlike, birdlike and reptilian movements occur. In
the orgasm reflex, Reich compared man to a jellyfish,
opening and closing in a basic pulsatile pattern. The jellyfish
is beautifully centred, but it cannot function on land. In
moving from lying to standing we recapitulate the movement
of life from the waters on to land.

Millicent Linden, in a book of exercises to improve posture
and increase the flow of life through the body, writes of this as
follows:

Life came from the sea and slowly conquered the land,
always ascending in form and defying gravity. The

most profound skeletal changes in the upward trend
occurred when we went from a four-legged to a two-
legged mode of locomotion. The adaptation of the
human body to the requirements of the upright
posture, although not perfect, is well blocked out. The
fundamental adjustments have already been achieved. If
man continues to exist he will continue to evolve. The
forces that wrought the present situation have not
abdicated their functions. Any improvement in man's
adaptation on the ladder of life, in the constant defiance
of gravity, would help characterise future man.[8]

We can understand how it is possible for a group of people to
be held spellbound, silent and in awe, at the experience of one
person at the centre, who, in the course of perhaps only half
an hour, recaptures some of this evolutionary movement flow
as he changes from lying to uprightness. Charlotte Selver, in
her work on sensory awareness, talks of the process of 'coming
to standing'.

Much of a person's body tensions are organised against the
fear of falling. The person who cannot fall easily will find it
hard to fall in love. Reich relates fear of falling to orgasm
anxiety, since both are based on contraction against
pleasurable streaming.

As I have shown clinically, orgasm anxiety is always
based on falling anxiety; the rapid and extreme
convulsion in the orgasm is experienced as falling if it
cannot take its course freely. In contrast the free,
uninhibited orgastic convulsion conveys the sensation
of floating or flying.[9]

Part of Reich's answer to the falling anxiety in an infant of
three weeks was to actually let the child fall in order to
accustom him to the sensation of falling.

Holding the child under the armpits, I would lift him
and then lower him, slowly at first and then
increasingly quickly. At first the child reacted with

crying, but soon he began to enjoy it. He even developed a kind of game from it: he made 'walking' movements with his legs. He leaned against my chest and looked up towards my head. I understood what he wanted: to crawl up on me; arrived above my head he would squeal with pleasure. In the succeeding weeks, the climbing up and 'falling' became a favorite game.[9]

Many adults reveal their fear of falling in their locked knees, tightened buttocks, tense ankle joints, and general rigidity. Lowen has developed a number of exercises aimed at helping a person to become aware of the unconscious ways he tenses himself against falling. Group experiences, where a person allows himself to fall and be caught by the group, not only build trust, but re-educate the body to its own currents of flow.

I worked with a woman called Dorothy who could allow herself to fall backwards and be caught, but who also was unconsciously holding her breath. When she allowed herself to repeat the falling experience and to breathe out on the fall, it became an alive experience instead of a mechanical one: now she felt strong inner currents of excitation that she had not felt since a child, pleasurable streaming from the centre of the body out towards the extremities. The excitatory currents are the same as the 'roller-coaster' sensations which children get from swings and are closely related to the streams of free-flowing energy that occur when the body is allowed to melt in orgasm. In orgasm the body is made as if weightless. For Dorothy, who had a dry, controlled, rather desert-like character, this experience put her in direct touch with her underground springs, the sap of her own vitality. Falling was thus the gateway to her own process.

Similarly, walking is another gateway to the exploration of one's process, the exploration of one's ground. Walking is really controlled falling. As we take a step forward, we destabilise the body from its uprightness and the body begins to fall. Putting a leg forward momentarily arrests the fall and, as the other leg moves, the body again starts to fall and is again prevented from falling by the onward movements of locomotion. A person, afraid to fall and tensed against gravity, therefore cannot walk freely. He has lost the pleasure of simply walking. Walking is always to get somewhere.

The simple act of sitting is, again, a way to feel one's ground. Take a simple example; a person lies back, relaxes and accepts support, breathing deeply. He is encouraged then to sit up, slowly, and to stay as relaxed as possible, supporting himself now in the sitting position. Very often, what happens is that the breathing is unconsciously restricted. The position is not a cramping one as it is perfectly possible to breathe as deeply when sitting as when standing; so there is no apparent reason.

The reason is that sitting up is more associated with the social role of being more adult, less animal, more controlled and more responsive to the demands of others. Standing, for many people, is similarly a statement of tense preparedness to act with control upon the world. It is well-known that standing has become a mainstay of the bio-energetic approach; the basic entry to the feeling of one's ground. As Lowen has explained:

> Grounding is not a term that Reich ever used to my knowledge, nor is it a concept that he worked with actively. Reichean therapy takes place with the patient lying on a bed and makes no attempt to explore with the patient the functions of standing, holding one's ground, moving forwards . . . Grounding as the term is used in bio-energetics means having one's feet solidly planted on the ground or being fully in contact with the ground. It does not describe a mechanical one but an energetic one. To be grounded a person must feel his feet touching the ground. This is not possible unless there is an energetic charge in the feet and an energetic interchange between the feet and the ground.[10]

Some of the deepest experiences people have contacted, which help them to connect with the process of their own withheld life, have arisen out of new qualities of standing and walking. We have to help people re-experience their body stance, re-align the body, so that it stands as though for the first time with all the surge of achievement and vitality that belongs to the erect position. Sometimes just the experience of standing in a new way becomes intensely alive. So much so that a person can pour with sweat just standing on the spot; the body pulsating gently, or sometimes vibrating strongly, as the muscles release some of their normal store of dammed-up energy and this becomes available to nourish the whole person. A walk, as though for the first time, becomes a practice ground for trying out the pleasure of new steps, a testing place for whether one can allow the flow of anxiety to wax and wane without contracting or falling over. These are birth moments in human experience. Such simple actions, in a sensitive context, with slight guidance, can give a person the experience of a flow of life he is normally never in contact with. They transform him. He looks transfigured. He begins to re-organise himself and his life.

Stanley Keleman introduced me to the concept of the imaginary body. The imaginary body is the potential body that is blocked from expression by the tensions and habit patterns by which we learn to structure ourselves. Experience outside the usual structuring allows in new life. A person has a taste of life outside the usual structures he shackles himself by. The imaginary body is his glimpse of what he could become, a direction in which he can transform himself. It may take many such experiences, repeated in the context of ongoing work on oneself, before the imaginary body becomes the real body, the body of a person who has become alive again.

Here again I am not talking about explosive discharge, nor the agonies of primal abandonment, but of the experience of integration and self-formation that comes from containing and breathing into a feeling. It can then acquire the capacity to nourish internally and transform a person's life. We can see it whenever someone succeeds in making the transition from hysterical acting-out and over-emotionalising to the state of being filled with the depth of oneself that transforms the breathing. When this happens the breathing loses all panic, all contractedness, all pressurisation and self-torture. I can hear the ocean in it. It moves through the body like tides, with an inevitability that has the millennia of evolutionary time that it took to evolve a body that can participate in its own process without standing against it or walling off from it. Ola Raknes wrote:

> Those who are used to taking note of their own bodily sensations will certainly be able to sense the streamings which go through the whole body. With a full and deep breathing these wave-like movements give a feeling of being alive through and through. Those who have relaxed bodies and unclouded minds have these sensations as the regular and permanant background to all that they experience, and it is this which gives colour, taste, and freshness to their whole life.[11]

We are talking of a kind of therapy that touches the primary dimensions of human experience. The task of all true therapies, and the aim of the core teaching in all true religions, is to reconnect us with the depth of ourselves.

CHAPTER 8

FACING AND SOUNDING
Eye-contact, voice and language

It is said of Freud, who was in the habit of sitting behind his patients when they took their analytic session, that he chose this position as he was embarrassed by too much direct eye-contact. There is no doubt that he listened with great receptivity, but he seemed unable to face his patients in the sense that I am using the term here.

Facing is very much concerned with qualities of eye-contact. Reich was led to his discovery of muscular armour, the breathing blocks and the vegetative currents in the body by painstaking work in facing people with what he saw in them. At first his method was confrontational. He would point out the character defences, mimic the facial expressions, imitate the tone of voice and so on, until so much feeling was generated that muscle tone, breathing rhythm and emotional flow were all powerfully affected. Fritz Perls developed some of these character-analytic methods in his techniques of gestalt therapy, one of which puts a person on the 'hot seat' and faces them with their particular character attitudes and body configurations.

Reich's work, however, moved beyond this. He did much more than attack and confront the character defences that a person presented. He reached out to make contact with the buried life-expression and to encourage that to sparkle more strongly. A good illustration of this way of working is given in an account, by a therapist, who took personal therapy with

Reich and describes his experience. Reich had already worked in various ways on the emotional expression in his eyes and had released different levels of rage, longing and anxiety. However there was a particular quality of excitation in his eyes that Reich had glimpsed but not been able to draw through. The account goes on:

> After a few weeks it came. During the session it suddenly appeared and hit the therapist (Reich) and he shouted excitedly and with satisfaction, 'There it is!' Again the patient looked at him in quizzical, skeptical, eyes-and head-cocked way as if to say, 'What! Are you off your nut again?' But the therapist was not to be diverted and he kept pointing to the patient's eyes and saying that there it was, until the patient began to feel it himself. A gleam, together with the shifting of the eyes and head, had brought up a new expression out of the depths into the eyes and this had caught the therapist's eyes and being. It was a flirtatious, come-hither look, a sort of wink, with a raising of the eyelids, eyebrows and forehead and a moving of the eyeballs to one side, accompanied by a suggestive tilt of the head in the same direction. As the therapist continued to imitate this expression and the patient began to make better contact with it, the whole face participated in it, at first with blushing shame-facedness and then to the tune of a hearty laugh. The therapist had got to the patient's secret and 'understood!'. It was a meeting of minds and emotions. No words were necessary. The patient soon brought out the rest of the hidden impulses. He made 'yoo-hoo' calls and whistles. Then came the talking. With a significant smile, later with sobbing and quivering, he recalled his abortive attempts as an adolescent at flirting; his burning desire to attract girls in this – held back and repressed by his moral training and fear of discovery and punishment.[1]

This work on the facial expression opens up the patient's

emotional life very deeply. He can surrender more freely to his feelings, and his sexual life and working life improve considerably. The account continues:

> One day a 'miracle' happened. Suddenly the patient was startled and opened his eyes wide with astonishment. While he was looking at the therapist the latter's face had suddenly become soft, and glowed with light. The patient soon realised that it was his own eyes that had opened up to orgone excitation and lumination and he was therefore able to 'see' better and thus to have his own orgone energy excitation contacted by the energy excitation of others . . . What this means for coming generations is stupendous, for there is no doubt that most people do not really 'see' because of their armouring. They miss the brightness of life – that is its orgonotic lumination and pulsation and, therefore, its poetry and music and beauty. The patient, at any rate, was definitely improved in his seeing, with a good deal of the fear and hate gone out of his eyes. He saw the world differently, as a good and pleasurable place to be in and as a future place of 'heaven' and not the 'hell' that it had been before.[1]

This breakthrough was not the result of 'massage' on the eyes (though that may be valuable), or of simply encouraging expressive movements with the eyes (though this is very important). It was the direct result of the exchange of looks between the two people in the room, a reaching out on the part of the therapist with his own aliveness to contact and excite into activity the aliveness buried in the person he was working with. Without this willingness to read the secret expression and to nurse it into life, any therapeutic encounter is gravely weakened. It is like blowing on the flame when the fire is nearly banked out with ash and trying to fan it into greater life.

Searching out the secret can easily be misunderstood to mean demanding that someone bare one's soul: 'I insist that you face me.' It can become like the teacher who demands of the recalcitrant child that he look her in the eye. In general there are two extreme positions that people take up in regard to secrets; sometimes the therapist is over-eager to dig out the hidden aspects of the patient or client and tends to adopt the attitude, 'Tell me your secrets and then I will know you trust me.' The patient on the other hand may well feel the opposite view: 'When I trust you I will tell you my secrets.'

Alexander Lowen has given a powerful reminder of the importance of facing the person one is trying to help, in the case-history of a man called George.[2] Lowen had been working with him by bio-energetic means for some two and a half years, yet he felt at a particular point in the therapy that, in spite of all the good analytic work and hard intensive work on the tensions, he was pretty well back where he started. Some crucial insight had been missed. Lowen describes how they had talked about the fear of death and then something occurred to him which explained the key to the client's anxiety and his personality. Lowen looked at the patient as he was lying there and said:

> George, I think you've given up – a long time ago. How long ago did you realise that you'd given up?

Patient: When I was a very small baby, a very small child. I sensed it quite a long time ago.

Dr Lowen: Then what was all that effort that followed that? Since you'd given up, why make the effort?

Patient: It was not wanting to face the fact that there was this will to die and this struggle keeping myself from accepting that I did want to die.

After it was over he realised that 'You can do anything you want. You can analyse as much as you want. You can do as much physical work as you want. Nothing will fundamentally change until that key has been turned and that door has been opened.'

Lowen concludes that this central insight, the digging out of the secret death wish, is quite crucial.

> With all of that hard work and with all of the good
> analysis, it is my feeling that the therapy could not have
> moved ahead if I hadn't turned that key and opened up
> that whole polarity in which his life was oscillating.
> And that nothing else would have been possible if that
> polarity had not been touched.

Let me give an example, from my own work, of the importance of this work to do with facing the person who is there. Jessica was a beautiful woman with an alive sexuality and a very clear intellect. In the first interaction we had, she spent the first quarter of an hour talking about her background and some of the problems she faced in her social life. After this I asked her to lie down so I could relate to her non-verbal expression and see how she breathed. When she lay down the most pronounced rigidities were around her jaw and neck; she was holding her head very stiffly. Her breathing was fairly deep but very measured (she had been practising yoga for some time). I put my hands on each side of her head and rested them there. This had a very powerful effect on her, as usually her head was only reached through words. People made love to her body and spoke to her head. Her breathing deepened and some crying came through, at which point she curled up, screwed her eyes up tight and said, 'I don't want to look, I don't want to look at you.' I allowed her to stay in the contraction for a short while, so as to experience what she was doing. She then said, spontaneously, 'I think I ought to face you', and sat up.

We then began to unravel what the not-looking was all about. Earlier, in describing some of her social problems, she had used the expression 'I switch off if I don't want to see something hurtful.' I began to relate this verbal expression to the feeling I had about her eyes; her eye contact was very direct, she looked straight at me, yet I felt something clouding her expression. Suddenly I had the image of a dipped beam. It was as though she used her eyes like headlights, but on dipped beam.

Now the experience of sharing with another person very sharp images of just how they are functioning in the here and now, of facing them with this kind of truth about themselves, generates a lot of excitement. Of course, it has to be done in a non-critical way. In a sense one has to show love for the character defences, in order to tease them apart and to help a person see that, though they were necessary to that person, maybe one can function without them for a moment or two at least. Thus, in the exchange of excitement that is generated by focusing intimately on a particular character expression, something 'miraculous' happens; the quality of aliveness changes and more life comes through. It is like the sun appearing momentarily from behind clouds.

With Jessica, as our interchange went on, there were moments when her eye-contact fleetingly changed – as though just for a second or two she allowed herself to go on to full beam. When this happened, two other things happened with it: her breathing deepened and became freer and her posture changed, her head tilting up and her chin thrusting forward slightly. It became clear that she allowed her sexuality into her body (she was very alive in dancing) but denied it to her head (which had to be kept cool and rational). Her character pattern became clear in that moment; she was a gypsy philosopher. Her head was public and must be kept rational and not passionate; passion could be allowed only to her body in private. But, in those moments when her eyes came on to full beam, she became a more integrated person. Her face showed what her body felt and her eyes blazed with a vital strength she would not normally allow through into her head.

No deep emotional outpourings took place in this session, yet the work went a long way down and it was very moving to make contact this deep so early. At the end of the session she said that she had learned more about herself in that hour than from fifteen years of relationships with men.

Facing is concerned with recognition, with how we see people, with the qualities of lumination that develop when people really face each other and with the forms of illumination that flash out of such contact. Insight develops in step with outlook. If a person can let his inner self be seen by another, he begins to become recognisable to himself and can then look within, not in the sense of any sterile introspection but in the sense of learning to love and accept who he is, and so recognise himself. Clear seeing between people thus encourages deeper being. If we remember the close relationship between these two functions in infancy, we should not be too surprised at their recurrence together in the therapeutic work.

Another way for the inner self to be shown is through expression and communication in language. The capacity to speak is one of the key qualities of being human. When a child learns that it can shape the flow of air that comes out of its mouth to form sounds that symbolise the world around it, its range of expressiveness is enormously enhanced and undergoes a qualitative change. From Helen Keller's experiences before she had understood the relationship between symbol and sound we can learn how crucial is the ability to vocalise experience in a meaningful way.

Leopold Stein has suggested that speech evolves from the combination of sucking movements and breathing sounds.[3] The expired breath, passing through the larynx, gives a basic vowel sound which is shaped by the tongue and the cavity of the mouth. The smacking and sucking movements of the lips and tongue provide the primitive consonants, which in early language appear as clicks. The inversion of a click by blowing out the air instead of sucking it in, forms a consonant.

Some insight into the relationship between speech and thought is provided by young children who constantly confuse thought with speech. Thus Piaget explains:

Stern noticed that his four year old daughter confused thought with the voice. She said expressly that we think

with the mouth and tongue. This spontaneous remark
of a child gave us the idea for a systematic inquiry on
this point. We asked sixty children between the ages of
four and twelve what one thinks with and whether one
can see and touch thought. The result of this inquiry
was very clear. All the children under about seven
answered like Stern's little girl, 'We think with our
mouths'.[4]

Rhythms of breathing, shaped by the mouth, thus come to
symbolise the complex thought processes of the mind. Francis
Mott explains the relationship in this way.

Speech appears as an effort to copy in the respiratory
tubes the configurational affect generated in the cerebrospinal tubes. The air in the respiratory passages and
the mouth cavities becomes the analogue of the cerebrospinal fluid. The movement of the air through the
trachea is the analogue of the rhythms moving up the
cerebrospinal tube. The cavities of the mouth and nose
are the analogue of the cerebral cavities. Vowels and
consonants stand in relation as nuclear and peripheral
units of cerebrospinal affect . . . Speech is thus an
outward copy of an internal process. Its values are configurational. It is an effort to express in a column of
vibrating air what is going on in the vibrating cerebrospinal fluids. The very origins of voice seem to me to
stem back to the hollow vertebral column in which the
waves of thought are beating out their patterns, which
the sound waves of the voice strive to imitate.[5]

We can look at the functions of contact and the blocks to
contact in language in three ways:

1 Learning to speak and the blocks to language
   development.
2 Voice production and the tensions that restrict the
   voice.
3 Styles of language.

As regards the first developments in the process of learning to speak, speech is a social act. By listening and repeating the speech sounds of its parents, a child learns that babbling is an act of communication. Speech is playing with sounds and discovering that sounds are tools that can work for you. A child soon learns that the sound 'milk' will usually persuade its mother to bring a refreshing drink. By learning to interact playfully with others through sounds, it learns to talk to itself, at first aloud and later internally. Dialogue turns into self-dialogue and self-dialogue flows back into more dialogue. Silent thinking, it has been shown, is accompanied by micro-movements of the larynx, so thought is mostly sub-vocal speech.

Yet some children are mute. In some forms of autism, in the absence of any demonstrable brain damage, the child remains silent throughout the period of speech development and may never learn to talk, since once the critical period for language is passed it is apparently very difficult to acquire the skill of speech. It is sometimes possible to teach such children rudimentary forms of speech by behavioural conditioning; they start to emit pieces of language in response to rewards or punishments. This cannot disguise the fact that the spontaneous desire for speech is still absent. The autistic child declines to speak as part of its general withdrawal from contact, just as it avoids meeting people with the eyes and encapsulates itself in a private social world.

There has been discussion as to whether or not autism is a form of childhood schizophrenia. Schizophrenic children more usually show disordered and fragmented language and not the total block of the mute autistic child. The schizophrenic child, that is, attempts the social function of language and in so doing lays itself open to mental invasion. Laing has documented extensively the way that words are used as subtle ways of controlling the identity of the child in the families of people who later became classed as schizophrenics.[6]

An adult schizophrenic patient described in Frieda Fromm-

Reichmann's book, had been mute for years.[7] Every week his psychiatrist visited him in hospital, and every week the patient refused any verbal communication. At the end of six months the patient greeted the therapist by saying, 'I see you have a new tie today, Doctor.' From then on verbal interchange could develop. In this situation language was intact, only the contact function had been broken.

Barbara Roberts described her work with autistic children in an article in *Energy and Character*.[8] She described a girl of eleven who was totally mute. Yet when her therapist put his hand on hers she was willing to communicate in language through writing.

Jan Foudraine worked with chronically institutionalised schizophrenics, some of whom had no intelligible language. He found that he could establish a meaningful dialogue with them if he did not initially require them to talk sense, but if he himself was prepared to move towards them contactfully without treating their unintelligible sounds and word-fragments as gibberish.

> The psychiatrist is forced to abandon his attempt to induce the client to conform to the generally received and accepted use of language. The psychiatrist is asked to come down to the level occupied by his client, to respond to the level of communication 'beneath' the level of verbalised expression . . . A lad who talked quite unintelligibly surprised me on one occasion by saying something I thought I could understand. After I had put my notion directly into words he said, 'A bird is known by its note, a man by his talk', and then resumed his unintelligible language in a somewhat less unintelligible manner.[9]

His book is full of examples of how to use unintelligibility as a communicating bridge. 'Talkability' arises when the non-communicator is prepared to venture out by himself to make contact from his side.

Some time ago a BBC *Horizon* programme gave the life

story of a man called Joey who had been in a hospital for spastics since birth. Due to an injury then, which damaged the motor nerves controlling the speech organs, he had never uttered any intelligible sounds. In the same hospital it happened there was one other patient who could understand these otherwise meaningless sounds. However this second patient was too uncoordinated to be able to write. By acting as interpreter for Joey, he made it possible for a third man, who could write but could not understand the inarticulate sounds, to write down what was said. In this way Joey was able to write the story of his life in totally coherent prose. So even when there is brain damage, the function of language may survive intact, waiting for someone able to build a communicating bridge.

The second category is where we find that the way we actually manufacture the sounds of communication is also a function of the development of contact. In order to speak articulately and expressively there must be a rhythmic coordination between the organs of speech and the breathing. The column of air resonates in the chest, the throat and the cavities of the head. If any of these are blocked, the smooth flow of voice is broken up and some form of voice inhibition results.

The most obvious disturbance to the voice is stammering. Stein distinguishes two primary forms of stammering which he calls 'clonic' and 'tonic'.[3] In the tonic stammer, the speech organs seize up or freeze, refusing to utter a particular sound over which the person blocks. In the clonic stammer, certain sounds are reiterated b-b-badly. The second form is more socially discomforting than the former, so tonic stammers tend to replace clonic ones. The stammerer then learns to substitute the words he or she blocks on, so as to cover up the specific areas of tension.

Stein's way of treating this is to encourage the tonic stammerer to revert to the clonic stammer and to then play with the repeated sounds deliberately. He is drawing on a process which Glynn Seaborn Jones has called 'voluntarisation'. In effect the patient goes back and learns to babble again and is thus given a second chance to integrate the movements of sucking and breathing.

John Pierrakos has made a special study of disturbance in voice production. The following are the major disturbances which he describes.

1 The flat voice indicates that the expression of feeling is suppressed and kept within a small range. One has the impression of lack of depth. The rhythm is monotonous, the resonance poor. The oral character falls into this category. There is a lot of 'empty talk' to gain affection. One of his female patients used to talk incessantly with a flat monotonous voice at the beginning of therapy. She admitted subsequently that this was a gimmick to gain affection and avoid going deeper into her emptiness.

2 A voice limited to one register with a narrow range. This voice is predominantly high-pitched for fear of contacting deeper sexual feelings. This is particularly the case in hysterical structures, where there is an abundant supply of energy and blocking of emotions. The passive-feminine individual has a voice that is soft, high-pitched and which almost sounds feminine, as if he were keeping the emotions away from the chest and abdomen. It says, 'I comply, I am aware of you, don't hurt me.'

3 The mechanical voice lacks resonance, is monotonous and dry and cold. Schizoid patients talk this way. Their breathing is split and the diaphragm and abdomen are severely contracted. The range of the voice is extremely limited.

4 The affected voice is an attempt by the individual artificially to modulate his voice to cover his lack of feeling. It has an artificial quality. Many people consciously assume different roles to avoid expressing

their true feelings . . . In this category could be placed the masochistic character who uses the voice to express constant complaints and whines in order to provoke a reaction and obtain release of his locked emotions.[10]

The third category of developmental function in contact is the form the communication finally takes; the style of language.

Talking between therapist and patient has been a traditional mode of interchange. But talking can often be a way of avoiding facing the other person with the truth about oneself. It was Laing who documented most extensively the ways in which neurosis expressed itself as a particular form of human bondage, the bondage of words.[11] A disjunction is something that separates and pulls people apart. What Laing is saying is that language, as used in normal human interaction, has a blocking function; it splits us apart and it mirrors the distortions of contact between people. But the process is self-reinforcing in a positive feedback sense. The distorted knots of language make contact even more difficult and the more difficult contact tightens the double-binds of language. Thus neurosis is an in-turned and tightening spiral of fragmentation. The blocked body-stream and the knotted word-stream reinforce and reflect each other.

But there is a creative function in language also. O'Connell recognises this when he writes, 'as language can be a form of hypnosis when its limits are not appreciated, the precise use of language can be paradoxically one of the paths to liberation'.[12]

Language is used precisely in this sense when it is able to bring feelings into focus. What is the opposite of a disjunction in language? It is a conjunction, when suddenly fragments of experience that were separated can flow together. We make contact by looking at each other face-to-face, by listening to each other, by touching each other when the heart is in it and by a certain kind of 'being alongside' which resists definition. If we see 'one of the basic purposes of therapy as being a return to contact with others',[12] then therapy becomes less of a treatment and more of a particular form of dialogue. What a person needs first and foremost is to be recognised where he is and who he is, which brings us back to the need for facing.

The therapeutic encounter provides the opportunity for a person to discover whether his experience of himself can be understood by anyone else and can, in any way, tally with how another person experiences him. The severest forms of mental illness are failures of communications, and communication is the most potent form of change. The gestalt therapists have recognised what they call the 'paradox of change'. It is close to what Krishnamurti has always taught about the confusion between 'what is' and 'what ought to be'.[13] The harder we work to 'solve' a neurotic problem, the more tenaciously it maintains its ground.

> Change occurs when one becomes what he is, not when he tries to become what he is not . . . experience has shown that when a patient identifies with the alienated fragments, integration does occur. Thus by being what one is – fully – one can become something else. The therapist himself is one who does not seek change, but only seeks to be who he is. The patient's efforts to fit the therapist into one of his own stereotypes of people, such as helper or a top-dog, create conflict between them. The end-point is reached when each can be himself while still maintaining intimate contact with the other. The therapist too is moved to change as he seeks to be himself with another person. This kind of mutual interaction leads to the possibility that a therapist may be most effective when he changes most, for when he is open to change, he will be likely to have his greatest impact on his patient.[12]

Thus the contact of therapy has to supply what the first relationships did not, a joining of the inside and the outside. A person in therapy seems 'to have to unite his perceptions with the attitude of another before he can fully perceive himself; the self cannot come into being without using the other as a lever ... it is not that two heads are better than one, but that two heads are needed for one'.[12]

In the field of this kind of relationship, feelings are more than discharges of energy; they become communications again. As deadened feelings spring back into life, insights start to spring in. They carry a particular charge which is unmistakable; there is a frisson of authenticity, a flash of recognition, when a coupling of images occurs and the emotion generated can be both fully shared and fully integrated, for 'to carry experience itself alive into the heart is an extraordinary achievement'.[14] The coupled image is a mating between the words that come out of a person's mouth and the flow of energy in his cells. It is the reverse of the 'knot'. If a knot is a blocked word-stream reinforcing a contactless body, the coupled images of insight arise when words are generated from feelings that can be fully faced for the first time.

Winnicott has described how crucial dialogue between people is for any meaningful self-dialogue to be developed. He describes how with a patient 'We discussed the way in which talking to oneself does not reflect back, unless this is a carry-over of such talking having been reflected back by someone not oneself.'[15]

I was doing some work with a client called Paul on his problem of joining his heart to his head. We worked on his breathing and he got in touch with very deep grief and sobbing. The sobbing went on for a long time; he was deeply into it. After a while I got in touch with an unending quality in it; it seemed he could stay in it for hours. It often happens in therapeutic work that people go just for the emotional release and as long as emotions are flowing they think that everything is fine. But abreaction is not necessarily enough. It is necessary to keep a feeling for the total emotional quality of each expression and to look for places where contact with it may be broken or withheld. In Paul's case I felt he was at some level blocking off from his own grief and therefore was getting stuck in it, beginning to drown in unendedness. I asked him to share with me what the grief was about. Now he was able to build the bridge back between the world of the hurt child and the world of the adult that he was, for he described the content of the grief which was present-day material, related to his current girlfriend. The depth, quality and degree of hurt in the crying all came from infancy, but the triggering situation was an adult one. If he had been allowed just to regress it would have been easy for him to have used the childhood pain as a way of avoiding facing the present-day hurt. But as soon as he could share the content, give voice to the grief as well as pouring it out in the sobs, he re-humanised his feelings and allowed the hurt in his heart to join up with the memories in his head.

When people are moved they do not just cry out, the sounds take shape as words, the cries become meanings. Memory comes from a Greek word meaning 'to care for'. Memory comes alive, as distinct from being an intellectual trace, when you care for your experiences, when you take time to digest what has happened to you, when you get the taste of your own life-course back into the body. Memory, so the biologists are beginning to discover, can leave some kind of trace in every cell. It is the dissociated intellect which divorces the past from the present, as two separated pools of time. Dreams reveal that there is no true distinction and all experiences can still work in us if we let them. The problem of therapy is not to cut the past away like dead wood but to re-work it, to regenerate it, so that the body can become charged with the significance of what it has truly lived.

Reich used to say that character was frozen history; as the character softens, history melts and becomes fluid again; time past ceases to be a rut people are trapped in. Your experience is what you welcome into you; the rest is happenings. The more you have to shut out, the harder it is to hear the sound of your own voice. When every feeling is meaningful, and all meanings are fully felt, then the neurotic chain is broken that splits the body from the mind, and locks the inside within the outside. It was John Pierrakos who wrote:

> The voice expresses or blocks vibratory movements from the core of the organism. What moves a person is his inner attitude. The pulsatory movements of life, of which the energy field is an expression, combine with the physical movements of the body in unitary functioning. When both are free, the organism resonates and is set aflame. The body is then experienced pleasurably, its movements are harmonious, its voice is melodious and free to move in a wide range. One can say that the ability to express the full range of one's feelings vocally as well as verbally is a measure of health. In life, to voice one's feelings, to speak up, is man's birthright. To swallow one's feelings and be silent is to hold inwardly and cramp the soul. This process is equivalent to chronic suffering, to giving up and slowly dying.[10]

Therapy is a journey towards the joining of what was split, the coupling of broken images, the fusion of the body-stream and the word-stream. 'The work is not something a therapist does to a patient so much as it is the study of ways of being together with this person so that ultimately he can be together with other persons.'[10]

If personality is linked to sound, then this kind of interacting is less of a dialogue, in any conventional sense, than a 'sounding out' of experience, a sensitivity to its reverberations, a facing of its meanings. Only by this means, I believe, can anyone be helped to develop the capacity to contain the powerful energies of strong feelings. Sounding out one's own truth in this way, through honest encounter with another person, is an essential need if one is to succeed in grounding oneself in one's own life-time and body-space. When this can happen, a kind of organic intelligence gets born, which has nothing to do with reasoning or the manipulation of concepts; it is when the person and his experience are not separated any more.

CHAPTER 9

BORDERLINE PATIENTS AND BOUNDARIES

On the edge of psychosis

Basic to vegeto-therapy and bio-energetics is the view that the discharge of feeling and the mobilisation of energy is an essential tool in the softening and dissolving of the neurotic character patterns and muscular armour. Reich's discovery of the *physiological* basis of the Freudian 'stasis neurosis' in dammed-up biological energy, trapped behind repressive defences, opened the way to a deeper understanding of ways of releasing bottled-up emotions. From the original cathartic approach of Josef Breuer, working with hysterics, there is a direct line through the work of Reich to the 'primal scream' therapy developed by Arthur Janov.

Many of these cathartic and emotion-releasing techniques have found their way into the practice of humanistic psychology and to the newer styles of group therapy popularised by the 'growth movement'. Gradually it was discovered that, whereas powerful techniques of provoking anger or fear, sadness or excitement, may help break down the tight armouring of a rigidly organised compulsion-neurosis for a borderline psychotic person, such methods are fraught with grave hazards. The very encouragement of 'letting go', surrender to the involuntary and giving up of ego-control, which proved so helpful with rigid neuroses, were found to be questionable at the least and in some cases totally damaging and destructive, causing ego-fragmentation and precipitating psychotic breakdown with this type of person.

Nic Waal, one of Reich's leading co-workers in Norway, wrote to me many years ago[1] that, when working with pre-psychotics, it was necessary to do 'ego-building' before proceeding with deep vegeto-therapy if one wanted to avoid the risk of psychotic breakdown.

Arthur Janov has distinguished three 'lines' or levels of working with people. The first line is the level of pure visceral sensation and primitive gut-feeling; the second line is the level of expressive emotion; the third line is the level of ego-integration through insight and word-language. It is Janov's view that in working with psychotics one must first strengthen the third line. This is equivalent to Nic Waal's term 'ego-building'.

The term 'grounding' was introduced by Stanley Keleman[2] to describe the process of being rooted in organic process; it was used by Alexander Lowen to describe both the physical actions of getting more closely in touch with one's muscles through toning-up exercises[3] and the process of releasing powerful emotions through expressive actions like kicking and hitting the couch.

An expressive action is distinguished from an impulsive action by the coexistence of strong feeling and a measure of conscious control. The essence of 'freaking-out' is the abandonment of any degree of ego-regulation and the surrender to an eruptive flow of feeling. If this happens in the context of a therapeutic session, the ego-control is delegated to the therapist or group leader and recovered at the end of the experience. We can visualise a spectrum of control taking the following form: in the case of the compulsive over-controlled person one helps him to develop what is missing – the spontaneous flow of involuntary feeling and action; in the case of the impulsive under-controlled person, one has to help develop the ego-control.

In the language of transactional analysis, this is the balance of the adult and the child. Bernard Rosenblum, the American orgonomist, once said to me that he saw two kinds of people in therapy: adults who needed to find their child and children who needed to find their adult.

The two uses of the term 'grounding' – to cover the discharge of excitation into feeling which earths the emotional energy, as lightning earths the atmospheric charge, and grounding in the sense of improved reality sense – reflect this polarity of child and adult. The id grounds itself in pleasure and the surge of strong emotional life; the ego grounds itself in reality which includes the ability to contain and hold feelings and, if necessary, to postpone pleasure now to obtain greater pleasure in the future. Alexander Lowen developed these principles of 'pleasure' and 'reality' in his first book, and described the 'holding' function of the ego as a container and focuser of feelings.[4]

In working with pre-psychotic people, or people in actual psychotic states, it is possible to work expressively and with the skills made available by vegeto-therapy, provided that the process of ego-building goes constantly hand in hand with the emotional work. In order to make this clear I will describe a few examples in relation to the expression of a few basic emotions.

Reich describes, in his brilliant case history of a schizo-phrenic, many dramatic occasions of emotional break-through, including outbreaks of murderous rage. Reich was clear, however, that such breakthroughs required perfectly clear contact between patient and therapist. He wrote:

> When deep emotions, especially hatred, break through the armour, a procedure which is absolutely necessary for cure, we know that we have created an artificial situation, involving genuine emotional forces. We know the emotions are potentially dangerous, but the process of breaking through was deliberate. Usually we have the patient well in hand, and we have prepared the emotional breakthrough for days or weeks with the greatest care.[5]

Elsewhere in the same article he explains this point in more detail.

I let her develop her rage by encouraging her to hit the couch. This is a dangerous procedure if the patient, especially the schizophrenic, is not in perfect contact with the physician. In order to secure this contact, one must explain to the patient that he must stop his rage reaction instantly when asked to do so. It is the task of the physician to decide when the point in emotional release is reached where the patient is in danger of getting out of control. Only very skilled orgone therapists can accomplish this task. Therefore, I warn physicians who have not been trained in the techniques of medical orgone therapy, and trained orgone therapists who do not have the necessary experience, against tackling schizophrenics. One cannot proceed in such cases without releasing the rage, and one cannot release the rage without much experience gained previously in less emotional situations.

Alexander Lowen has discussed the therapeutic benefits of the release of rage in promoting the ego function in schizophrenics.

Some of the manifestations of schizophrenic illness must be understood as attempts at the restoration of the ego function. The destructive outbreaks must be so construed. They represent the release of aggressive impulses which, while irrational and dangerous to the environment, tend to promote both ego strength and integration in the schizophrenic. I have always believed that much could be accomplished if the schizophrenic could be allowed to smash some old furniture in a carefully controlled setting. Many schizophrenics relate that following such an outbreak they feel much better. Of course, such measures must be part of a broader therapeutic programme.[4]

John Rosen took up the challenge of confronting his psychotic patients' aggression by involving himself in wrestling with them. He described this in his book *Direct Analysis*.[6] James Willie, a medical orgone therapist, made use of full size male dummies as controlled targets for releasing aggression in working with schizophrenics.[7]

Recently I met a man, whom I shall call Malcolm, in a bio-energetic group. He was in a pre-psychotic state. He described how he was caught in an impasse between feeling that he was imploding inwards towards devastation and the sense of being blown to pieces inside and exploding outwards in destructive outbreaks, especially where he lost control in primal groups and had to be forcibly restrained by the other members. Twice his experience of loss of control had been followed by several weeks of enforced hospitalisation. The challenge he presented was how to create a space between implosion and explosion where he could focus and direct his rage.

In working with Malcolm I decided to use the principle of voluntarisation; that is to set up an initial contract with him to facilitate the gradual building of ego control in the release of rage. Step by step I led him into the controlled expression of powerful anger, which he expressed through hitting. Instead of splitting himself between holding his aggression in and being powerless to express anger (implosion), or bursting out with rage and being powerless to control his destructiveness, he began to fuse the ability to feel angry and the ability to decide how much anger was safe to express. Thus in the course of several therapeutic experiences in the group he learned to own his own power, to harness it and to channel it, rather than to disown it, or be thrown by it.

Terror is a basic feeling that is deeply repressed in schizophrenia. The blockage of eye-contact has the function of preventing the perception of the inner excitation. In Reichian work, both the facilitation of the expression of fear through the opening wide of the eyes and the release of fear through screaming may occur frequently. In working with schizophrenics, the same process of voluntarisation can be used to acclimatise a person to deeper and deeper levels of contact with his own fear so that he can let this out at levels of excitation that he can tolerate, without being flooded by it. To be flooded with fear is intolerable for the schizophrenic and leads to a deepening of the split to shut down the facing of the inner terror.

'The biosystem', Reich wrote, 'has a very low tolerance for sudden increases of the emotional, i.e. bio-energetic level of functioning. Disorientation, hallucinations, speech deterioration and murderous impulses are likely to appear with a sudden increase in energy level if the tolerance is low.'[5]

Reich describes, in the case of the schizophrenic woman that he treated, how he worked with her facial expression to mobilise gradually the underlying life.

> I let her move the skin of her forehead, roll her eyes in all directions, express anger and fear, curiosity and watchfulness. This is not manipulation and has nothing whatsoever to do with any kind of manipulation. We do not manipulate mechanically; we induce emotions in the patients by letting them imitate wilfully this or that emotional expression.
>
> She objected very strongly to showing the expression of anxiety in her eyes. This objection is usually more intense in schizophrenics than it is in neurotics. The reason, based on several cases of schizophrenia, is the following: raising the eyelids, opening the eyelids wide and showing anxiety, releases a sensation of severe terror with the feeling of oncoming disaster. Sometimes panic sets in. Some patients have the feeling that they are dying, 'going off' and that they will be unable to 'come back again'. It is essential to be very careful at this point.[5]

Reich would work with his schizophrenics by encouraging the voluntary wilful taking-over of the voluntary function of 'going off'. In this way he helped people not to terrorise themselves by their own unperceived responses. He taught his schizophrenics how they went off, and also how to come back.

In moving away and back, within the limits that the person could tolerate without splitting off, he taught self-regulation. Stanley Keleman has called this principle 'playing the accordion'.

Another principle that Reich used in all his work (but one suspects particularly so with schizophrenics) was to take the organism as far as it is willing to go, and then a little bit further. He continues his description of working with the eye-block with his schizophrenic patient: 'I worked very cautiously on her expressions in the forehead, stopping her whenever she showed too strong anxiety. After some time, she could move her forehead more easily and she felt freer.'[5]

In the same article he describes how the work with eye-contact leads directly into the fear, in the case of a different patient.

> A man with clear-cut psychotic mechanisms used to react with severe anxiety after turning his eyeballs upward. He felt as if he were being choked to death. One day, I let him turn his eyeballs upward again. This time the reaction was particularly strong. In the course of the anxiety attack, he stared into one corner of the room, tipped his eyelids wide open, began to scream and pointed in terror toward the corner – 'Don't you feel it', he screamed, 'There, it's right there, coming out of the wall, staring at me.' Then, with a sudden jump, he jumped up and ran with terror into that corner from which he felt the stare had come. I led him into this reaction several times. It subsided gradually, and finally disappeared altogether.[5]

Again, as in the case of the rage-reactions, the most essential safeguard here is the presence of the therapist. He can balance his sense of the capacity of the person he is helping to keep contact with, the present-day reality of the room and the therapeutic setting, with the infantile terror that surfaces. The adult learns to admit the throttled-down child. The terrified and victimised child learns he has an adult inside him (and represented outside him in the person of the therapist) who keeps in contact, maintains self-perception and is available to help integrate the previously shut-down experiences.[8]

If life within the armour is felt to be in some sense paradise lost, then many will try a multiplicity of ways to re-experience this. To some, maybe the psychedelic high offers the hope of paradise regained. The search for pleasure impels many people who take psychedelic trips. The schizophrenic trip on the other hand has little to do with pleasure. Indeed there is a specific pleasure anxiety, as part of the general intolerance of sudden increases in excitation. The psychoanalyst Rado wrote:

> Schizophrenic disorders may be viewed as showing
> what happens to central integration in the person
> whose pleasure resources are inherently deficient . . .
> Absence of sufficient pleasure slows down and hinders
> psychodynamic integration, as the absence of an
> essential enzyme slows down and hinders biochemical
> integration.[9]

The understanding of the energy dynamics of the pleasure function was the cornerstone of Reich's whole endeavour. *Character Analysis* was founded on the insights of the orgasm theory. Vegeto-therapy grew out of the discovery of the streaming sensations that people experienced when they relaxed their bodily tensions in a state of high charge. Not surprisingly, this understanding gives Reich's view of the function of pleasure in schizophrenia a special importance.

Schizophrenics often complain about being possessed by weird forces, or electric currents, or of being influenced from afar by some kind of electrical machinery. Victor Tausk, in a classic paper as early as 1919, set out five characteristic effects of what he called the 'influencing machine':

1 It makes the patient see pictures. When this is the
   case the machine is generally a magic lantern or
   cinematograph.

2 It produces as well as removes, thoughts and feelings by means of waves or rays of mysterious forces which the patient's knowledge of physics is inadequate to explain . . . Its function consists in 'draining off' thoughts and feelings by one or several persecutors.

3 It produces motor phenomena in the body, erections and seminal emissions that are intended to deprive the patient of male potency and weaken. This is accomplished either by means of suggestion, or by air-currents, electricity, magnetism, or X-rays.

4 It creates sensations that in part cannot be described, because they are strange to the patient himself, and that in part are sensed as electrical, magnetic, or air-currents.

5 It is also responsible for other occurrences in the patient's body such as cutaneous eruptions, abscesses and other pathological processes.[10]

Reich's schizophrenic patient had vivid experiences of the 'forces' that she felt as an energy radiating from the walls of the room. The forces are often mystified into the excitatory sense of life derived from God, or the sense of being persecuted by the devil. Reich points out that 'the common functioning principle of both God as well as the devil is the basic biophysical functioning of the organism, the biological core, whose most significant manifestation is the plasmatic current, and its subjective perception as a melting sensation of love, as anxiety, or hate'.

The schizophrenic both desperately needs the integrating power of his own pleasure feelings streaming through his body and is terrified of being taken over by the involuntary flow of life. As Reich, step by step, increased the breathing level in his patient, he found that she got nearer to experiencing her own internal bodily excitation. The schizophrenic life-style is sustained by the flight from bodily excitation into cerebral over-excitation. Reich writes:

She had come closer to the natural forces, the 'melting'

sensations within herself. If this was correct the delusion of 'forces' from 'Beyond' had lost some of its energy and thus had weakened. She came closer to reality by coming closer to real forces of life, the orgonotic sensations within herself.[5]

These realisations led Reich to formulate three factors that would decisively affect the prospects of her therapy.

1 The more and better contact she made with her plasmatic bio-energetic streaming sensations, the less the fear of the 'forces' would be. This would also prove my contention that the 'forces' in schizophrenia are distorted perceptions of the basic orgonotic organ sensations.
2 This contact with her body sensations would help to establish some degree of orgastic satisfaction, and this in turn would eliminate the energy stasis which operated at the core of her delusions.
3 The undistorted experiencing of her body sensations would enable her to identify the true nature of the 'forces' and would thus slowly destroy the delusion.[5]

We have already seen that, in the case of both anger and fear, the experiencing of the flow of affect, if it happens with ego-participation, can be a powerful way of grounding a person who has fled from feelings into their head. At the same time this work needs to be done with considerable caution and great respect for the pace and energetic level of the person one works with, owing to the danger of a person reacting by intensified splitting to the increased level of excitation. Reich is under no illusions that the process of helping his patient towards accepting a flow of pleasure will proceed easily.

Before [better contact] could be accomplished, the patient would have to pass through a series of dangerous situations. Delusions and catatonic reactions were to be expected with each breakthrough of strong orgonotic streamings in her body. She would perceive

these sensations with terror, she would block them off
by bodily rigidity, and the blocked-off plasmatic
currents would be transferred into destructive impulses.
Therefore the 'secondary' impulses which derive from
the blocking of the original basic emotions, would have
to be handled carefully, and would have to be 'let out',
slowly, step by step. This danger would become
especially great when the first spontaneous orgastic
contractions of her organism would begin to occur.[5]

Pleasure in fact needs to be finely tuned to the energetic
capacity of the organism. The analogy is that of warmth for a
person with frostbite. The frozen tissues need warmth, but too
much warmth too quickly will damage the tissues and
produce an adverse reaction. 'While warmth offers promise',
Lowen wrote, 'it also poses danger. The thaw may produce a
flood which will overflow the banks.'[4]

A woman in a group, whom I shall call Rachel, had
recently had a strong psychotic reaction, with depersonalisation, unreality, flight and suicidal feelings. It turned out that
the precipitating trigger for her crisis was the receiving of a
massage from a well-meaning person with therapeutic
intentions. What the massage did was to create too sudden a
thaw, to open up her boundaries, weaken her already weak
ego sense, and precipitate her into an identity crisis. Even very
light massage can be, in such circumstances, an intense
provocation. In working with this person shortly after the
psychotic reaction, I asked her to teach me the kind of body
work that, whilst it could be pleasurable, also confirmed her
sense of her own boundary. She taught me that firm touch,
which gave her a clear experience of the edge of her body, was
the right kind of experience at this time. We also worked with
the flow of pleasure through active movements which gave
her a sense of herself as agent, rather than just as passive
recipient. I found many of the concepts derived from contact
dance[11] very useful in this work. Albert Pesso has also devoted
an entire book to the discussion of different qualities of ego

participation or surrender in qualities of movement.[12]

Contrastingly, whereas Rachel had been precipitated into a fairly psychotic space by being unexpectedly unbounded, Morton Herskowitz has given an enthralling account[13] of how he brought someone out of a catatonic state of mutism by providing nurturing body contact. Everything depends on the presence of the helper and his sense of the other person's private space, boundary and inner reality.

The man was in his early thirties and was seen in the emergency room of a general hospital.

> The patient sat on the examining table staring into space. His face was pale, with pallor most marked in the region of the forehead. His lips were pressed together, not tightly, and there was slight circumoral pallor. His body was of the asthenic type, held still, but not rigidly. The extremities were warm. Movement of the chest with respiration was barely visible. . .
>
> The therapist, always seeking to establish eye contact, sat facing the patient, and took his hands, stroking them softly. After ten or fifteen minutes the patient began to regard his hands with an uncomprehending look, sometimes tracing the outlines of the fingers of one hand with the other. The therapist repeated, 'That's your hand, Joe. That's your hand'. . . The gentle and unenforced contact melts the patient a little and he gives a few tearless sobs and breathes somewhat more freely.
>
> A move to touch the patient's lips gently with a finger was met with physical withdrawal. It was clear that a new equilibrium had been established with increased reactivity and increased anxiety.
>
> After a time the patient did not move away when the therapist stroked his forehead and periocular area for several minutes. He became involved with a pillow lying on the examination table, touching the pillow cover then the pillow inside, apparently unable to

establish the connection between them. The therapist
pulled the pillow out, and then replaced the cover,
repeating this several times with an explanation. This
seemed to quiet the anxiety and the patient could now
be induced to lie down with his head on the pillow.

The therapist laid his cheek upon the patient's and
cuddled the patient to him. In this manner the patient
fell asleep and slept for five to ten minutes. He awoke
with a start and asked, 'Where am I?'. . .

When asked if he would like something to drink, he
asked for a glass of milk and after drinking it, he was
discharged into the care of his family physician.[13]

This was purely an example of emotional first aid. Eva
Reich[14] has described the possibilities of short-term help in
general practice, and Herskowitz's work with the catatonic
man is an excellent example of what she talks about. In
discussing his work with this man, Morton Herskowitz
emphasises several points.[13]

1 He relates the perceptual block to the loss of ego
   boundaries and diffusion of the energy field.
2 He works with the eye segment 'by attempting direct
   eye confrontation with the hope of eliciting a
   response in the patient's eyes, by stroking the
   patient's forehead, by giving simple explanations for
   simple acts, and by examining simple relationships
   in an attempt to stimulate the brain to recognise
   what it already knew when it functioned as a
   thinking organ'.
3 He uses non-provocative body contact to melt the
   catatonic defence down gradually: 'the attempt to get
   the patient's energy moving involved the principle of
   super-imposition of energy fields' – in this case the
   direct excitation of the patient's energy system by the
   therapist's.
4 He paces this contact at a rate the patient can accept:
   'at this point the therapist's stroking and vocal

contact enabled the patient to gradually tolerate a
larger energy movement and increased contact. The
final gentle contact and cuddling permitted the
expansion of the patient's energy system to the point
of sleep and produced relaxation of the acute
armouring.'

The nurturing contact that Herskowitz made possible may
suggest that he encourages regression. He acts towards this
thirty-year-old man in some respects as though he is a needy
infant. In other respects, however, through the eye contact,
voice contact and adult style of communication, he treats him
as an equal. His work has the effect, whether intended in this
way or not, of bringing the adult and the child in this man
somewhat closer together. But the whole question of the
advantages and disadvantages of regression will be discussed
at greater length shortly.

Fritz Perls[15] has described how the ability to withdraw from
a close relationship is almost a prerequisite for the ability to
enter into it. There is a pulsation between contact and
withdrawal, just as there is between waking and sleeping. The
schizophrenic tends to move to the extremes, either being
helplessly dependent on a symbiotic relationship without
which he feels he has no reality or life blood, or freezing
himself into an emotional desert in a desperate attempt to
cling to a precarious independence.

Cornelius and Marianne Bakker have written a fascinating
book[16] which explores human territoriality. The book is
concerned with how we make our boundaries. They describe
territory as 'that area of an individual's life which he
experiences as his own, in which he exerts control, takes
initiative, has expertise, or accepts responsibility. It is the
realm in which a person has a sense of independence and feels
free to act on his own initiative.' Among the areas in which a
person needs to feel secure, in order to have a firm sense of
identity, is his personal space.

Each person maintains a certain distance between

himself and others, depending on the type of relationship and the situation. There is an invisible barrier surrounding each individual, the penetration of which he responds to with a vague sense of discomfort and an automatic attempt to re-establish the previous distance.

They continue:

Schizophrenic patients require a greater distance for comfort than non-schizophrenics. It is important to remember that approaching an animal closer than the 'fight distance' often reacts in an attack if no opportunity exists for that animal to retreat. The same response occurs with human beings who feel extremely threatened and see no way out. In approaching this type of individual, therefore, it is crucial to leave him ample room to move away. Awareness of these spatial aspects of man's territoriality is of practical value to the person who deals with psychiatric patients. Considerable trouble can be avoided by carefully assessing the degree of closeness which each patient can comfortably tolerate, always leaving him an avenue of escape.[16]

Professor Nikolaas Tinbergen,[17] the ethologist, understood this principle. His lifetime of work understanding behavioural signs in wild life had taught him respect for the meaning of human body signals. His way of making contact with autistic children was as follows. He walked into a room full of autistic children and understood their avoidance of eye contact as a signal that they were avoiding approaching him. He respected that signal and proceeded to occupy himself in the middle of the room, whilst avoiding any attempt to initiate contact. After a time the children read his body signals to be that of a strange adult who was not demanding that they respond to him. (In the behavioural treatment of autism, by contrast, children are punished for avoidance of contact and rewarded for going through the motions of contact.) Tinbergen is showing us that it is possible to resonate with a withdrawn child without escalating the threshold of approach so fast that it runs away for that reason. The withdrawn children began to approach the non-approaching Tinbergen. At first they would make slight nudging movements, like a hand brushing a knee, still not looking at him. He would make a responsive nudge back. Eventually they would give him a quick glance and would immediately avert their gaze. Tinbergen did likewise. When the children discovered that they had in the room an adult who was non-intrusive they came increasingly out of their barricaded autistic habit-patterns.

Jan Foudraine, whose work will be described more fully later, also learned this in his dealings with chronic schizophrenics. He describes a particular patient, Walter.

> It became clear to me that in the whole range and depth of our contact I have got much too close to him. I see with my own eyes what the 'terror of closeness', this panic that is bound up with our deepening contact, really means. Walter can feel himself dissolving once more and melting symbiotically into me. In the course of a dramatic session I explain to him that at last I understand this terror he has of merging and melting away. Matching his deed to the word, I push my chair as far as possible away from him into the corner of the room and it seems to me that he suddenly quietens down. He starts to nod approval. 'Yes, it's much better like that, we must keep our distance. Your eyes are blue and mine are brown.'[18]

Contrastingly, other work with autistic children by Burton Schaffner seems to be successful by virtue of the fact that it dissolves some of the boundaries. Based on his work with rhesus monkeys (paralleling that of Harlow and Harlow), he found that if autistic children are placed in an office chair and swivelled round and round for about a minute, there is, immediately afterwards, eye-contact, person-to-person contact and impassioned gestures to repeat the experience. His theory is that this motion stimulates the inner ear – one of the earliest active sense organs. To many others the experience would be one of disorientation or dizziness.

The ultimate form of privacy and inner personal space, according to the Bakkers, is the realm of thought and fantasy. They discuss the need for not feeling invaded by over-demanding people.

> Personal ideas must be shared voluntarily if one is to preserve a sense of integrity. Interestingly, the most severe psychiatric disorder, schizophrenia, has as its most ominous symptom the patient's feeling that he has lost all privacy. He complains that his thoughts are controlled by others and that his every idea is immediately read by those around him. He feels like an open book, not by choice, but because powerful forces have penetrated his innermost being.[16]

There is another major dimension of human territoriality, described by the Bakkers as 'action territory', which they define as 'the area in which a person considers it his prerogative to act, exert control, make decisions, exercise his expertise and take responsibility, in other words an area of action which a person claims as his own'.

Showing how the loss of action territory can precipitate a psychosis, they give the instance of a young woman, living in a very critical family, who was continually undervalued.

> She seemed to have no psychological space or action territory whatever in this family, except for one small niche that over time she had carved out for herself. Every night after dinner she cleaned the kitchen and did the dishes . . . Her mother appreciated the help and vaguely recognised that it was of some importance to her daughter.[16]

One evening, in a tense family situation, or possibly by accident, she drops a plate which lands on two crystal glasses and shatters them. Her mother gets angry and shouts at her, 'You stupid thing, you can't even wash the dishes without breaking them. I will have to do them myself from now on.' The girl flies into a rage, breaks some more plates deliberately, rushes out of the kitchen into her bedroom and suddenly switches her freaking-out reaction into a freaking-in. When the parents got to the room:

> Her speech was totally incoherent. They tried to calm her . . . but no degree of comforting had any effect. Eventually they called the doctor and the girl was admitted to hospital where during the first days she uttered incomprehensible sentences, repeating over and over that she was dead and that the people around her were dead, a sentence no one really understood.

The Bakkers go on and explain the implication of their example in terms of action territory: 'If an individual has an exceedingly small territory he cannot take any risk with it, for when he loses it he may have nothing left, and having no territory is equivalent to not being alive.' Indeed they go much further and make the statement that the sense of personal identity is founded on the establishment of individual territory, both internal (personal space) and external (action territory).

Growth is an expansion of the body; psychological growth is an expansion of territory, an enrichment of one's inner life, the acquisition of new and personally meaningful skills, and the willingness to share one's life-space with others. 'Love, work and knowledge are the well-springs of life', which Reich took as his motto. In pursuit of our love, our work and our knowledge, we are aggressive in the straightforward meaning of the word that Reich used – to move forward expansively. The Bakkers define aggression in a precisely similar way.

> In no way does aggression imply destructiveness. . . It is a phenomenon which lies at the root of life itself. Life is dynamic, it moves, it grows and expands beyond

141

narrow boundaries. Aggression does not refer to
anything that is either good or bad in itself; it is simply
an integral part of the living community of man.[16]

If aggression is the attempt to move a person's boundaries
outwards, regression is defined by the Bakkers as the act of
moving boundaries inwards, with a resulting loss of territory.
To give up your individuality, to lose your mind, to lose touch
with your body, to have your personal space invaded by others
and your thoughts read – all these are regressive situations in
the territorial use of the word. The Bakkers point out that this
is in many respects different from the use of the word
regression in the psychiatric sense. In schizophrenia we have
the paradox that territorial regression and the loss of
boundaries is a basic characteristic of such a state, yet in
psychiatric work regression is sometimes recommended as a
form of therapy. I will now attempt to throw some light on
this apparent contradiction or paradox.

In an earlier chapter I distinguished between tactical and
strategic regression. In tactical regression a person makes a
contract with a therapist or a therapeutic community to
surrender his normal attempts to cope in the adult world, and
to go back to a much earlier developmental stage in order to
experience re-parenting. The aim of tactical regression is to
grow up by first giving up the unsatisfactory style of being
pseudo-grown-up. Jacqui Lee Schiff, who has mounted
community re-parenting programes for psychotic adolescents,
claims that:

> Psychotic regression will usually be to an age prior to
> the beginning of the pathology, prior to one year of
> age. The person will then proceed through the
> developmental sequence of maturation at an average
> rate of one developmental year per three to six weeks.[19]

The best known and most fully-documented instance of
therapeutic regression is that of Mary Barnes, who spent
several years at Kingsley Hall, a community set up by R. D.

Laing. Here she lived out different stages of infantile disturbance and finally learnt how to re-grow into a more integrated and non-psychotic person.

It is difficult to distinguish how far it is the reliving of childhood traumas in itself which is the therapeutic factor, and how far it is the deep and powerful relationships that are formed with the re-parenters, that is the really decisive healing element. Joe Berke, the therapist who saw Mary Barnes through her long journey, and co-authored the book about this experience,[20] described the role of regression as that of positive disintegration (in contrast to an unsupported schizophrenic breakdown, which usually leads to negative disintegration).

> A great deal of what might be called by a psychiatrist 'regression' is a person's natural attempt at self-healing. Our work, and what we consider the proper work of the therapist, is to help a person along the road of his or her distintegrative experience – provide the essential services, food, a warm place, a nice atmosphere – and let the breakdown and recovery happen without interference. Then the return trip – the integrative phase – will be a very healing experience.[21]

Strategic regression, as I call it, is a different matter. Here the goal is not to grow up, but to go back to a womb-like state as a matter of preference. There are at least three ways in which this can occur.

In the first case a patient regresses without a contract. Jacqui Schiff insists that all regressive patients should be told not to do this and that this message be reinforced. She regards this kind of regression as quite unproductive and stresses that 'it is important for the person (the therapist) to incorporate clear prohibitions against regressing without a contract and a structure adequate enough to provide care'.[19]

Sometimes a person who is undergoing a supported regression attempts to exceed the terms of the contract. A critical time in the experience of Mary Barnes was when she tried to demand from her community that they tube-feed her. She was refusing to take food through the mouth and had the fantasy that tube-feeding was a closer re-experiencing of the umbilical situation. The therapist dealt with this situation by making a clear decision; tube-feeding was not possible (or even desirable?) and Mary must agree to take nourishment as a condition of their being able to continue helping her. If this seems like the therapist controlling the patient, we need only reflect for a moment on the vast powers to manipulate therapists that uncontrolled regression can offer to people. The Bakkers point out that there is a considerable overlap between the psychiatric and the territorial meaning of the word 'regression' and they add:

> A reduction in social functioning and a return to child-like behaviour usually results in a loss of territory, but this sequence does not always hold. In many instances a person uses child-like behaviour to gain territory. Sometimes such behaviour functions as a weapon; and although it may seem to be regressive in the psychiatric sense of the word, in territorial terms it turns out to be aggressive.[16]

Similarly, Jacqui Schiff says that 'in relation to the external environment, regression is an attempt to elicit a symbiotic response which will get the Child taken care of in some manner, though perhaps not the kind of care that is needed'.[19]

In contrast to the therapeutic use of regression and the manipulative use of it, there is a form of regression which creeps up insidiously and leads to an excessively unbounded state physically. It corresponds to what I have earlier called 'spacing out'. Aaron Esterson uses the term 'reversion' to refer to this process. Since Esterson was, with Laing, one of the founders of the 'anti-psychiatrist' group that pioneered the foundation of Kingsley Hall, his remarks are particularly important.

Reversion may be seen as a form of regression carried past what seems to be the individual's personal historic starting point. While regression is an emotional and experimental going-back in personal time, reversion involves entering a world without time. There appears to be a varying period after biological birth during which there is no continuing experience of person continuity in space and time. In reversion the person may experience himself carried back to this period and to the period spent in the womb before biological birth.[22]

Esterson describes reversion in a way that corresponds closely to the state I describe as disembodiment earlier. On the spectrum of arousal, there is a pulsation between the 'I' and the 'Self' which was well described by Ronald Fischer.[23] The grounded mystic is able to surrender his sense of having an independence and to dip deeply into the experience of oneness, merging and the cosmic sense of self. The schizophrenic on the other hand has only a frail ego, which dissolves easily and plunges himself into a universal but fragmented sense of *the inability to differentiate*. Sometimes he seeks this state actively; sometimes he falls into it; sometimes he guards against it with all his powers. Laing has described the polarity between *engulfment* and *petrification*:

> Instead of the polarities of separatedness and relatedness based on individual autonomy, there is the antithesis between complete loss of being by absorption into the other person (engulfment) and complete aloneness (isolation).[24]

Laing sees the schizoid person as devoting his whole effort to preserving his self.

> This as we have pointed out is precariously established; he is subject to the dread of his own dissolution into non-being; into what William Blake described in the last resort as a 'chaotic non-entity'. He is prepared to write off everything he is, except his 'self'. But the tragic

145

paradox is that the more the self is defended in this way, the more it is destroyed. The apparent eventual destruction and dissolution of the self in schizophrenic conditions is accomplished not by external attacks from the enemy (actual or supposed) from without, but by the devastation caused by the inner defensive manoeuvres themselves.[24]

It is part of this paradox that reversion offers both the glimpse and promise of preserving a deeper and more fundamental self, and, once the pulsation between inner-withdrawal and outer-connectedness is lost, it creates a cocoon of unearthliness that wraps the schizoid individual around like an impenetrable cloud. Let us listen to Esterson again, describing both the hope and the danger of uncontrolled reversion.

Reversion may occur in the course of a project of self-discovery, as in yoga exercises, or during psychoanalysis, where the logic of the enterprise requires the person to allow himself to enter the pre-personal and non-personal regions. Or it may be the outcome of personal fragmentation in a social situation that is experienced as unlivable due to mystifying interpersonal pressures. Or it may result, for instance, from the action of chemical agents, such as mescaline, LSD, and the like. . .

In the timeless world of reversion there is no experience of self and not-self, no distinction between here and not-here, no perceptual discrimination. The person is, therefore, helpless and socially dependent. The experience is non-egoic and pre-egoic. By egoic experience I mean 'I' experience, . . . the pattern of experience and being of a discrete self experiencing discretely in respect of others. . .

A personal or egoic self distinguishes constantly between self and others. During reversion the capacity to discriminate perceptually is lost in varying degrees.

For instance, in complete reversion the 'I' becomes

lost without trace in what may be termed the 'primary matrix of experience'. The person experiences total dissolution of himself, i.e. of personal self and personal identity.[22]

Where a person follows a spiritual pathway with proper preparation, guidance and discipline, there becomes possible what Esterson calls a successful reversion, which he likens to a regressive–progressive movement in which the person uses their ecstatic experience of transcendental truth as a way of facilitating a new personal *emergence*.

Where reversion is used negatively, it becomes a withdrawal from relationships and a defence against personal experience (including early personal experiences recontacted during regression). Esterson writes:

> For instance manifestations may be experienced which have been variously termed 'archetypal', 'mystical', 'spiritual', 'transcendental', 'mythological', 'cosmogenic' and so on. These phenomena must be evaluated dialectically if the experience is to be assimilated by the person. *Otherwise he may become assimilated by the experience. . .*
>
> Thus reversion involves considerable risk, and if undergone by a person who is not sufficiently already truly centred it is liable to lead to personal catastrophe. It is often experienced as a rebirth, but a rebirth is a birth, a new beginning – an infancy, not manhood or womanhood. In my view the ecstasy of reversion should not be regarded as a position that can be reached by repeatedly repeating the experience.[22]

The problem in therapeutic groups is that these are sometimes set up in order to help people who are over-identified with a rigid worldly ego to loosen its grip on their consciousness. But if people come to such a group, whose need is diametrically opposite – to form an intact personal core of identity or to establish a fuller or more grounded personal territory – then the risk of precipitating psychoses for such people from the group experience will be great. Esterson's view of these two types of people is expressed in terms of the analogy of passing through a rent in the fabric of a veil in the Jewish temple which hides the Holy of Holies.

> There are two forms of danger, both the result of a rent so to speak in the veil's fabric. . .
>
> On the one hand there is the person so afraid of what may emerge through the rent he is engaged in a defence that results in him being so radically alienated from the possibility of experiencing the worlds of phantasy and the transcendental. At the other extreme is the person so totally immersed in emerging phantasy and transcendental experience, that he is radically divorced from the shared world of social reality. To be healed each must discover that from which he is divorced, and he must do so in a way that allows the integrity of the veil to be reconstituted.[22]

Laing in his later period seemed to some to confuse the disoriented schizophrenic state with the clarity and orientation of the mystic. A group who contributed to a symposium on anti-psychiatry in 1970, feeling that Laing's confusion here was in contrast with his earlier insights in *The Divided Self*, wrote:

> Laing implies that the person in a schizophrenic state has abandoned his ego, has gotten rid of it and has therefore approached the truth of the mystic . . . The schizophrenic in fact has to first get his ego back together again before he can start to lose it in a mystical way. But while one is in this state of fractured ego it is easy to think of oneself as having lost it. And thus on an intense acid trip one is very likely to say 'I'm the budda' or something to that effect. But it is only to be lost a short time later.[25]

Coming to the other side of the dynamic, Esterson's term

'emergence' is in contrast to the experience of merging. It restores the lost half of the pulsation between the inner and outer.

Getting the ego back together may be helped by rebuilding the banks of the nervous system, as in mega-vitamin therapy, or by the skilled grounding of energies in therapy that focuses on re-embodiment. It may be helped by that form of skilled regression that allows a person to slough off a false-self like a dead skin and, under protracted conditions, grow a new ego to act as a healthy membrane at the interface between the person's inner life and outer world.

But there is a third form of regression that we meet in this survey of treatment possibilities for schizophrenics. That is the regression induced by institutional care. Jan Foudraine, a Dutch psychiatrist, has devoted a whole book to a critique of institutional care for psychotic people, believing that the help provided by most hospitals perpetuates a conspiracy of symbiotic-interdependent relationships that reinforce passive dependency and regressive inactivity and increase the initial weakness of the ego.

Foudraine's work is of the profoundest importance to anyone who seeks to provide non-symbiotic help to a person in a schizophrenic crisis. It is essential reading to those who need concrete support for the belief that it is possible to effect even long-term chronic schizophrenia by a wholesale re-designing of the milieu in order to strengthen and re-inforce the latent adult in each person. Foudraine believes that there is sense latent in the apparent 'nonsense' of schizophrenic conversation. He gives many examples of this approach, with rich human detail, and proves that it is possible to carry out meaningful creative relationships with people, who for decades have opted out of all meaningful creative relation-ships. The title of his book, *Not Made of Wood*, speaks for itself.[18]

Foudraine's approach is totally consistent with the work of the Bakkers, though his is focused specifically on schizo-phrenic states, and their approach was not. He helps the schizophrenics recover their lost territory, to expand it and to re-root themselves in the social world. He sees the central task of therapy as to strengthen the weak ego and to encourage the resumption of responsibility, self-directedness and self-formation. At first his 'patients' were incredulous that he credited them with a long disused capacity for maturity. So were the staff, long trained to regard their chronic care patients as semi-vegetables.

In building his relationships with these people, Foudraine respected their territorial integrity, the boundary of the self that his work was trying to reconstruct. He worked at the interface of dependence and independence, recognising that the twin rocks that shipwreck so many attempts at the therapy of schizophrenia are those same rocks that Laing pointed to: the rock of engulfment into symbiosis; and the rock of retreat into incommunicability and isolation. 'In approaching a person living on the edge of disintegration', he writes, 'it is essential to strike a balance between giving too little and too much support.'[18] Theodore Lidz similarly emphasises:

> One must not love the patient in the sense of their being a diminution of the boundaries between the therapist's self and the patient's. He must get the patient to utilise his own perceptions of things, not depend on the therapist's to validate his own perception which has been denied over and over again in the family.[26]

There is no contradiction between the ego-approach of Foudraine and the energetic approach of Wilhelm Reich. Both are aware of the duality of conscious and unconscious processes. We have seen how Reich's work relieved the pressures of the id and so made it easier for the ego functions of motility and perception to integrate themselves in a more ordered way. We also saw how Reich paced his work skilfully to avoid fragmenting the ego with too strong a surge of emotional material. Foudraine found a variety of methods of strengthening the weak ego and learned that it was then able to involve itself actively, without too much dependency, in the process of making sense of the turbulent inner life. 'When one has seen autism of many years' standing', he wrote, 'melt like snow under the sun and the "defective condition" unfold in the relationship with the psychotherapist in a rich diversity of emotions, one is no longer satisfied as a psychotherapist with the terminology employed in psychiatry.'[18]

As Walter, Foudraine's autistic patient said, as the snow began to melt: *'Help me become a man, keep your distance, and leave most of the psychotherapy to me.'*

CHAPTER 10

INNER GROUND

Essence and existence

Wilhelm Reich distinguished between a tertiary, secondary and primary layer in people's emotional drives.[1] The tertiary layer was the level of character defences, substitute contacts and the conformist social veneer, well-adapted to the culture pattern. The secondary layer was the repressed unconscious with its forbidden drives, frequently destructive or confused. The primary layer was made up of spontaneous impulses to reach out and make contact.

The primary layer of expression is that which is described by John Pierrakos[2] as containing the 'core feelings'. It is the blockage and frustration of these which produces the destructive and raging middle layer. Psychoanalysis knew only of two layers, which it called the 'conscious' and the 'unconscious'. The unconscious was the territory of the id, with its nightmares, its polymorphous perverse sexuality and its impulses to destroy. It is no wonder that the early Freudians concluded that 'an adequate degree of repression is necessary for a healthy mind'.

Reich claimed that if the destructive impulses of the secondary layer could be released from repression and dissolved, the healthy expression of the primary drives in each person would manifest themselves spontaneously. He observed this in therapy when he worked with the fundamental expressive language of the body at deep levels of plasma relaxation.

Experience with people in groups and of people who have gone through therapeutic systems that emphasise tapping the primal pools of pain, like primal therapy, do not always or necessarily confirm Reich's finding. Thus nowhere in the literature on primal therapy do we find a clear description of the qualities of vegetative aliveness and contactful warmth that Reich described for people responding from their primary feelings. This need not surprise us, since Janov has focused principally on the brain rather than on the expressive language of the body, as it is understood by those who work with bio-energy directly.

I believe it is possible, in some of the cathartic therapies, to go on for a very long time with the discharge of bad feelings, without necessarily contacting the good ones. Some people, who may have masochistic inclinations, may be attracted to the raw discharge of painful feelings as an end in itself. I have known people who did this so violently that it led to intestinal inflammation and ulcer formation. It is possible, in other words, to get stuck in the second layer.

One of the reasons that Reich succeeded in eliciting the deeper vegetative streamings and plasma currents from the primary layer is his extraordinary sensitivity as a therapist and his own deep sense for natural life expressions. He recognised how easy it was to use fear to block rage, or rage to block fear, so creating vicious cycles with no natural point of closure, and his skill as a therapist allowed him to interrupt these and lead a person towards deeper sources and resources in himself.[3]

Freud, in his book on the ego and the id, understood the task of describing how the ego arose by diffentiation from the id. Freud looks on the nucleus of the ego as being formed by the systems of external perception and consciousness which he refers to as the *superficial system*. Freud recognises that the ego is much more than this, since it also includes factors of internal perception. He writes:

It seems that another factor, besides the influence of the system Perception, has been at work in bringing about the formation of the ego and its differentiation from the id. The body itself, and above all its surfaces, is a place from which both external and internal perceptions may spring. The ego is first and foremost a body ego; it is not merely a surface entity, but it is itself the projection of a surface.[4]

Alexander Lowen, in a very clear account of the Freudian view of the ego, in the chapter on 'Somatic aspects of ego psychology' in his first book, comments on Freud's statements in these words.

The ego is a surface phenomenon, both physically and somatically. The system perception-conscious lies at the surface of the cerebral cortex. This enables us to comprehend Freud's statement that the ego is a projection of a surface onto a surface.[5]

Not only is the ego a function of the cortex, the outer rind of the brain, but brain tissue itself is formed from ectoderm, the outer of the three embryonic layers.

The study of character was part of Freudian ego-psychology. The relationship between the concept of character and the concept of the ego has been well expressed by Lowen.

The relationship between the ego and the character is involved. The ego is fundamentally a subjective perception of the self, whereas the character and personality are objective appreciations. But the patient's description of his own ego is noteworthy for its unreliability. The patient thinks of his ego in terms of his ego ideal, which expresses some inherent capacity rather than an actual function. Thus the analyst has to construct the true ego from a determination of the character structure and an appraisal of the personality.[5]

Lowen goes on, in a footnote, to quote Otto Fenichel's statement that character consisted of 'the ego's habitual modes of adjustment to the external world, the id and the superego, and the characteristic types of combining these modes with one another'.[5]

The history of psychoanalysis is the story of the attempt to resolve the problems of human emotional suffering by analysing the contents of the mind. By the process of free-association the contents of both the conscious and the unconscious mind could be drawn from a patient in the form of a stream of consciousness, dreams, images, memories and verbal communications. One of the difficulties the psychoanalysts ran into was the blockages that people put in the way of such a free flow of consciousness. The mind blocked itself with mind games. These came to be studied as the character traps. Ways of working with character, such as transactional analysis, try to use mind-methods of pointing out the mind-traps.

When Reich developed character-analysis, he discovered that ego states are rooted in bodily attitudes and that consistent work on character-attitudes led to the emergence of spontaneous bodily movements. Eventually he moved more and more to working directly on the bodily tension states. A therapy like gestalt therapy, which was an outgrowth from Reichian character-analysis, focused some attention on the body but continued to work primarily through the analysis of the various mind games, projections, introjections and retroflections, that people used as character-disguises at the tertiary level of defence.

Philosophers and psychologists have argued for years about ways of defining mind and the relation of mind to body. Pioneers in the growth movement sometimes duck neatly out of this dilemma by using a term like 'bodymind' to describe the complex interaction between psychic and somatic events.

In the light of the way that ego and character are defined above we could take the view that *mind is the outside of the body*. This is true in many senses. It is physiologically true in that mind activity, thinking, is a function of the cortex, which is an outer surface; it is psychologically true, in the light of Freud's statement that the ego is a projection of a surface on to

a surface; it is true in terms of the fact that most of the
information that circulates through our minds has come from
distance receptors, particularly the eyes and ears, and that the
chief way we make clear what is in our mind is by speaking it.
Written language enables a person to express the contents of
his mind to the ends of the earth and for centuries into the
future. Even those of occult persuasion should agree, since
'the mental and emotional bodies' of occult tradition are
usually portrayed as envelopes surrounding the physical
body. In psychic research thinking is sometimes regarded as
some kind of radiation emitted by the organism. A person
may sit in a cloud of psychic impressions, a combination of
emanations from a number of sources.

But if the mind is the outside of the body, we can say that
the body is the inside of the mind. Every ego-state reflects a
bodily attitude; every character expression has a physiological
anchoring. We see regularly in therapeutic work how a person
who tries to share, through the mind, what is going on in his
life, is sometimes speaking from his character-trap. Interrupt-
ing the verbal communication, in such cases, elicits the true
message hidden within, or underneath, the surface expression.
In Stanley Keleman's expressive phrase, the body begins to
speak its mind,[6] using, of course, a non-verbal language.

It is not difficult to realise why, compared with the
machinations of the mind, the body is fundamental. This is
how Rajneesh puts it in answering a question as to why
tantra puts so much importance on the body.

> You were born as a body; you live as a body; you
> become ill as a body; you are treated, given medicine,
> helped, made whole and healthy, as a body. You
> become young as a body; you will become old as a
> body; you will die as a body. Your whole life is body
> centred, centred around the body. You will love
> someone. You will make love to someone, and you will
> create other bodies: you will reproduce other bodies. . .
> You can go beyond, but that journey has to be through

the body, by the body and you have to use the body. But why do you ask? Because the body is just the outer thing.[7]

How can the body be the 'outer thing'? Wilhelm Reich distinguished between the flesh and the body. He wrote:

In the distinction between the 'body' and the 'flesh' in early Christianity, our present orgonomic distinction between the 'primary' naturally inborn drives ('God') and the 'secondary' perverted evil drives (Devil, sin) was anticipated. . . The sharp antithesis of 'god' (spiritual-ised body) and 'devil' (body degenerated into flesh) this tragedy is plainly known and expressed.[8]

The body is an outer thing because it is lit up from within by what Reich calls a healing power. We are talking here about matters that are beyond normal physiology, which does not recognise a specific life energy, nor is it able to come to terms with that depth quality that moves the tissues and makes the protoplasm sparkle. What lies at the heart of the body? The literal heart is a physiological pump. Surgeons can now transplant it. We need a word for the living force that vitalises the flesh. We could call it soul. Such a word need not have specific theological associations. Negroes speak of soul music. Morton Schatzman has written a book called *Soul Murder* which deals with the crippling psychosis suffered by Daniel Schreber. 'The term "soul murder" ', Schreber writes, 'is already in current usage and refers to the idea widespread in the folk lore and poetry of all peoples that it is somehow possible to take possession of another person's soul.' Schatzman writes:

What is called psychosis may be, at least sometimes, an attempt gone awry to awaken from a daze in which one was put as a child. Schreber's father, it seems, had put his son to sleep, in a sense, in early childhood. The son partially awoke to this awareness while thought mad. 'At the time when my nervous illness seemed almost incurable, I gained the conviction that soul murder had been attempted on me by somebody.'[9]

We say, of someone in a psychotic state, that he is 'out of his mind'. It would be more accurate to say that he is out of his body. In many schizoid or schizophrenic states there is the feeling that the body has become an object, the core of the person, the basic identity has no room inside it, feels banished, cannot put down roots into flesh.[3]

Schatzman's story of how Schreber was crippled by the paranoid upbringing from his father is an extreme version of the process of human armouring that Reich called 'the murder of Christ'. The mind deadens, the body stiffens or freezes, the soul has difficulty glowing. Reich's description of a healthy child makes clear his view of the inner soul quality that lights up a happy person.

> The child of the future is gentle, loving, giving freely and gladly. Its movements are harmonious and its voice is melodious. Its eyes sparkle with a gentle glow and look into the world with a quiet deep gaze. It is soft in its touch of hands. It can stroke so that the stroked one begins to radiate his own life energy. This is the badly misinterpreted 'healing power' of Jesus Christ. . . The healing power of Christ, later on so badly distorted by armoured man into mercenary cheapness, is a well understood and easily observable quality in all men and women who are endowed with natural leadership. Their strong orgone energy fields are capable of exciting the sluggish 'dead' energy systems of the wretched and miserable. This induced excitation of the weak living system is experienced as relief from the tenseness and anxiety, due to the expansion of the nervous system, and even provides a quiet, kindly, lovely glow of true love in an otherwise hateful organism. The excited bio-energy in the weak is capable of expanding the blood-vessels, of inducing better blood supply to the tissues, of improving the healing of

wounds, of counteracting the stale, degenerative effects of stagnant life energy. . .

Nothing whatsoever can destroy this glowing silent force. It penetrates everything and governs every move in every cell in the living organism. . . This glow in the feel of the skin is to the true physician a sign of the health of a human being, just as its absence is a sign to him of the presence of sickness. In fever, this glow grows fierce since it fights the deadly infection. It is the glowing of the life force which continues after the death of the body. It is the glow of the soul.[8]

In using this language, which transcends normal physiology, Reich is not committed to any specific beliefs or religious doctrines. He is, however, introducing a deeper dimension, the primary dimension of existence, the dimension of a person's inner depth.

John Pierrakos, who together with Alexander Lowen was one of the founders of bio-energetics, felt that working with the body, deep though that process, was not deep enough. He wrote:

My experience with patients showed the need to reach deeper than the functions of the body, the negative unconscious and the analytic mind. To lead to true integration, the healing work needed to centre on the life-affirming consciousness that is the human core. Excluding the person's spirituality from therapy came to seem like shearing off a pyramid.[10]

We are not talking about ideas of spirituality, in any mystical or disembodied sense. Reich has shown how most organised religions talk about the ideal of the spirit, but will kill the spirit whenever it lights up in a boy's or girl's eyes. Rajneesh writes:

The closer a thing is, the more difficult it is to see it; the closest almost impossible; because eyes need a certain space, perspective, to see. I can see you but if I go on

coming closer and closer everything will be blurred:
your face will be blurred, lines will lose their shape, and
if I go on coming and coming and just put my eyes on
your face, nothing will be seen – your face will become
a wall. But still I can see a little because a little distance
will be there.

   Not even that much distance exists between you and
the real. It is just touching your eyes. It is just touching
your skin – not only that, it is penetrating the skin. It is
moving in your blood. It is beating in your heartbeat. It
is you.[11]

Stanley Keleman said to me, a few years ago, that he had given
up working on character defences and body blocks. He had
begun to work directly on the core. To work in this way is to
tap a true healing ability. I am talking about what goes on
when we touch people. Body therapists learned long ago to
leave behind the taboo that prevented the psychoanalysts from
any warm physical contact with those they sought to help and
have brought in many skills and repertoires of physical touch,
massage and manipulation, aimed at softening the bodily
rigidities and giving a person more contact with their inner
energy flow.

   To touch another person involves much more than
technique. There are times when technique can kill the spirit
of what it seeks to transmit. Thus to push hard on the armour
may break through a key resistance, only to have a person
tighten up somewhere else. Many years ago Alexander Lowen
taught us that it is possible in this way to chase the tensions
round the body. Again, Rajneesh has written beautifully on
the trans-physiological dimensions of touching.

   You can eat things without tasting; it is not difficult.
   You can touch someone without touching; it is not
   difficult. We are already doing it. You shake hands with
   someone without touching him because to touch, *you*
   have to come to the hand, you have to move to the
   hand. You have to become your fingers and your palm

as if you, your soul, has come to the hand. Only then can you touch. You can take someone's hand in your hand and withdraw. You can withdraw; then the dead hand is there. It appears to be touching, but it is not touching.[12]

Anne Parks, in teaching her style of deeply intuitive massage, used the phrase 'calling a person into his body'. It is a kind of summoning. Stanley Keleman once said that, when his therapy went deepest, he found that he was functioning like an energy reservoir which could call people into the world. Because many people banish themselves from the body, they are not at home there. And sometimes all the warmth and contactfulness from a therapist may not be enough to summon them.

A woman called Caroline came to me for therapy because her emotional and sexual life was confused. She had learned that her body was something that was responded to by people who had no feeling for her inner-ness and for her quality of experience. She had come to distrust it deeply as a bridge for feelings. Her thoughts were confused, her energy level was low. In spite of this, she made clear eye contact. The therapy worked at trying to revive the flow of feeling in her tissues. It tried to warm up the skin surface, improve the circulation, and mobilise her breathing. In spite of some progress I felt dissatisfied with her response. It was as though an invisible wall existed, like gossamer, to ward off deeper contact. Her feeling at a deep level was, 'So what. You can touch my body, you can work on my breathing, you can search for my energy, but I will not let you really meet me. I let you look into my eyes, but even though they remain clear, I am invisible to you because I am not in them.' She did not say these words. Rather this was the intangible feeling I was picking up while working with her. I learned from Alexander Lowen's work with a patient called George[13] how important it is *not* to proceed with the body work at such times unless there is contact with the inner attitude of the person.

In a totally out of character session, I stopped all attempts to work on energy flow or bodily contractions. I gave up even sitting face to face with Caroline and trying to work directly with her expression. I lay down on my back and began to talk to her about my feeling that at the deepest level she did not trust anyone to reach her. Nor did she trust that there was a deep enough self to reach. I admitted defeat in trying to reach the inside of her experience by touching her on the outside, through working with the body. With many people the body work opens the way to deeper contact and opens up the inner glow that Reich describes. With Caroline it was the other way round. Her experience of the session was that for the first time in her life her soul had been recognised. She had remembered who she was. She had come into the room to listen to what I had to say and to begin to answer from a usually, withheld dimension of herself. The session was a turning point which resulted in a progressive thawing out, over the next few months, of her bodily withdrawal signs. She began to become much warmer. Her breathing became more lively. These changes happened spontaneously, from inside out, because of the quality of touching that happened, when physical touch was abandoned as too great a source of threat to her.

It made me realise that just as the mind is the outside of the body, and the body the inside of the mind, so the body is the outside of the soul and the soul is the inside of the body. Caroline experienced herself before the turning-point session as an outside without an inside. After that session she became an insider who was re-growing an outside.

I asked rhetorically earlier what lies at the heart of the body. There are three ways we can use the word heart. There is firstly the physiological meaning, a pump circulating fluids. Secondly there is the heart centre in the body, the centre of feeling. Finally there is the heart, in the sense of the inner essence.

The heart in the second sense begins to be contacted in any therapy that works with 'opening the feelings'. You can work down towards the feelings by loosening the cramps in a person's mind, or you can work up towards the feelings by improving his contact with the ground and his body.

Alexander Lowen has described the pulsatile movement of life energy in the body.

> Human life pulsates between its two poles, one located in the upper or head end of the body, the other in the lower or tail end. We can equate the upward movement with a reaching toward heaven, the downward movement with a burrowing into the earth. We can compare the head end with the branches and leaves of a tree, the lower end with its roots. Because the upward movement is toward light and the downward one toward darkness, we can relate the head end with consciousness and the lower end with the unconscious.[14]

If a person is free to flow freely towards whatever he or she is moved towards, without characterological compulsions or bodily armour, then whatever s/he experiences will be deep. But such a state is extremely rare, because when it occurs it is an experience of enlightenment. Most of us are blocked from rooting ourselves in our own depth by the conditioning of childhood and of centuries. In Indian religion the term karma is used for this conditioning. Karma is the treadmill of habitual thought patterns, of stereotyped body movements and mechanical life-patterns. In this sense, *karma is identical with armour*. When Reich described the deep surrender of a spontaneous orgasm he was describing a momentary experience of enlightenment. The capacity for deep surrender, if it could be carried into life as a whole, is the foundation of an unarmoured life.

This identity of armour with karma, and of the dissolution of armour with the transcendence of karma, is one that is implicit in the teachings of Bhagwan Shree Rajneesh.

> Wilhelm Reich says you have not known sex at all unless in sex you can attain a deep orgasm. It is not

only a release of sex energy; your whole body must become relaxed. Then the sex experience is not localised at the sex centre, but it spreads all over the body. Your every cell is bathed in it, and you have a peak – a peak in which you are not a body. If you cannot attain a peak in sex, a peak in which you are not a body, you have not known sex at all. That is why Wilhelm Reich says a very paradoxical thing. He says sex is spiritual.[15]

Tage Philipson, who was the first Danish psychologist to practise vegeto-therapy, wrote a two-volume book called *Love Life: Natural and Unnatural*.[16] In it he took the view that sexuality and love are inseparable in a healthy organism. Love begins in the heart, at the centre of the organism, and swells out to the periphery. It may be expressed sometimes in genital sexuality, and at other times it is expressed in a person's whole manner of being in the world. Where sexuality is cut off from love, there is a short circuit; the energy does not well up from the depth but follows superficial pathways, bypassing whole segments of the body.

Lowen has produced an interesting diagram to illustrate the effects of blocks between the sexual, feeling and intellectual centres. It is reproduced in Figure 10.1. He describes the schema as follows.

If we can conceive of the body as being divided in its midsection by a ring of tension in the diaphragmatic area, the two poles would become two opposing camps rather than opposite ends of a single pulsation that moves between them. Now it is a fact that some degree of diaphragmatic tension exists in most people. I pointed this out earlier in connection with the loss of belly feeling, *hara*, due to a restriction of deep abdominal respiration. It is also true that some degree of 'splitting' is common to most people in Western Society. The effect of this splitting or dissociation of the two halves of the body is a loss of the perception of unity. The two opposite directions of flow become two

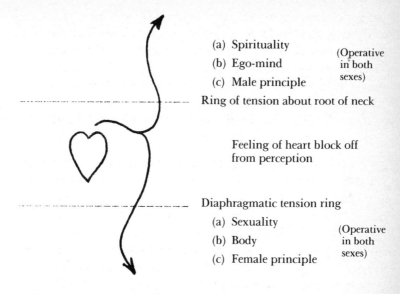

(a) Spirituality
(b) Ego-mind   (Operative in both sexes)
(c) Male principle

Ring of tension about root of neck

Feeling of heart block off from perception

Diaphragmatic tension ring

(a) Sexuality
(b) Body   (Operative in both sexes)
(c) Female principle

Figure 10.1   Tripartite division of the body

antagonistic forces. Sexuality would be experienced as a
danger to spirituality, just as spirituality would be
viewed as a denial of sexual pleasure.[14]

In connection with my embryological view of the bodily
organisation that I developed in earlier chapters, I put
forward the view that the armouring process leads to an over-
balance or imbalance in different organ systems of the body.
We can think of this as a preference for a mesodermal,
endodermal or ectodermal style of existence. More simply, we
could talk about gut-experience, head-experience, and spinal
experience, according to whether people are most comfortable
with internal body sensation, ideas and images, or motor
activity through the back and limbs.

In thinking about the nature of the tension areas that block
off contact between these three key functioning systems, I
realised that that pathway from head to spine, associated with
the energisation of the spinal neural pathways, and also with
cerebrospinal flow patterns, is blocked principally by the

tension at the base of the neck in the nuchal area. This spot has been called the *paranoid button.* The pathway from head to gut, on the other hand, passes through the throat. Tensions at the top of the gullet (in the area where *globus hystericus* symptoms are found) are the key blocks to the flow of feeling down the alimentary canal (called the 'id canal' by Gerda Boyesen). The flow of energy from the front to the back of the body and vice versa, or more specifically from the gut to the spine and back, seems to be mediated by the transverse muscle that is both rooted at the back of the abdominal cavity near the lumbar spine, and regulates the degree of intestinal openness or closure, namely the diaphragm. I came to look on the two neck tension zones and the diaphragmatic block as being the linchpins of the whole armour process. I include the deep-seated eye-blocks in this understanding, for Reich has shown that deep withdrawal in the eyes is anchored physiologically in the base of the neck. The eyes can be looked on as the top of the spine, since the flow of energy up the back in an alive person will express itself as a wave that rises through the top of the head and lights up in the eyes.

When I formulated the view that the neck (the diaphragm of the head) and the diaphragmatic muscle (the neck of the abdomen) were the focal tension rings, I had overlooked Lowen's clear diagram that is given above. So I take this as some measure of confirmation for this view.

I prefer the concept of a bridge that is not used to the concept of a split. People learn to keep energy over-stored in some parts and under-available in others. There is a fear to integrate again. They need help in coaxing energy across the bridge of the diaphragm and along the pathways in the neck. Before these zones of contraction relax, what we see are three types of people: head people, with a reduction of feeling and activity; body people, with an over-focus on compulsive sexuality or compulsive activity; and people who are over-wrought emotionally and are caught up in waves of passionate attachment or protest that do not gratify them at a deep level. These are people with storm-tossed hearts.

Lowen has a second diagram which portrays his view, not in terms of anatomical pathways, but by the use of Reich's functional schema for unity and antithesis of functions (see Figure 10.2). What is interesting here is the distinction between 'body', on the right of the schema, and 'energetic core of the body' at the base. To work with the energetic core is to transcend physiology, even if work with the body is the vehicle with which one approaches the deepest dimensions of a person. Lowen is here distinguishing between the inside and the outside of the body, not in the anatomical sense but in the existential sense. He quotes Jung as saying:

> If we can reconcile ourselves with the mysterious truth that spirit is the living body seen from within and the body the outer manifestation of the living spirit, the two being really one, then we can understand why it is that the attempt to transcend the present level of consciousness must give its due to the body. We shall also see that belief in the body cannot tolerate an outlook that denies the body.[14]

Lowen goes on to say that Jung's statement that what is called the spiritual life is really the inner life of the body, as opposed to the material world which is the outer life of the body.

To the divided person, spirituality and inwardness must

UPWARD FLOW	DOWNWARD FLOW
(a) Spirituality	(a) Sensuality
(b) Conscious	(b) Unconscious
(c) Ego	(c) Body
(d) Heaven	(d) Earth

Energetic core of body
heart and solar plexus

Figure 10.2   Energetic unity and antithesis

lead away from sexuality and the body, just as sexual expression must pull him down into the flesh and away from spirituality. But both the sexuality and the spirituality of such a person will lack heart. It will lack soul. It will not vibrate with the quality of surrender to the depth. It will show neither biological surrender in deep orgasm, nor what Rajneesh calls 'existential surrender' to the whole of existence. The process of blocking off from nature is a learned process. Consciousness is needed for it. It is the mind and language and the whole conditioning routines of a culture pattern that become anchored in our heads and then rooted in our physiology. No muscle tenses chronically without messages from the brain to tell it to contract. That is why Stanley Keleman looks on the brain as a muscle.

Morton Schatzman writes in his book on Schreber:

> Certain heard words, especially if heard often and in childhood, may be encoded and transformed, stored, and later in disguise, retrieved and re-experienced. I think everyone, some of the time, and some people nearly all the time, recurrently experience in and with their bodies literal meanings of certain oft-repeated speech they heard in childhood. That is they retranslate words back into the same modality of bodily experience from which those who spoke the words derived them from within their own bodies . . . Possibly some day we shall speak of linguasomatic, or psycho-semantic, not psycho-somatic illnesses.[9]

When Rajneesh was asked for some practical advice on how to open and develop the heart centre, the advice he gave was on how to get out of this kind of head-conditioning. Many of the dynamic meditation forms used in his ashram, as well as the numerous forms of body work that he has incorporated from the West, have this as their aim. It is not that in deep bio-energy work one wants people to be without heads, to be ego-less and free-floating, or irrational and mindless. Rather it is a question of moving down away from superficial character-reactivity, going through the seething layer of the projections and introjections, the guilts and the blames, and contacting what the Buddhists call 'clear-mindedness'. A clear mind can only come from a clear heart. Rajneesh puts it this way:

> When you have a heart that is alive, your mind's quality will also change. Then you can go to the mind; you can function through the mind. But then the mind will become just an instrument: you can use it. Then you are not obsessed with it, and you can move away from it any moment you like. . .
>
> And another thing: you will come to know that you are neither the head nor the heart, because you can move from heart to head, from head to heart. Then you know that you are something else, X. If you remain in the head and never move anywhere, you become identified with the head. You do not know that you are different. This movement from heart to head and from head to heart will give you the feeling that you are totally different. Sometimes you are at the heart, and sometimes you are at the head, but you are neither heart nor head.
>
> This third point of awareness will lead you to the third centre, to the navel. And the navel is not really a centre. There you are. That is why it cannot be developed: it can only be discovered.[15]

There is a good reason why opening up the heart opens up the abdomen. It is because an open heart leads to a deepening and a welling-out of feeling. I am not talking about explosive discharge, or the agonies of primal abandonment, but of the experience of integration and self-formation that comes from containing and breathing into a feeling, so that it can acquire the capacity to nourish internally and transform a person's life. We can see it whenever someone succeeds in making the transition from hysterical acting out and over-emotionalising, to the being-filled with the depth of oneself that transforms the breathing. When this happens the breathing loses all panic, all contractedness, all pressurisation and self-torture. I can hear the ocean in it. It moves through the body like tides. It has an inevitability that corresponds to the millennia of evolutionary time that it took to evolve a body that can participate in its own process. Ola Raknes wrote:

> Those who are used to taking note of their own bodily sensations will certainly be able to sense the streamings which go through the whole body with a full and deep breathing. These wave-like movements give a feeling of being alive through and through. Those who have relaxed bodies and unclouded minds have these sensations as the regular and permanent background to all that they experience, and it is this which gives colour, taste and freshness to their whole life.[17]

He is talking of the primary dimension of human experience. The task of all true therapies and the aim of the core teaching in all true religions is to re-connect us with the depth of ourselves. Paul Tillich has written that 'We are in constant motion and never stop to plunge to the depth. We talk and talk and never listen to the voices speaking to our depth and from our depth.... Like hit-and-run drivers, we injure our souls by the speed with which we move on the surface.... We miss, therefore, our depth and true life.' He points out that 'depth psychology' can lead us from the surface of self-knowledge into the realms of unconscious wishes and impulses. The bio-energetic work on the body can extend and carry this process further. He writes:

> It can help us to find a way into our depth, although it cannot help us in an ultimate way, because it cannot guide us to the deepest ground of our being and of all being, the depth of life itself.[18]

Religion has used the word 'God' for the inexhaustible depth and ground of being. Reich used the word in precisely this meaning when he wrote:

If you know the ocean, be it asleep or stirring or fully
awake, you know God and you know what all the
Christs in the history of man have talked about. If you
do not know the ocean, you are simply lost, no matter
who you are. You may know about the ocean as if in a
mirror only if you are afraid to drown in its depths, but
you can never stop being a part of the ocean, emerging
from its depths, and returning to its stillness. And in
coming from and returning to the ocean, you take its
depth with you: not a little bit of depth as against the
great ocean depth. Not a milligram of depth as against
a thousand tons of depth. Depth is depth, no matter
whether in a gram or a ton. It is a *quality,* and not a
quantity.[8]

From Caroline, who came to me for help in her closed down
state, I learned a great deal. She did not respond to bio-
energetic exercises, or to peristaltic massage. Her body was
there, but she had gone away. She was not at home. Much of
the session time was spent in facing together what it felt like
to be not available, to build the invisible curtain that screened
her from contact with others and more importantly from
contact with herself. 'We can discover our souls', Tillich
wrote, 'only through the mirror of those who look at us.'[18]

I understood better how the interaction between us had
ultimately brought the life flowing back into her veins and
meaning back into existence on re-reading the final sections of
Lowen's book on depression. He wrote there that the central
issue of therapy is how to restore an individual's lost faith.

This is not easily done, and I have no facile answers to
this question. One cannot preach faith. This is like
preaching love, which sounds great but is really only a
rustle in the wind. One cannot give another person
faith; one can share one's faith with another in the hope
that the spark will ignite the embers in the other's soul.
And one can as a psychiatrist help another person
recover his faith by finding out how he lost it.[14]

INNER GROUND

This area of contact and experience is needed to overcome the experience of groundlessness, of being a straw in the wind. All the work on providing grounding for the body through postural work, stress positions, cathartic release of blocked emotions, have their place. But they are only the outer ground. We need to deepen and enrich this process by paying attention to how a person builds his life-space or organises his life-time, what sense he has of his ability to form himself by participating more fully in his own process.[19] [20] [21] We need to help him find his inner, ground, his *essence*,[22] the source from which his own healing energy wells up with the power to integrate him anew in spite of whatever he learned about how not to feel alive.

CHAPTER 11

THE WOMB, THE TOMB AND THE SPIRIT

Life beyond the body

This chapter seeks to share some viewpoints on the relationship between birth and death which I developed as part of my personal journey towards creating some meaning in the face of a bereavement.[1] The chapter began as two lectures given at the Boyesen Institute of Biodynamic Psychology in London, but it was written in a small German village; it was completed after a visit to Uberaba in Brazil. It seeks to throw a little fresh light on a journey that is longer than man.

As the search for ever earlier levels of trauma is pushed backwards in time, from the age of four, to two, to before speech and before birth, to the third trimester, to implantation, to conception and perhaps to a previous life, it becomes clear that we are facing an infinite recess. There simply is not enough time in this life to work through the traumas of all the previous ones. I have the greatest respect for some of those who have directed us into ever deeper levels of regression, but I believe their reasoning is faulty. It is based on what Stanley Keleman calls the myth of the Garden of Eden. Return to the womb, to oceanic sensations, to a totipotent state of feeling, is ultimately a flight from death. What lies behind us in our history is a blaze of light accompanying embryogenesis,[2] but we cannot recapture it by strategic regression to the bliss of an untraumatised foetal state.

The way forward is a path inspired by hope and threatened by horror. Darkness threatens us on many sides, whether in

173

the form of old primal pains resurfacing, or the social convulsions erupting increasingly in many parts of the world in
the last quarter of a century, or the fact that the clock at the
Bulletin of Atomic Scientists stands at four minutes to
midnight.[3]

Rebirthing, primal integration, bio-energetic work, are all
helpful not because they take us back but insofar as, in spite of
their rationale of reliving the past, they are able to move us
forward and to progress.

There are events that are so terrible that working them out
cathartically is a gross inadequacy and reliving them could be
to quadruple the agony. How does one help a woman whose
son of thirteen was killed in a car accident to cathart her grief
when she has been crying without relief for more than a year
already? One cannot go back and recreate his life. Going
forward for this woman involved heeding a signal sent to her
in a dream. One night she could not sleep. She saw his coffin,
but it was empty. 'I know it's empty', she said, 'because he's
not in it, he's waving at me to tell me he's all right.' Refusing
to acknowledge this signal sent to her in a dream had
maintained this woman in a depression for twelve months.
When she was able to accept her dream she was able to move
beyond the grave of depression she had dug for herself and to
begin to live again in spite of her tragedy.

The movement of life follows the arrow of time; it is
directional. The direction is forwards. But the arrow of time
points towards finitude, towards death and towards non-
existence. Martin Heidegger defined life as a 'being-towards-
death'. The search for pleasure, social, sexual or foetal, may
distract us from this realisation. The work of Reich founded
the wave-like movements of protoplasm and affirmed the
primacy of pleasure, but avoided the fact that the onward
wave movement rolled inevitably towards shipwreck. The
body of the amoeba alone is immortal.

Regression therefore is an attempt ultimately to reconstitute
oneself in a womb-like environment, to take on the
protectedness of the foetal state.[4] Progression is the thrust

from foetus to child to adult and onwards into a state culminating in death. Who wants to progress, though, if death is the final solution? In a nuclear age when mass extermination hangs over us all, it is understandable that regressive therapies and paranoid cults should mushroom and flourish. The way back is seen as the way forward and the way forward is seen as the way back.

How would it seem, though, for a foetus poised before the transition out of the only known world of the womb? When I was in Iceland, in August 1981, I discovered the modern Icelandic play *Yolk Life*, written by Oddur Bjornsson.[5] The stage is the womb. The *dramatis personae* are two foetal twins, non-identical, eight months after conception. The curtain opens on darkness. As it lightens electronic sound effects of abdominal rumbling noises are heard. The theatre of psycho-peristalsis begins. Oddur Bjornsson writes in his introduction:

> At first sight the idea itself appears to be somewhat difficult to stage, but the play has been produced with considerable success. Two things appear to be most important in the play. They are partly mankind's dependence on, and limitation by, his immediate environment, and partly the two opposing characters played off against each other. One of the twins is obviously a rationalist, although not completely lacking in imagination, an egoist who accepts his environment as being the only one he can come into contact with. The other twin, however, is more complex. He appears to be weak and dependent but possesses a certain intuition which requires expansion. After all he does have this strange feeling of a life after the embryo existence.

Here is the final speech in the play by Foetus One.

> Couldn't you imagine a big world, a world which was a hundred thousand trillion times bigger than us, where

the light would not be so dark and darkness as bright,
where there would be others like us and not like us,
where there would be pianos and dogs, playwrights and
proper chairs to sit on, mail order catalogues and men
like those in the ghost story and what are they called
again . . . women? that can multiply! And more head
space, so one can stand up straight. Beethoven, so one
can play all the pianos. Primuses that can be thrown
out of windows. Bedpots, and photographers with eye-
glasses. And and all possible kinds of things. And and
also all impossible kind of things. Eh? Can't you
imagine that. Oh, can't you really imagine that!

Foetus Two gives a very short answer, his brother's stupidity
completely overwhelming him: 'No.'

The play ends in darkness and silence.

We are left with this dilemma. From inside the womb, or
spaceship or world or body, the argument between the two
twins is unresolvable. But everyone in the audience is outside.
Everyone outside the womb, or spaceship or stage or body,
knows that one twin is right and one twin is wrong. It
depends on which side of the interface you are on. From the
pre-natal side of birth, there is no way of telling. From the
post-natal side, clearly the ending of womb-life is not an
extinction but a phase transition; a watershed or a gate
between worlds.

In learning to cope with bereavement I learned the
difference between warm grief and cold grief. Cold grief was a
sense of blackness; a bleak hopeless despairing in which I
killed my breathing. Warm grief carried within it a sense of
awe with the possibility of healing in it. So warm grief carried
within it the possibility of relief. I learned there was a choice I
had in how to breathe and in how to grieve.

Anthony Bloom, the Metropolitan of Sourozh, describes the
difference between the event of death and the response to
death. The first is extrinsic; it happens to us, out of the blue.
People we love can be struck down in an instant, without

warning. The second death is intrinsic; 'it consists of all the negative attitudes and feelings that suck away vitality from within: resentment, bitterness, remorse, regrets, lack of peace'.[6] Unresolved grief has been linked to cancer formation. Cancer has been linked to the loss of sense of a future. In grieving over a loved person who has died, we mourn not only the past but the dead future. Cold grief locks us in inescapable despair; warm grief can carry with it a sense of gratitude out of the blackness of the void.

Something similar happened to me as I noticed how my intellect dealt with belief or disbelief in any continuity beyond the threshold of death. If I believed, as my rationalism had conditioned me to, that death was final and exterminated everything of value, I noticed my heart contracting and a sense of bitterness growing. If, on the other hand, I entertained an 'as if' notion, that some form of continuity was possible, my heart felt more open and expanded. How my intellect insisted on not cheating itself with superstition or false hope! It was then I rediscovered what Pascal had first formulated in the seventeenth century: he who believes in mortality may live with a closed heart for thirty years, and if death is the end he will never know it because he will be dead. If death is not the end, he will be confronted with the results of thirty years or so of dying the second death, the death of hope. He who believes on the other hand in some form of immortality – survival, continuity, call it what you will – can live with an open heart for the rest of his life. If death is the end he will never be disillusioned, because he will be dead; and if death is not the end he will be confirmed in his faith in ongoingness and continuity. 'To which view shall we be inclined?' asked Pascal. 'Reason cannot decide this question. Infinite chaos separates us. At the far end of this infinite distance a coin is being spun which will come down heads or tails. How will you wager? Reason cannot make you choose either, reason cannot prove either wrong.'[7]

Robert Jay Lifton has argued that the choice for continuity, which is an act of faith, is close to what Eric Erikson calls basic trust. Lifton writes:

> Erikson emphasises the issue of basic trust as the earliest
> developmental crisis, and he sees the legacy of this
> earliest time as having vital importance for adulthood.
> But the establishment of trust itself involves the
> confidence in the integrity, connection and movement
> of life, pre-requisites for a viable form of symbolic
> immortality. Where this confidence collapses
> psychological impairment ensues.[8]

Clearly the debate between the materialist and the spiritualist, the extermination believer and the survival believer, is the same debate as that between the man who calls heads and the man who calls tails in Pascal's wager. It is also the same debate as that conducted by the twins in the womb in the Icelandic play. But whereas everyone in the audience knows which twin is right in relation to birth, there is no audience available to tell us which twin is right in relation to death.

But supposing that birth, viewed from inside the womb, is sensed as death; could it be that death, from outside the body, would be experienced as birth? Let us explore a little further into the symmetries of birth and death.

In an earlier chapter I gave an account of embryogenesis, which was first published under the title 'Incarnation'. Incarnation means being embodied. Dis-incarnation means being disembodied. Reincarnation means being re-embodied. Professor Stevenson, in his five volumes of research into cases suggestive of reincarnation,[9] has accumulated the evidence for the fact that some individuals appear to recall having lived before their present life. The continuity of an individual life appears in this perspective as something existing prior to birth as well as after death.

Genetics has described the process of embryogenesis in ways that suggest that the process of morphogenesis, the forming of bodily shape, is directed by formative forces. They are still searching for what these forces might be in chemical gradients. Harold Burr has suggested that these formative

forces were electromagnetic in nature.[10] Glen Reich, a
biochemist at London University, has developed the
hypothesis that there exists in all biological tissues an
electromagnetic system which has an endogenous functional
capacity to regulate biochemical processes. His work is
linked to the findings of Kirlian photography. An article in
the BMA *News Review* on Kirlian photography was subtitled:
'Kirlian photography, the plaything of occultists, is now
attracting the attention of medical researchers who are finding
that it is a useful diagnostic tool.'[11]

In May 1982, I went to visit Hernani Andrade, the director
of the Institute of Psycho-biophysics in Sao Paulo. After fifty
years of the most carefully documented research he developed
his theory of the biological organising matrix, which was
republished in *Energy and Character*.[12] In this theory he
postulated the existence of a bio-magnetic field that was
associated with bioluminescence. Such a field, he suggested,
was not created by the tissues of the body; rather the
organisational form of the tissues of the body were formed by
this field, in the same way that the patterns of iron filings are
shaped by an external field.

In June 1982 I visited Hiroshi Motoyama, the director of the
Institute of Religion and Parapsychology in Tokyo. Professor
Motoyama has demonstrated that there is a step-down process
from non-physical energies to physical energies, in which the
body functions rather like a transformer.[13] Thus energies,
'formerly the playthings of occultists', which are invisible and
intangible may be stepped down until they become visible and
tangible. Motoyama measures the invisible flow of energy
through the meridians of acupuncture, visibly, on electrical
apparatus. Also, in the University of Colorado, Valerie Hunt
succeeded in measuring the effects of the energy centres of the
body (the chakras) on an oscilloscope.[14] Thus it should not
surprise us to learn that some physicists have suggested that
the formative forces that provide the matrix for morphogenetic organisation have qualities reminiscent of light,
which is of course an electromagnetic radiation.

Here is a clairvoyant describing embryogenesis in terms of the irradiation of light from a biological organising matrix which she describes as a 'mental body'.

> The general appearance of the embryo mental body in the case under investigation was that of an opalescent ovoid bubble with a hole in the top. Down this passage there was a constant interplay of force which looked like a stream of brilliantly coloured particles of light. In the middle of this bubble was the shadowy human form, and the descending stream passed into the top of the head . . . The whole phenomenon was surrounded by dazzling and blazing light which increased in intensity towards the centre of the causal body. The down poured force kept the atoms of the mental body in constant motion, and as it struck the matter of which the mental body was composed, it formed a vortex into and through which the rest of this matter was continually being drawn. This movement, however, did not affect the general shape, which remained ovoid as previously described. Although the human form was visible within the ovoid, it must not be thought of as hollow, but rather as a solid though translucent mass of rapidly moving matter. Every atom of the body passed through this vortex, and the down-flowing stream which produced it, was magnetised by it, glowed more brightly and then gradually became less brilliant as it flowed away into other portions of the body.[14]

Whilst the source may not be acceptable, the description tallies with reports from many other sources, which perhaps lends 'verisimilitude to an otherwise unconvincing narrative'. The description however sounds remarkably similar to descriptions and diagrams of the human aura.

So, if life-energy is, as Reich postulated, associated with lumination, death would seem to be characterised by the extinction of lumination. It was Dylan Thomas who counselled us in his magnificent poem to 'rage, rage against the dying of the light'.

Cells, in a state of health, luminate and pulsate. Hands give off a vital field that can be measured on X-ray films and which can change the molecular bonding in water. The whole body luminates in love-making. Healers have fireworks coming out of their fingers that can be recorded unmistakably in Kirlian photography, as well as felt subjectively as the heat that precedes tissue regeneration and renewal.

It is less well known that dying itself is associated with both external and internal impressions of light. Many observers with psychic awareness have described seeing light leaving the body through the top of the head when observing someone who dies. The light is described as vaporous, cloudlike, luminous and phosphorescent. Nandor Fodor describes it as like a floating flame.[15] Bendit and Bendit write in a chapter called 'The act of dying':

> It seems as if what takes place is the reverse of what happens at the beginning of incarnation . . . Here we have the withdrawal of the nucleus [of the energy field] prior to the dissipation of the material originally gathered together, and subsequently held in proper form round its focus.[16]

From the experiences reported by those who have clinically died and then made an unexpected recovery, we have reports that resemble the ecstasy of meditation. Illumination is the central feature of these reports. Assagioli defines illumination in these words.

> An inner perception of light which in certain cases is so intense as to be described as a dazzling glory and an impression of fire. It is from these characteristics that the term 'illumination' has arisen, the term by which superconscious states are often designated. In many cases this illumination extends to the external world which is perceived as transfigured and bathed in an ineffable light.[17]

There are further parallels with other sources of light - the stars. Astrophysics predicts that the fate of many stars is that they collapse in stages to a singularity of such intense density that no light can escape. The star has become an invisible gravitational sink called a 'black hole'.

Certain astronomers are suggesting that white holes also exist. They are sources of intense, outpouring radiation and particles of unknown origin. The suggestion has been made that in a parallel universe, our black holes appear as white holes, and vice versa. The sink in one world is a source in another. In remembered states of foetal awareness, the imagery of the black hole occurs frequently in people who do not study astrophysics. The black hole is a foetal view of the birth canal, the sink down which it dies out of uterine existence. From the post-natal side of the boundary, those in the birth room witness an event called crowning, the emergence into their world of a new source, the newborn baby, who is often appropriately wrapped in white.

We experience the death of our body like the death of a star as approaching the stage of becoming a black hole down which we will be sucked out of existence. At funerals (in Europe) people dress in black to record an extinction; in China they dress in white and, as Buddhists, believe in reincarnation. In clinical death experiences people report visions of white light after they have separated from their body.

It is inevitable that we have to look at some of the pathologies surrounding birth and death, where part of the process is incompleted. I shall refer to this as *umbilical castration* and *etheric parturition*.

The unborn child is connected to the mother's placenta by the umbilical cord. The act of birth ends with the third stage of labour when the placenta is expelled from the mother's body. It is also separated from the baby's by the cord being cut. Le Boyer recommends that the cord should only be cut after it has finished pulsating. The dead placenta and the dead cord are jettisoned and the living body of the baby is delivered as contents from the container of the womb to begin its new existence.

Francis Mott has used the term 'external placenta' for the earth on which the new-born baby is grounded, once its free floating uterine existence has been left behind. Severing the cord severs the interface between the oceanic life of the womb and the terrestrial life of post-natal existence. There is no real way back, though in psychotic states or in other forms of involuntary regression one may cling to conditions that are womb-like. We could refer to such states as being *womb-bound*

R. D. Laing in his brilliant book *The Voice of Experience* has a chapter called 'The tie and the cut-off' in which he deals with a variety of ways in which people may feel a sense of umbilical castration or umbilical impingement.

> If we feel a relationship as an attachment and the attachment is a tie, it is almost impossible not to feel tied to something, thread, string, rope, a chain or steel or daisies.
>
> Attachment may be felt positively or negatively as being tied to the other by something or other. The tie may be pleasant or unpleasant, desired or undesired, welcome or imposed, two ways or one way. Innumerable variations of this theme are expressed in a host of metaphors. He's a noose around my neck. She's my lifeline. He's my anchor. He's still tied to his mother's apron strings. Friends are connected by invisible threads.[18]

The umbilical cord is a lost foetal attachment. We develop the arms, legs, genitals and eyes for making new bondings to the body of the earth and the body of another. These bonds can be atrophied, rigidified, or can pulsate with the same kind of sensitive flowing life that characterised the umbilical connection. But unlike the cord, a permanent attachment for nine months, these other bonds are temporary. They show rhythms of contact and withdrawal.

Laing speaks of another type of cord connecting the energy body to the physical body. Many people with paranormal vision have described a light-body or centre of consciousness, associated with the physical body like a double, and in life so intimately associated with it that for most purposes we think of the two as one. Andrija Puharich calls this the psi-plasma body.[19] In so-called out-of-the-body experiences, the double and the normal body become dissociated in space-time and in consciousness. Laing writes:

> Many people say that they have seen or felt a cord, a chain, a strand, a tape, a hand, an arm, a thread, a string, a shaft of ribbon, a pipeline, a long neck, a beam, a shaft, a flower, a coil of light, a sunbeam, sometimes pulsing, connecting them to their doubles or subtle other selves.[19]

This is how Robert Crookall, a geologist, botanist and psychic researcher, described this cord.

> The 'cord' is described as relatively short and thick when the 'double' is within a few feet of the body and getting thinner and thinner as they separate, until it is like a spider's web. When the 'double' is near the body it absorbs much cosmic vitality, the prana of the Hindus, and this is transmitted via the cord extension to the physical body. A number of people who had out of the body experiences independently stated that they saw this vitality pulsating in their 'cord'.[20]

Sylvan Muldoon wrote:

> When the astral body is in coincidence with the physical, you are physically alive. When the astral body moves out of coincidence you are physically dead unless the astral cable, running from the Energetic (= Astral) body, is intact. That is the purpose of the astral 'line of force', to deliver the breath of life to the physical body, while the finer astral body is being protected.[21]

In an account in *The Physician,* quoted by Crookall, the separation of the two bodies at death was described as follows.

> Immediately previous to the final dissolution, I saw, playing energetically between the feet of the elevated spiritual body and the prostrate physical form, a bright stream or current of vital electricity (the 'silver cord'). This taught me that death is but a birth of the spirit from a lower into a higher state, that the correspondence between the birth of a child into this world and the birth of the spirit from a material body into a higher world, is absolute and complete, even to the umbilical cord, which was represented by the thread of vital electricity which for a few minutes connected the two organisms.

These cords are reported from all cultures, literate and illiterate, and by all ages. They are independent of religious belief. They appear to be reports by people with paranormal vision of objective events.

The physical body thus acts as a placenta mooring the non-physical body to it. The body of light is tied to the body of matter by this cord. Death always involves severing the cord. The body of matter, as placenta, as matrix and container for the double, dies. The body of light is seen as a separating form.

> The feet become cold first. One sees right over the head what may be called a magnetic halo, an ethereal emanation, golden in appearance. Now the body is cold up to the knees . . . The emanation is more expanded . . . and attains a position near the ceiling. The person has ceased to breathe. The emanation is elongated and fashioned in the outlines of the human form. It is connected by the silver cord beneath with the brain. The thinking faculties are rational, while nearly every part of the person is dead. The golden emanation is connected with the brain by a very fine life thread. On

the body of the emanation there appears something
white and shining, like a human head; next comes a
faint outline of the face; the neck and shoulders
manifest, and then in rapid succession, all parts of the
new body. . . The fine life-thread continues attached to
the old brain. The next thing is the withdrawal of this
electrical principle. When the thread snaps the spiritual
body is free.[22]

From this point of view life on earth can be seen as pregnancy.
Death appears as full term. Suicide begins to look like an
abortion. Just as a postnatal person who may be unwilling to
end prenatal existence can be said to be womb-bound, a post-
mortal person who is unwilling or unable to come to terms
with the surrender of pre-mortal existence, is referred to as
earth-bound.

If the energetic double, freed from its physical coupling,
attaches itself to a physical location, we talk of it as a ghost.
Many researchers have suggested that the ghost is an earth-
bound person who through stress, or predisposition, is unable
to accept the fact of his transition through the interface of
death. Once again, there is no way back. A ghost may haunt
you, or its old haunts, but it cannot root itself to the physical
earth any more than pre-natal regression can tie an adult back
into the actual womb.

Birth, death and orgasm all involve tremendous boundary
interactions. In birth we enter the gravitational field of the
earth after nine months afloat in amniotic fluids. In orgasm
we surrender to tremendous involuntary pulsations as we
enter or are entered by the body of another. In death we
become divorced from the matrix of matter and the placenta of
the earth. All three can involve convulsions. It is not
surprising that we carry forwards and backwards in time our
association between these three experiences.

Fear to die in the event of birth, experienced as birth
anxiety, can lock a person into a contracted state that prevents
surrender in orgasm. It can be projected forwards on to death.

186

Reich wrote: 'The fear of death and dying is identical with unconscious orgasm anxiety and the alleged death instinct, the longing for dissolution, for nothingness, is unconscious longing for orgastic release of tension.'[23]

Birth, if it is non-traumatic, may be experienced by mother and child as like an orgasm. Paul and Jean Ritter were the first as far as I know to highlight this relationship. Death too, if clinical death accounts are to be relied on, may resemble orgasm. Freud argued that immortality was a fantasy based on projection from womb life:

> It was not for a long time that I learned to appreciate the importance of phantasies and unconscious thoughts about life in the womb. They contain an explanation of the remarkable dread that many people have of being buried alive; and they also afford the deepest unconscious basis of this uncanny life before birth.[24]

Thus said Freud in 1909. Over seven decades later we do not need to be so dogmatic. Laing's perspective would seem to be more open-minded, and more in touch with the growing edge of both quantum physics and quantum bio-energetics:

> It seems to me to be strictly impossible to tell, from the observation of someone dying, whether mind, soul or spirit is extinguished as the brain dies, or whether he, she, it or they vacate the brain and body. Neither construction contradicts objective facts.
>
> It is impossible, therefore it is not. It is not, because it is impossible. . . The prevailing scientific view is that visions at death and after death do not occur, because they cannot. Memories of before birth, or between lifetimes and of other lives are false, because they cannot be true.[18]

Maybe we put a taboo on death in the same way as we put a taboo on sex and a taboo on birth, not wanting to moderate the expansion of consciousness and the extension of boundaries involved in rejecting Freud's conclusion. Technocratic obstetrics kills the natural life impulses in the birth process; pornographic sexuality by cerebralising sex, destroys the natural simplicity of orgasm; and mechanistic science kills death by reducing it to a purely physical event.

The symmetry of birth and death is also found in breathing. The newborn baby has collapsed lungs that have never contained air. We hear the birth cry, but not what precedes it, the first intake of air. This inspiration is the first act of postnatal life. If the cord is cut early, and no other source of oxygen exists, the baby must inspire immediately or else it will be dead. But the inspiratory rush of air can be felt as invasive and traumatic.[2] It can precondition a person towards reduced inspiration. In schizophrenic states there exists a condition of flattened breathing which has been called 'uterine respiration'.[25] People who do not want to breathe in are people who do not want to stand, to charge up, or to sustain themselves in a gravitational field. They collapse easily. At the other end of the breath-wave lies expiration. At death our last act is to let go of the air in our lungs. Samuel Beckett's play *Breath* packs the whole of life into a minute between the birth cry and the last breath. When someone dies, we say they have expired. Fear of death leads to rigidity, control and the holding of breath. It creates an inspiratory attitude to life. It holds people locked in tension against fear of bursting. Fear of life leads to collapse, resignation and depression. It creates an expiratory tendency, with greatly reduced inspiration.

Charles Kelley has related reluctance to breathe in with the blocking of fear and reluctance to breathe out with the blocking of anger.[26] Our breathing reflects how we were born and may condition how we die. Stanley Keleman has described two styles of dying. We could call them 'anger-dying' and 'fear-dying'. He calls them 'eruptive dying' and 'congealing dying'.

> In eruptive dying the contained organism is exploding, breaking out of its boundaries into the world. Strokes

and heart attacks are common examples of eruptive dying. The event is usually sudden, and is one style of dying, one way the organism terminates itself. The other way is the opposite . . . The body gathers itself, collects itself, withdraws from the social world. Here dying occurs as a series of debilitating or self-retreating events or as a shock, a deep withdrawal, moving towards complete inhibition. . . This style of dying I call congealing.[27]

These two styles of dying express the termination of the organism. Stanley Keleman's book *Living your Dying* looks at many ways we die by breaking through boundaries and initiating endings during our lifetime. The poet John Keats used to talk of 'dying into life'.

If we consider what dying can be for the essence of the person escaping the boundaries of the physical body, we can visualise a third style of dying, ecstatic dying. 'Is there a person alive', Keleman asks, 'who wouldn't like to go to their dying full of excitement, without fear, and without morbidity?'

Clinical death experiences suggest that people do not want to come back from their visions and their illuminating experiences. Expiring seems to be inspiring. This has nothing to do with masochistic or self-sacrificing attitudes. I believe we should make the utmost of life in the body while we have it. Cutting it short by our own folly or suicidal wishes could be the worst possible preparation for any kind of satisfaction in life out of the body. In occult tradition, suicides are particularly likely to end up as earth-bound. Chuang Tsu wrote:

The true man of old slept without dreaming and woke without anxiety. His food was plain and his breath was deep. For the breath of the true man rose up from his heels while the breath of common men rises from their throats. . . The true man of old knew nothing about loving life and hating death. When he was born he felt

> no elation. When he entered death, there was no
> sorrow. Carefree he went. Carefree he came. That was
> all. He did not forget his beginning, and did not seek
> his end. He accepted what he was given with delight,
> and when it was gone, he gave it no more thought . . .
> The wood is consumed, but the fire burns on, and we
> do not know when it will come to an end.[28]

So far I have tried to show that there is a balance in the way we lead our lives, from birth to death; perhaps a circular progression is a better analogy. I would like to extend this way of thinking further into the environment in which we find ourselves. We live in two worlds, a visible and an invisible. Reich described these two worlds as the world of nature, caught within a membrane or structure, and the mass-free world of orgonotic streaming.[29]

A visible sun awakes in the morning. But there is an invisible sun that we can detect only through radio emission. The earth actually floats in the invisible field of this sun. Physicists call it the 'magnetosphere'. Reich called it the 'orgone envelope' of the earth. Our auras, the orgonotic envelopes of our bodies, are affected (invisibly to ordinary eyes, since they do not see auras) by the invisible influence of the solar wind.

There is a world of matter and secondary radiations and a world of energetic waves that is more or less understood by physics. Beyond the electromagnetic spectrum that defines the physical world lie the non-physical levels of reality. Decades of evidence from the most recent wave of paraphysical research have established the objective reality of non-physical events such as telepathy, remote seeing, precognition, distant healing, out-of-body experiences and psycho-kinesis. Much of this research comes from that most materialistic of countries, the USSR. Twenty years ago the aura was an occult notion held to only by mystics. Reich died in prison for his claims about orgone energy fields surrounding the living body. Today that bastion of orthodoxy, the medical profession, is poised on the verge of recognising the reality of what the mystics call the aura.

We are again faced with the question of which is primary. Does the world of matter generate invisible fields or is it that the invisible fields generate the world of matter? Reich, in *Cosmic Superimposition*, has postulated the emergence of mass particles from a mass-free, energetic continuum. 'The "energetic orgonome" leads to the formation of "material orgonome".'[29] An orgonome is a basic living form characteristic of biological systems. Reich gives many examples: the seed, the egg, the embryo, the human body. The energetic orgonome corresponds to the aura. The material orgonome corresponds to the body. Reich appears to be seeing the body as a condensation of the aura, rather than looking on the aura as an evaporation from the body.

In the first part of this chapter I described the observations of seers who saw energetic streaming during embryogenesis. In addition to the three cell-layers of the associated lifestyles,[30] we have the organising fields or biological organising model, as postulated in a recent article by Hernani Andrade.[12] The three embryonic germ-cell layers are called the ectoderm (outside), mesoderm (middle) and endoderm (inside). We need a similar word to donate the morphogenetic field which, according to Andrade and Burr, organises the topology of the body. I suggest the word 'morpho-derm'. Specifically this means the non-physical force field which shapes and leads to the formation of a cohesive body.

There is support for such a view in quantum physics where, instead of consciousness being looked on as a byproduct of a piece of matter called the brain, it is coming to be looked on as an organising field at the roots of existence which may function as a force acting on the very particles that the world is made of.

The speed of physical light is a boundary term for the physical universe. At the speed of light, mass becomes infinite and size dwindles to zero. These are the conclusions of Einstein's special theory of relativity. The physical world is a world that travels at speeds from zero to light speed. Einstein's equations also have a second solution in which mass is negative; it corresponds to no known physical reality. The two solutions of Einstein's equations lie each side of the threshold of light. We could call them the 'sub-luminal' and the 'supra-luminal' universes; or the universe of physical matter and the universe of psi-matter, in the words of Puharich;[19] or the mass-bound and the mass-free world, in the language of Reich.

Consciousness is mass free. Telepathy is unbounded by the body and its speed of transmission is instantaneous. It beats the light barrier. It is supra-luminal. Clairvoyance carries information from one space to another, instantaneously, as two American physicists demonstrated very practically a few years ago.[31] In spiritual healing, according to Leshan, without direct contact even of energy fields, or bodily radiations, contact between persons can be established which transcends all laws of physics and allows changes in the health of tissues to take place.[32]

Chico Xavier, the world famous Brazilian healer, in his book *Evolution in Two Worlds*,[33] paints a picture of two contiguous domains of experience; he calls them the domain of matter and the domain of spirit. In life these two domains are so enmeshed together that we see their superimposed images as one. Brain and mind appear to fuse to a pulsating lump of grey matter in the head.

Ultimately those who postulate a fundamental unity at the roots of existence may well be right; both what the physicists call matter and what the mystics call spirit may be different levels of vibration of one fundamental oceanic energy. Reich recognised how 'The "soul" represents the orgonotic excitation, and the "flesh" the confining tissue.'[29] But the tissue itself is a set of structures that ultimately dissolve into quantum excitations that are relatively stable in time.

The watershed between body and soul, between denser and finer levels of vibration, is the border of detectability by the five physical senses and their mechanical extensions. What we can see with our eyes, hear with our ears, touch with our hands, photograph with our cameras, and pick up with electronic equipment, is physical. Everything else either does not exist, or it does exist and is beyond current methods of physical detection.

When the clairvoyant talks of other planes of existence, at higher levels of vibration, and of subtler bodies than the physical, his view does not cancel or deny any known physical fact. Some such outlook, however, would seem a necessity to begin to make sense of the rich evidence we have for non-measurable levels of experience. I would now like to dwell on some of the more human aspects, and in particular those of enlightenment and how it relates to embodiment.

A tree has roots and it has leaves. The roots go down into the soil and take up minerals from the earth; the leaves reach up into the sky and take light from the sun. The tree is soundly embedded if it is well grounded (*enracine* in French). It is enlightened through photosynthesis and the respiratory function of the leaves. What it takes from the light and air and what it takes from the soil create the body of the tree. In Hebrew culture the tree is a symbol for the body of a man. In Chinese culture man bridges the polarity of earth below and heaven above. The real tree inhabits two worlds, the world of soil and the world of light. The allegorical tree joins heaven and earth.

The development of consciousness, the growth of a more human and ultimately more spiritual awareness, is a process of progressive enlightenment. I do not mean any mystical state of perfection and I do not mean a ritualised religious quest. We can use the word in its perfectly ordinary meaning; to be more enlightened is to be more humane, to function more from the strength and the clarity of the heart.

Development in the material sense means the building of a body, of a working life, of a family, or structures for life support. A well-embodied person manages to use the structures of his life to support and nourish the growth of his spirit; they are not in conflict; the body personal and the body social function as a womb for the spirit. But a person building

what Reich called muscle armour, creates patterns of rigid-
ification and densification of tissue that progressively encase
the heart and shut out the light. The body then becomes a
tomb for the spirit.

I have known people hammer on their heads or tear at their
chests in a compulsive effort to break through the wall of
contracting flesh that blocks their sense of vitality and life.
Reich wrote:

> Orgastic longing, which plays such a gigantic role in
> the life of animals, appears now as an expression of this
> 'striving beyond oneself', as 'longing' to reach out
> beyond the narrow sack of one's own organism. We
> 'yonder', to use an apt phrase, for the beyond of
> ourselves. Perhaps here lies the solution of the riddle
> why the idea of death so often represents the orgasm. In
> dying too the biological energy reaches beyond the
> boundaries of the material sack which holds it
> prisoner.[23]

Orgasm is the life event which typifies the 'yondering'
tendency most clearly in fully embodied people. Reich's
therapy, in softening the armour, makes possible pulsatile
orgastic movements that lead sometimes to a deep sense of
their cosmic connectedness in people. Small changes in
rhythms of breath can alter the tonus of muscles and the firing
frequencies of the nervous system, to permit rigid body
structure of the over-embedded person.

What of the state called 'disembodied'? True disembodiment is a phase transition, the parturition called death that
cuts the energetic bond between body and spirit, between
material orgonome and energetic orgonome. But to say that a
person is disembodied means that the coupling between
matter and spirit has become tenuous while he is still alive.

Sleep is one such tenuous state. In sleep there is evidence
suggesting that the coupling becomes temporarily loosened.
Only the etheric cord is left to join the subtler essence of the
person to his physical form. In dreams we dissociate.

The person known as psychotic, dreams awake. He acts split; that is, dissociated. He is partly out of his body. Fear has made him jump out of his skin. We say he is partly out of his mind. Alexander Lowen, in talking of the dissociation in the schizophrenic state, writes of it as follows.

> All writers agree that in depersonalisation the individual reports a loss of contact with the body or with significant parts of it. There are accompanying sensations of strangeness and of unreality. Sometimes the person has the feeling that he is looking at himself from outside the body, or from a distance . . . We do not simplify the problem by describing it as due to a disturbed imagination. To explain this disturbance we would still have to account for the original feeling. In this problem of depersonalisation, we face a phenomenon which transcends psychology and physiology.[34]

Lowen goes on to describe the experience of being 'beside oneself' or having a double self. 'One of the doubles', he says, 'was the body, fully alive and functioning normally. The other was a spirit-body (the so-called ethereal double).' His discussion of these processes continued as follows.

> The process whereby a double self is created is more complicated. When the atmosphere about a highly excited organism becomes strongly charged, cohesive forces seem to develop in it. Ordinarily all living organisms show an aura about the body which is a natural phenomenon existing about all charged systems. My associate, Dr John C. Pierrakos, has made an intensive study of the energy field about the human organism in both health and disease. It seems that in very highly charged states the organism can move out of its aura or field which then remains behind in the form of the body, and follows the body as a shadow. Once set up as a nucleus, it will retain its form and

195

cohesion so long as energy streams from the body into
it. [The observations assembled by Carrington and
Muldoon would suggest that the energy streams from
the aura into the body also, and that this is the primary
direction of energy flow.] By virtue of the energy bridge
between the two systems, the perception of the self is
doubled. The field phenomenon collapses and
disappears as soon as the subsidence of the excitation
withdraws the energy into the body proper. . .

The schizophrenic personality is anti-material, anti-
everyday reality. We can describe it as a withdrawal, but
it is tantamount to material death. I could therefore
agree with another schizophrenic patient who told me
that her body was dying. When this happens the spirit
or free-energy tends to leave the body. . .

I know as I write this that many readers will become
skeptical. Some will question while others will turn
against all bio-energetic interpretations. This was a
reaction which greeted many of Freud's most valuable
contributions. They will ask if I have seen these
'ethereal doubles', if I believe in spirits. I can only say
that it is not a question of belief, of spiritualism, or
parapsychological phenomena. We are attempting to
understand an illness, the symptoms of which, if they
are taken seriously, are incomprehensible from the
viewpoint of the reality of our everyday lives.[34]

We will return to Lowen's concepts of the spirit-body and the
process of energetic doubling in a section on possession and
psychosis below.

In his book *Cosmic Superimposition*, Reich postulated a
very basic principle in nature, which led to fusion. The basic
characteristics of superimposition were: two directions of
energy flow, convergence and mutual approach of the two
energy streams; superimposition and contact; fusion and
sharp curving-in of the path of the flow so as to create a
nucleus of bounded form or structure.

Two years later Paul Ritter suggested that if the orgasm were looked on as an event between two people, it could be described in terms of three fundamental phases of a single process. He termed the three phases attraction, fusion and liberation. Energetically we can represent the process as in Figure 11.1. Stage 1 shows the approaching energetic events; stage 2 shows their merger, coupling or fusion; stage 3 shows the ending of the superimposition and the liberation of the now-dissociated processes.

We can use these concepts to represent the relationship between spirit-body and material body. Let us take the upper line to represent the energetic orgonome, or what Andrade calls the 'biological organising model'. The lower line would represent the energetic condensation of the fertilised cell, the material orgonome, with its DNA content, in a totipotent state, before differentiation and morphogenetic organisation has begun. The second part of the diagram represents the coupling of the life process, the superimposition of matter and spirit, the incarnation of mass-free energy in the condensing and focusing plasmatic sac. In the third phase we have liberation, the separation of the essence of the person from his existence in a body which returns to dust. The upper line represents the continuity of the energetic orgonome (the survival of the spirit body); the lower line represents the decomposition of the material orgonome.

Stepping away from the body into the more energetic

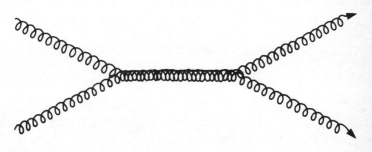

Figure 11.1   Attraction, fusion, liberation

medium, I would like to look at dreams, visions and hallucinations, which later will lead into the areas of psychosis that we met in the previous chapter.

If I see a ghost, am I seeing what other people can't see, or am I projecting on to the world outside me a confused image from my own brain? If I dream, am I experiencing a particular state of resonance in my brain, or is the non-physical part of me experiencing some kind of reality in a non-physical domain? What happens when two people who have never met and who live in different cities both dream that they meet each other one night and then dream that they arrange to meet in a third city two weeks later, not in a dream, and then, not in a dream, actually do so? (This happened to two people I know who started a twenty-year partnership.)

A dream may be a series of images evoked from the excitatory patterns in the brain. It may also be something else; an out-of-the-body experience that is not grasped as such. In occult terminology such an experience is spoken of as astral travel, travel of a subtler body on a subtler plane of existence. A dream might of course contain mixtures of both types of experience.

If a person has a vision which is confirmable, such as dreaming a set of events which subsequently take place, we say that he is psychic. If a person has a vision which is not confirmable, i.e. he says he sees things that we say we cannot see, we call him psychotic.

Laing quotes Gilchrist, telling the story of William Blake:

On Peckham Rye (by Dulwich Hill) it was, as he in after years related, that while quite a child, of eight or ten perhaps, he had his first vision. Sauntering along, the boy looked up and saw a tree filled with angels, bright angelic wings bespangling every bough like stars. Returning home he related the incident, and only through his mother's intercession escaped a thrashing from his father for telling a lie.[18]

Laing comments at some length.

Lying or not, children today are liable to be given treatment, if not a thrashing, for less than saying that they saw angels in trees.

A young child may be allowed one or two hallucinations if he or she seems normal otherwise, but more would suggest the need for observation at least.

Today, I would guess, Blake's vision is more likely to be disbelieved than believed. It may be tolerated. It will be allowed, if it is not forbidden. Angels do not exist, therefore he could be lying. He could have hallucinated them. Angels can only be hallucinations anyway, if they are anything. There may be something the matter with him. Should we not then have him looked at, examined, looked into. May there not be changes in the EEG?

Angels transgress the frontier of the objective world. The objective world is the preserve of objective objects and objective events. In that objective world angels are ipso facto, de facto, per se, as such, impossible, therefore they do not exist. From the objective biological point of view one can only ask the basic question: have angels biological utility? Have angels, that is hallucinations, survival value? Are they signs of pathology? Do they remit spontaneously? Have they good prognosis? Shall we allow them?[18]

'Hallucination' is derived from the Greek word *aluein* which means a homeless wandering, a restless roaming. We may project images from the past, or from our personal unconscious, out on to the world. A man terrified of snakes may hallucinate snakes when he sees a rope. We may also be able to introject into our here-and-now reality psychic events which are not of our creation and be troubled by them. Real ghosts do actually seem to haunt some people. The psychotic wanders out of his mind; the astral traveller wanders out of his body. Many psychically sensitive people, misunderstood because what they see is non-physical, may end up in institutions for the psychotic. Society may actually be disturbed by those who see what society has decided they cannot see because it is not there. Many psychotics who may have split off from everyday existence because of intense stress may also have genuine glimpses of other domains of existence that the normal ego barriers would otherwise have filtered out.

The evidence of the last few years has accumulated to show that psychotic states are reactions to stress acting on a person who is vulnerable to dissociation. In my book *The Charge of Consciousness*,[35] I went into great detail to describe the emotional dynamics, the biochemical reactions and the energy field metabolism of schizophrenic states. The stress drives a wedge between body and soul and creates some degree of disembodiment and depersonalisation.

Frank Lake, Stanislav Grof and others have identified birth trauma as one of the major stressing events that may set up a tendency for later psychosis. But we can distinguish two different forms of response to the stress of a tense birth. In the first of these the person's identity is out-of-the-body; he feels spaced out, euphoric, identified with Christ, senses himself as a spiritual astronaut or a cosmic visionary flooded with light. In the other state his identity is dead-to-the-spirit, he feels ground-down, burnt out; his imagery is of the black sun;[36] his body has become hell and he longs for death to liberate him from the tomb of the body. It is the difference between an acute schizophrenic episode and a severe depression.

A person who is naturally psychic is sometimes called a sensitive. If he can ground his heightened openness to other levels of reality he may become a healer or a seer. If he cannot ground it he can easily be confused with the out-of-the-body psychotic and may even be treated as one.

Many children are naturally psychic. It is part of a sensitivity they enter the world with. There is rich evidence suggesting the foetus is highly psychic.[37] Consciousness in the foetus has but recently reopened its association with matter in the events of incarnation. But children are frequently laughed at, ridiculed and humiliated for their psychic gifts. This can lead to a premature close-down. From now on the taboo on spirituality may be as strong or stronger than the taboo on sexuality. Arthur Guirdham in his book *Obsession*[38] has argued that obsessional neurosis may have its origins in the premature clamp-down and shutting-out of psychic vision or spiritual insight. The publisher's summary of the book is hard to improve upon.

> This book is a new approach to the understanding of neurotic disease. . . To the author, a consultant psychiatrist of forty years standing, the explanation of many of those who reveal obsessional symptoms is that they are suffering from repression of their psychic gifts.
>
> Obsessional states are a direct protective reflex following the perception of evil. This is first revealed in the night terrors and involuntary tics of childhood. The victims of obsessional states are often markedly psychic. Many are clairvoyant and telepathic. Their obsessional tendencies are related to the repression of these gifts. . . The obsessional patient is two persons in one: that is he is, on the one hand, a mystic with psychic gifts and, on the other, an exponent of an orthodoxy with ritualistic tendencies. The latter are a mask and an atonement for his psychic endowments. He combines in one personality the role of persecuted heretic and inquisitor, or gifted mystic and repressive priest.[38]

In treading the embodied road of evolution through the twin worlds we face two threats: the threat of being enmeshed so much in matter, compacted behind too much density of structure, so that the spirit starts to suffocate; this is the plight of the obsessional person trapped in his rituals. The other threat is the threat of being trapped out of matter; sent spinning off, free-floating, into space without ground or centre, on a cosmic trip to a far star, with no clear way of navigating back.

In *The Charge of Consciousness*[35] I looked on its process as one of gating. I described a number of boundary-functions in the brain that acted as gates to perception, feeling and action. The obsessional person is over-gated; he suffers from tunnel vision, compulsively bound actions, restriction of feeling, blocking-off of sensitivity, narrowing of perceptions. These over-gatings are precisely what Arthur Guirdham is calling the defence against psychic openness.

In the over-excited states of schizophrenia, we have under-gating. Too much psychic material is pouring into the consciousness without the ability to regulate it, sort it, digest it, integrate it, filter it or excrete it. Such a person sucks in what Frank Lake called 'negative umbilical affect'. Lake saw this as a literal taking-in of negative emotionality from the mother down the cord. But since the foetus is psychic we must also consider how foetal stress situations may weaken in some people the ability to gate-out wanted psychic material.

Obsession, I suggested above, can be looked on as a compulsive guarding of the self against psychic invasion. The obsessive person surrounds himself with rituals which protect him against named, or sometimes nameless, fears. Some of the rituals may be persecutory, as in the obsessional trials of witches in the Middle Ages. These acts of organised social compulsiveness protected people from psychic invasion by witches, so they thought. In similar fashion, Hitler's monolithic obsessional organisation for the extermination of the Jews had a protective function. The Jew, according to Nazism, was a threat to the Aryan blood.

The invasive agent that is feared in the obsessional defence is a possessing entity. The Jew was portrayed as a sexual possessor, a threat to the German woman. The witch was seen as a psychic possessor, someone who was believed able to take over control of one's body and soul. She was also seen as a sexual possessor, someone with the power to overpower male sexuality.

Morton Schatzman, in his fascinating study of the Schrebers,[39] shows how the paranoid father, by his oppressive rituals which he enacted on his son, was guilty of soul murder. The growing child had little defence against this kind of influence. His soul was possessed by the father. When he grows up and he is no longer forced to live the kind of life his father demands, he is still possessed. His behaviour is driven by the absent father. Dead fathers can in the same way continue, beyond the grave, by the well-understood processes in psycho-dynamics of introjection, to possess their grown children and to drive their behaviour along channels not of their choice.

Now what are we to make of a psychically open person whose absent father is actually sending telepathic messages as a way of strengthening a control system. The cord, of which Laing writes, which continues to tie people to each other in compulsive linkages, long after the umbilical cord is cut, may not just be metaphoric. People with low thresholds to thought-invasion may actually have negative affect from others who are actually negative to them pouring down their psychic plumbing. In the Polynesian system known as *huna* there is the teaching (also found in shamanism) that we are actually connected to each other by psychic threads (in *huna* called *aka* threads). Some people experience tugs and strains on their chakras when situated physically near and sometimes emotionally near (but physically far away) from others. Puharich has suggested that telepathic sending and receiving involves changes in brain capacitance related to the hyperactivity and hypoactivity of the vegetative nervous system and the setting up of psi-plasmatic warp-strains, a kind of invisible emotional push-pull system, rather as the gravitational influences between plants in general relativity are seen as warps in space time.[19] In psycho-synthesis those so tied are said to be 'corded'.

Television can broadcast a whole ethos of attitudes through its broadcasting channels. Subliminal advertising gets us when we least expect it. We live in a psychic sea of everyone else's thoughts and feelings; and we are part of the sea of negative or positive influence, both conscious and unconscious, which everyone lives and breathes in. Obsession is defendedness against unchosen influences to the point of loss of spontaneity and entrapment in oneself. Possession is defencelessness against unchosen influence. It is a form of selling the soul to the devil, or to the guru, in a way that we cannot disconnect from.

But possession is used one stage further to mean invasion of our personality, not by living forces but by discarnate forces. Guirdham's account is very clear.

> Possession implies the total subjugation of the human personality by another entity, usually discarnate. The possession entity is emphatically not another personality. This follows automatically in the case of possession by discarnatees who have already surrendered their human ego. The invading entity has a psyche, usually returned from the dead, but sometimes pertaining to the living.
>
> In the Middle Ages a good deal of illness both psychiatric and physical was attributed to possession. This belief has never entirely died. It was largely rejected for a couple of centuries and has recently been reconsidered. . . In Brazil especially a considerable circle of psychiatrists regard possession as a causative factor in psychotic disorders.[40]

I met some of the Brazilian psychiatrists in Rio de Janeiro in May 1982. I was impressed with their lucidity and their ability to combine a theory of psychic invasion by possessing entities with other more acceptable psychodynamic or biochemical theories. They have amassed a considerable body of data to support their claims and have developed techniques of *dis-obsession* which have proved effective, when normal psychiatric processes have not, for driving out the possessing entity and restoring sanity. The only account of this brilliant Brazilian work, in English, is the book by Divaldo Franco, *Obsession*.[41] The Brazilians use the word obsession in the *opposite* sense to the way it is used in this paper, as more or less equivalent to possession and not as a defence against it.[42]

An American psychiatrist who worked with this theory and who used the methods of dis-possession, is Carl Wickland. He describes how he views the possessing entities as invariably in some kind of earth-bound state.

Many are in a state of heavy sleep, others are lost or confused; troubled minds may be haunted by fear of the strange darkness, those conscious stricken suffer in anguish or remorse for their earth conduct; some, impelled by selfish or evil inclinations, seek an outlet for their tendencies, remaining in this condition until their destructive desires are outgrown . . . Lacking physical bodies through which to carry out earthly propensities many discarnated intelligences are attracted to the magnetic light which emanates from mortals, and, consciously or unconsciously attach themselves to these magnetic auras, finding an avenue of expression through influencing, obsessing, or possessing human beings. Such obtruding spirits influence susceptible sensitives with their thoughts, impart their own emotions to them, weaken their will-power, and often control their actions, producing great distress, mental confusion and suffering.

These earthbound spirits are the supposed 'devils' of all ages; 'devils' of human origin, by-products of human selfishness, false teachings and ignorance, thrust blindly into a spirit existence, and held there in a bondage of ignorance.

The physical conditions permitting this impingement are varied; such encroachment is often due to a natural and predisposed susceptibility, a depleted nervous system, or sudden shock. Physical derangements are conducive to obsession [i.e. possession], for when the vital forces are lowered, less resistance is offered and intruding spirits are allowed easy access.

This encroachment alters the characteristics of the sensitive, resulting in a seemingly changed personality,

sometimes simulating multiple or dissociate
personalities, and frequently causes apparent insanity.[43]

At the time of Christ, possession by 'devils' was the only
explanation of madness. Modern psychiatry has a simpler
explanation: disordered chemicals in the brain, or invasion by
thoughts from the unconscious. These two theories of
insanity are in no way mutually exclusive.

In psychotic states we know that the biochemical and
energetic gates that filter out psychic information are blown
wide open. The result is confusion between internal psychic
reality and external psychic reality. In the spaced-out blown-
open states of psychic unprotectedness, who can positively
state that negative influences may not enter and begin to
overpower the normal consciousness resident in the body?

Reich cautioned us to listen carefully to how the psychotic
describes his internal experience, when he wrote:

> The delusion of 'forces from beyond' is not merely a
> psychotic construction without a basis in reality; rather
> it describes a deeply felt reality, although in a distorted
> manner . . . In their delusions psychotics tell us
> important things about deep functions of nature. We
> must only learn to understand their language.[44]

I was struck by an unusual coincidence. In Guirdham's book,
The Psyche in Medicine, he gives an account of the physical
relationship between possession and emaciation.

> In addition to the classical symptoms of depression,
> agitation and self-accusation, the patients I have in
> mind showed two striking features: they were markedly
> emaciated and very hallucinated. With regard to the
> emaciation it is reasonable that depressed patients
> should show signs of malnutrition due to reduced
> appetite as well as an inability to assimilate what food
> is taken. On the other hand there are plenty of
> depressives who put on weight because the slowing up
> of their metabolic processes reduces their capacity to

burn up fuel. The cases I have in mind fall into a completely different category. The patients were so wasted that, in spite of a considerable intake of concentrated nourishing food such as eggs, milk and the like they resembled Belsen figures. I have known women of average height who have shrivelled to four stone and had wrinkled bodies and limbs like matchsticks. They also had a toxic appearance which very often justified the use of the word cachetic, which implies a tarnished café-au-lait complexion. This emaciation was due to possession. The latter was a secondary process grafted on to a pre-existing depression. We have already said that possession can induce guilt and depression. Contrariwise a patient can be depleted by depression... The loss of weight and toxic appearance referred to should be noted well. These are the commoner metabolic consequences of possession.[40]

In the ancient *huna* system of Polynesia, the healers were called *kahunas*. They worked with the orgone energy field of the body, and their word for what Reich called orgone was *mana*. They believed that transfer of *mana* was possible between people. A healer could help to augment and strengthen a person's natural supply of *mana*. A possessing spirit, on the other hand, could drain a person's energy and sap their strength and vitality, functioning like an energetic vampire. The *kahunas* had a quaint name for the possessing entity: an 'eating companion'. This is how Max Freedom Long describes it.

Since the kahunas of the healing orders were either trained psychics or used a psychic as an assistant, they were constantly on the lookout for spirits which had fastened themselves to the living and were causing some degree of illness or mental trouble. These spirits, because they invariably drew mana from the living to strengthen themselves, were called 'eating companions' by the kahunas and in all efforts to heal a patient they were watched for, and if found were removed, just as were the complexes. The observed technique for the removal was the accumulation of a very heavy shock charge of mana and the use of it, coupled with a type of mesmeric suggestion, to dislodge the obsessing spirit.[45]

Max Freedom Long distinguishes four grades of psychological disturbance; the third level includes deep neurotic, even psychotic or psychosomatic patterns of illness, while level four is illness brought about by discarnate influence.

Guirdham comments on the relationship between this kind of influence and the susceptibility to it.

It is not inevitable that a living person becomes a casualty from contact with a lower and evil entity, and succumbs to disease or accident. Disease arising from possession inevitably involves some degree of struggle between the individual and the possessing entity. It is always the role of the human personality to resist its own dissolution. Nevertheless it can happen that the invading entity finds in the person it enters the perfect pabulum for its development. The living individual can be taken over completely, not merely to commit isolated acts of destruction or homicide, but constantly and chronically, or at any rate for long periods, for the performance of evil.[40]

In the *huna* system there is a teaching about the low self, the middle self and the high self, which is extraordinarily close to the work of John Pierrakos in core energetics.[46] Pierrakos' work is about how to make contact with this high self. It is significant that, more than anyone else who came from the field of bio-energetics, he has focused tremendous awareness on the aura, or spirit-body. In the next section of this chapter there is a discussion of the energetic metabolism of the aura, and ways of strengthening it so that any possibility of the kind of psychic invasion described above is prevented.

Coming back to the energy field itself, Payne and Bendit have described in their invaluable book some of the properties of what I am choosing to call the 'metabolism of the energy field'.[47] It is clear from the account that follows that, just as in the physical body there is an ordered or a disordered metabolism, so this is also true of the energy-body. Indeed the two types of health bear a close relationship. This is how Benjamin Walker sees it.

The health of the physical body often determines the state of the astral double. In general it might be said that when the vital resources of the body are at low ebb, conditions arise that are conducive to dissociation. Extreme cold and fatigue, an accident especially to the head, injury entailing loss of blood, certain kinds of physical and mental shock, all serve to *shatter the cohesiveness and integrity of the individual.* A physically weak person exteriorises more easily.

Sylvia Muldoon was of the opinion that nervousness was the inability to hold psychic energy within the bounds of the body, the container being unable to hold the contents. The astral body gets over-excited and one becomes responsive to other ranges of existence outside the commonplace.

In the occult view, schizophrenia, like many other types of insanity, represents a pathological condition of the second body. The astral world starts making inroads into the waking consciousness.

Spontaneous exteriorisation, such as might occur during illness or accident, is one thing, but enforced dissociation is another matter altogether. A prominent psychic once said that those who dabble in these pursuits are likely to become afflicted with pathologies of the astral body.

If the astral body has once or twice been forcibly moved out of alignment by recourse to more drastic methods like psychedelic drugs, or some other xenophrenic inducing agent, the door to the outer dimensions that is normally shut tight during one's waking hours may be loosened, or worse still, remains permanently ajar, creating a leak from outside. Symptoms of such a state may include headaches, dizziness, loss of memory, hypochondria, fainting spells, paralysis, 'voices', hallucinations and nightmares.[48]

Payne and Bendit's account of the healthy metabolism in the energy field involves the creation of a balance between two streams of energy that converge on the chakras. They suggest that the chakra itself is a vortical energy form created by the interplay of these two streams of energy that converge on the chakras. They suggest that the chakra itself is a vortical energy form created by the interplay of these two streams of energy weaving together.

One of these, flowing in the spinal cord, is thrown out from the centre and flows towards the periphery in a widening spiral; this represents the *motor stream*. The second stream, impinging on the surface of the etheric body, spirals inward, narrowing as it goes; this is the receptive or *sensory stream*. These two spirals flow parallel to one another, but in opposite directions, and may be compared to interlocking screw-threads, in that one may be said to run in the grooves of the other. They give an impression of spinning, like the fluid in the vortex of a whirlpool.[47]

They distinguish between negative psychism, in which these two streams are poorly coordinated with each other, and positive psychism, in which they are well coordinated. The negative psychic state is one of vulnerability to invasion by the energetic fields of other people, or the hostile 'forces' that take over the consciousness in schizophrenia. The positive psychic state, although it is much more open than the usual mechanistic state of closure, still forms a boundary: it is as though the intact energy field emits a coherent radiant force that forms a barrier to any need to take flight into psychotic ideation when the normal rigid armour is not available.

> The chakras of the negative psychic are like a windmill, responsive to every breeze, whereas those of the positive are like an electrically-driven fan; capable of generating their own wind as well as being sensitive to draughts blowing upon them.[47]

Earlier in this chapter the polarity of the I and the self was used as a model for the pulsation between bounded and unbounded states. In spite of the great expansion of boundaries that must happen for a psychic receptivity or psychic outgoing radiation (healing force) to take place, in spite of the contact with the cosmic energy sources of the self, the positive psychic keeps an intact I. He loses the defended character-armoured ego, but retains the functional ego that is needed to integrate experience and to keep a coherent boundary.

> In the purely receptive chakras of the negative psychic, the incoming and outgoing streams are not coordinated with one another. The result is a lack of tone, of resilience, in the mechanism.
> When the intellect comes into play, the two streams become polarised, and lines of force are then created which help to maintain a stable relationship between the two streams. The difference is roughly that between the canvas cone used on airfields as a wind indicator, and a metal horn on a loudspeaker: the first goes slack when not filled with wind coming from outside, while the second retains its shape and does not depend on fortuitous external factors.[47]

The energy body in a sensitive person who is protected against shock and psychic injury is described as like a well-knit mesh; resilient, radiant and pulsating. If the psychic motor stream, the outflowing energy, becomes undercontained, then there is a surging in the energy-field which, whilst it may create a superficial firework display, is ultimately exhausting and depleting.

> The manic aura seethes and foams and throws off material, but this has no coordination or coherence and reflects the patient's jumble of talk and inconsequential behaviour.[42]

This is a centrifugal aura, throwing off sparks and ash like a catherine wheel. On the other hand the centripetal aura sucks in and absorbs like a piece of blotting paper.

> The channels through which the energy flows become slack like a canvas hose when the water-pressure is poor. The consequence is loss of vitality by leakage. The very fact that the pressure is low allows of such leakage, whereas the greater the pressure of vital energy the less permeable and the more continent the fabric becomes. A loose-knit etheric body is largely defenceless ... against the assault of psychic impacts.[47]

Payne and Bendit are describing hyper-arousal in the energy field. The same spectrum applies. The overgushing of the energy field breaks up the coherence of the mesh; the loose-knittedness prevents it from reforming. Both states loosen the bonding of the etheric matrix which joins and bridges the mental and emotional energy fields (the so-called 'astral body') to the physical organism and expose the person to the risk of unintended dissociation or involuntary disembodiment.

Dr William Tiller, who is head of the materials science department at Stanford University, has developed a sophisticated model trying to reconcile modern physics with some of the chakras and the endocrine glands. He sees the chakra-endocrine gland pair as a resonant energy transducer in the body. When the chakras are balanced properly, he writes:

> They create a spinning action at the inlet location. This

in turn leads to an energy vortex at the mouth of each centre. As the individual develops, the frequency of spin becomes faster and faster and a greater energy flux is processed by the individual. He begins to manifest greater and greater psycho-energetic capacities. At these higher energy fluxes, there is even a greater need for balance to occur between the different centres; otherwise energy surges can occur which will damage the weaker links of the system, and the imbalance in human behaviour patterns may be expected to ensue. . . . If one is in such an unbalanced energy function condition and one shocks open a particular energy centre, either by the agency of an accident, the taking of drugs, or severe emotional experience, then one may anticipate a type of personal havoc to follow.[49]

Psychic healers advocate a variety of breathing processes to try to steady the etheric bridge. These are better learned from an individual teacher. One may ask why people should need to learn to breathe. We have the same question in bio-energy work. It is not a question of learning deliberate techniques as a goal, although if breathing is very disturbed, conscious attention to the process of breathing may be needed on the way back to the recovery of spontaneous balancing of the energy field through natural breathing. But Payne and Bendit's account of the breathing needed to steady the etheric bridge would be hard to better from orgonomic knowledge.

The student should learn to breathe freely and fully, but not too fully, and deeply, but not too deeply; if he overdoes this, the result is giddiness and discomfort. The point is to learn to breathe with the diaphragm as well as the ribs. If one does this the upper part of the abdominal wall is seen to move with the breathing and the movement will not be restricted to the chest wall alone. A useful way to achieve this is to breathe in, filling first the upper part of the chest, then the lower, then to breathe out from below first, emptying the

upper part of the chest last. Gradually one should
accustom oneself to this as a normal way of breathing.
One may perhaps then become breathing-conscious, so
that as one realises tension and anxiety one feels the
change of rhythm and can then take steps to remedy
it.[47]

The outer ground is the body: it is built of flesh and bone,
blood vessels and nerve cells. It is an incredibly intricate work
of art and a fascinatingly complex piece of life equipment. It
walks the earth for seventy-odd years, and then perishes;
sooner if tragedy strikes younger.

The inner ground is who we are; it links us to a realm of
existence before the body is formed and which gives
continuity after the body has gone back to ash. The inner
ground of a person is not trapped by time or stuck in space: it
bridges all the boundaries.[50]

It is a very unusual idea to confine the journey of the
soul to a few years between birth and death. People still
live through journeys which take them to other life
times and other worlds. It is the pride of science to feel
able to say: all this is impossible.[51]

R. D. Laing

APPENDIX 1

THE EARLY INSIGHTS OF JOSEF BREUER

Some of the clearest insights into the choices of direction that therapeutic approaches were to take are found right at the inception of psychoanalysis. Josef Breuer, who collaborated with Freud before the turn of the century, is usually credited with introducing the *cathartic method* into psychoanalysis. His work provides one of the clearest sketch maps of the therapeutic terrain.

Breuer's understanding of the neurotic symptoms that he studied in his patients was in terms of currents of energy and channels of excitement. He compares nervous excitation with the functioning of an electrical system and argues that a surplus of excitation can spark over from one functional system to another.

Breuer distinguishes three types of activity through which excitation of the nervous system can be expressed.

1 *Ideational activity* – he contrasts waking consciousness with dreamless sleep as two extreme conditions of 'intra-cerebral tonic excitation'. Ideas, dreams, images, thoughts, perceptions, hallucinations are examples of this kind of activity.
2 *Motor discharge* through expressive behaviour of various kinds involving the body musculature.
3 *Vegetative affect* appearing as respiratory or digestive or cardiac distress.

It can readily be seen that these three forms of excitation correspond to the three embryological layers. We could perhaps call them the *thought stream*, the *muscle stream* and the *gut stream*, to emphasise both their germinal origins and their relevance to the processes of therapy.

The brain, in Breuer's view:

> behaves like one of those electrical systems of restricted capability which are unable to produce both a large amount of light and of mechanical work at the same time. If it is transmitting power, only a little energy is available for lighting, and vice versa. Thus we find that if we are making great muscular efforts we are unable to engage in continuous thought, or that if we concentrate our attention in one sensory field the efficiency of the other cerebral organs is reduced.[1]

Emotional stress, in Breuer's schema, is synonymous with an increase of excitation. In anxiety, rage, pleasure, pain, sorrow, something is stirred up. An emotional expression is a total organismic event in which the muscular system, the visceral system and the ideational system are all simultaneously involved. Thus Darwin, writing some twenty or so years before Breuer, on the action of emotions on the body, described:

1 Trembling of the muscles, which is common to many or most of the lower animals . . . I am assured by an eminent authority that young children do not tremble, but go into convulsions under the circumstances which would induce excessive trembling in adults . . . Of all emotions, fear notoriously is the most apt to induce trembling; but so do occasionally great anger and joy.

2 The manner in which the secretions of the alimentary canal and of certain glands – as the liver, kidneys or mammae – are affected by strong emotions, is another excellent instance of the direct action of

the sensorium on these organs . . . The great
physiologist Claude Bernard has shown how the least
excitement of a sensitive nerve reacts on the heart. . .
Hence when the mind is strongly excited we might
expect that it would instantly affect in a direct
manner the heart. . . the vasomotor system which
regulates the diameter of the small arteries is directly
acted on by the sensorium.[2]

Breuer, unlike Darwin, was deriving his concepts from
hysterical patients, not animals, and one of the characteristics
of hysteria is the phenomenon known as splitting, or dissociation. It is one form of blocking and one of its effects is to
break up the integrated nature of our responses. Breuer
recognised this, for he wrote that the nervous system:

forms throughout an interconnected whole; but at
many points in it great, though not insurmountable
resistances are interposed, which prevent the general
uniform distribution of excitation ... In the interests of
the safety and efficiency of the organism, the nervous
apparatuses of the complexes of organs which are of
vital importance – the circulatory and digestive organs –
are separated by strong resistances from the organs of
ideation. Their independence is assured. They are not
affected by ideas.[1]

He makes clear that the degree of such resistance varies
between people, and that there are those who appear to show
no nerves even in emotionally charged situations, and others
who develop palpitations and diarrhoea on the slightest
provocation.

However this may be, there are resistances in normal
people against the passage of cerebral excitation to the
vegetative organs. These resistances correspond to the
insulation of electrical conducting lines. At points at
which they are abnormally weak they are broken
through when the tension of cerebral excitation is high,

and this – the affective excitation – passes over the peripheral organs.[1]

An alternative channel through which excitation can be discharged is the motor system. Breuer distinguishes two ways in which this can take place: release through voluntary movements and expressions; and release through involuntary motor discharge. The first of these he describes as follows:

> Shouting and jumping for joy, the increased muscular tone of anger, angry words and retaliatory deeds – all these allow the excitation to flow away in movements. Mental pain discharges it in difficult breathing and in an act of secretion: in sobs and tears. It is a matter of everyday experience that such reactions reduce excitement and allay this in such phrases as 'to cry oneself out', 'to blow off steam', etc. What is being got rid of is nothing else than the increased cerebral excitation.[1]

These motor outlets are coordinated and integrated, in full emotional expression, but an excessively strong excitation, Breuer points out, can bypass or break through the coordinative centres and flow off in primitive movements. We have the equivalent of what he calls a short circuit. What we are dealing with is two levels of motor behaviour: the first pattern system controlled by the neo-cortex of the brain; the second mediated by the limbic system, the old reptilian brain. The limbic discharge is the earliest of the two developmentally, and is dominant in the foetal stage and in very early infancy; the voluntary motor discharge patterns do not develop in full until myelinisation is complete at a later stage. Breuer expresses it this way.

> In infants, apart from the respiratory action of screaming, affects only produce and find expression in uncoordinated contractions of the muscles of this primitive kind – in arching the body and kicking about. As development proceeds, the musculature passes more

and more under the control of the power of coordination, and the will. But the opisthotonus, which represents the maximum of motor effort of the somatic musculature, and clonic movements of kicking and threshing about, persist throughout life as the form of reaction for the maximal excitation of the brain – for the purely physical excitation in epileptic attacks as well as for the discharge of maximal affects in the shape of more or less epileptic convulsions (viz. the purely motor part of hysterical attacks).[1]

It is extraordinary that such a basic biological approach to the ways that people handle excitement should have been developed right at the beginning of psychoanalysis. The three areas on which Breuer focused – the stream of consciousness, the flow of muscular activity and the rhythms of vegetative life – are the dominant themes that underlie all later therapeutic work.

APPENDIX 2

REFERENCES

Introduction

1 Boadella, David, *Wilhelm Reich: The Evolution of his Work*, Routledge & Kegan Paul, 1985.

Chapter 1 Emotional expression and the body

1 Darwin, Charles, *The Expression of the Emotions in Man and Animals*, Chicago University Press, 1965 (first published 1872).

2 Freud, Sigmund, 'The origin and development of psycho-analysis', *American Journal of Psychology*, XXI, 1911.

3 Reich, Wilhelm, *Character Analysis*, Vienna, 1933; reprinted Farrar, Strauss & Giroux, 1969.

4 Laban, Rudolf, *The Mastery of Movement*, Macdonald & Evans, 1971.

5 Raknes, Ola, 'The orgonomic concept of health and its social consequences', *Orgonomic Medicine*, I, 1955.

6 Waal, Nic, 'A special technique of psychotherapy with an autistic child', in Gerald Caplan (ed.), *Emotional Problems of Early Childhood*, Basic Books, 1955.

7 Baker, Elsworth, *Man in the Trap*, Macmillan, 1968.

8 Lowen, Alexander, *Physical Dynamics of Character Structure*, Grune & Stratton, 1958; reprinted as *Language of the Body*, Macmillan, 1969.

9 Boadella, David, 'Stress and character', *Energy and Character*,

VI, 1, 1974; and 'Organ systems and life styles', *Energy and Character*, VII, 3, 1975 – VIII, 3, 1976.

10 Feldenkrais, Moshe, *Body and Mature Behaviour*, New York International University Press, 1973.

11 Alexander, Mathias, *The Use of Self*, Chaterson, 1932.

12 Lawrence, D.H., *Sex, Literature and Censorship*, Heinemann, 1955.

Chapter 2 Centring, grounding and facing

1 Mott, Francis, *Nature of the Self*, Allen & Wingate, 1959.

2 Boyesen, Gerda, *Entre psyche et soma*, Payot, Paris, 1985.

Chapter 3 Embodiment before birth

1 Nilsson, Lennard, *et al.*, *The Everyday Miracle*, Allen Lane, 1967.

2 Keleman, Stanley, *Your Body Speaks its Mind*, Simon & Schuster, 1975.

3 Laing, R. D., *The Facts of Life*, Allen Lane, 1976.

4 Hartmann, Otto, *Dynamische Morphologie*, Klostermann, 1950.

5 Schwenk, Theodore, *Sensitive Chaos*, Anthroposophical Publishing House, 1965.

6 Liley, A. W., *The Foetus as a Personality*, School of Obstetrics and Gynaecology, University of Auckland, New Zealand.

7 Heuer, Gottfried, 'Hypnosis, reincarnation therapy and biodynamic psychology I: A translucent turtle ascends to the stars', *Journal of Biodynamic Psychology*, 2, 1981.

8 Grof, Stanislav, *Realms of the Human Unconscious*, Viking, 1975.

9 Mott, Francis, *Bio-synthesis*, David McKay, Philadelphia, 1948.

10 Le Boyer, Frederick, *Birth without Violence*, Wildwood House, 1975.

11 Janov, Arthur, *The Feeling Child*, Simon & Schuster, 1973.

12 Luce, Gay, *Biological Rhythms in Human and Animal Physiology*, Dover, 1971.

13 Howe, E. Graham, *Cure or Heal?*, Allen & Unwin, 1966.

Chapter 4 Transitions to establishment

1 Dick Read, Grantley, *Revelation of Childbirth*, Heinemann, 1946.

2 Rank, Otto, *The Trauma of Birth*, Harcourt & Brace, 1929.

3 Janov, Arthur, *Imprints*, Sphere, 1985.

4 Kitzinger, Sheila, *The Experience of Childbirth*, Penguin, 1972.

5 Montague, Ashley, *Touching*, Harper & Row, 1971.

6 Casserley, Norman, quoted in *Life-News*, 22 Jan. 1975.

7 Grof, Stanislav, *Realms of the Human Unconscious*, Viking, 1975.

8 Vellay, Pierre, *Childbirth without Fear*, Hutchinson, 1959.

9 Benyon, Constance, 'The normal second stage of labour', *Journal of Obstetrics and Gynaecology*, 64, 6, 1957.

10 Petersen, Fred, *Experiences in Obstetrics*.

11 Lake, Frank, 'Birth trauma, claustrophobia and LSD therapy', *Energy and Character*, 4, 1, 1973.

12 Yunker, Barbara, 'Delivery procedures that endanger a mother's life', *Good Housekeeping*, August 1975.

13 Selinger, Zelig, in *Newsletter of the Institute of Bio-energetic Analysis*, 3, September 1975.

14 Ritter, Paul and Ritter, Jean, 'An orgonomic functionalist theory of birth', *Orgonomic Functionalism*, 1, 2, March 1954.

15 Reich, Eva, 'The prevention of neurosis, self-regulation from birth on', *Journal of Biodynamic Psychology*, 1, 1980.

16 Silvert, Michael, 'Orgonomic practice in obstetrics', *Orgonomic Medicine*, 1, June 1955.

17 Schwenk, Theodor, *Sensitive Chaos*, Anthroposophical Publishing House, 1965.

18 Bowditch, Valerie, 'Beginnings', *Handfuls of Light*, Abbotsbury, 1971.

19 Le Boyer, Frederick, *Birth Without Violence*, Wildwood House, 1975.

20 Sindenbladh, Erik, *Water Babies*, Black, 1983.

21 Morgan, Elaine, *The Descent of Woman*, Stein & Day, 1972.

22 Reich, Wilhelm, 'Falling anxiety in an infant of three weeks', in *Cancer Biopathy*, Orgone Institute Press, 1948.

23 Bevan-Browne, M., *Sources of Love and Fear*, Allen & Unwin, 1950.

24 Pearse, I. and Crocker, L., *The Peckham Health Experiement*, Allen & Unwin, 1943.

25 Mott, Francis, *The Universal Design of Birth*, David McKay, Philadelphia, 1952.

Chapter 5 Head, heart and *hara*

1 Hartmann, Otto, *Dynamische Morphologie*, Klostermann, Frankfurt, 1950.

2 Reich, Wilhelm, *Character Analysis*, Vienna, 1933; reprinted Farrar, Strauss & Giroux, 1969.

3 Sheldon, W. H. *et al.*, *Varieties of Human Physique, an Introduction to Constitutional Psychology*, Harper & Brox, 1942.

4 Boadella, David, and Smith, David, *Maps of Character*, Abbotsbury, 1986.

5 Keleman, Stanley, *Emotional Anatomy*, Center Press, 1985.

6 Pierrakos, John, *The Energy Field in Man and Nature*, Institute for the New Age of Man, New York, 1970.

Chapter 6 Waves of breath

1 Boadella, David, 'Styles of breathing', *Energy and Character*, 8, 1, 1977.

2 Johnson, Lillemor, *Integrated Respiration Therapy*, privately printed, Oslo, 1981.

3 Lowry, Thomas, *Hyperventilation and Hysteria*, Springfield, Illinois, n.d.

4 Grof, Stanislav, *Realms of the Human Unconscious*, Viking, 1975.

5 Davies, Will, 'Working with the in-stroke', *Energy and Character*, 15 1984.

6 Boyesen, Gerda, *Entre psyche et soma*, Payot, Paris, 1985.

7 Thorpe, W. H., *Learning and Instinct in Animals*, Methuen, 1956.

8 Reich, Wilhelm, *Character Analysis*, Vienna 1933; reprinted Farrar, Strauss & Giroux, 1969.

9 Mott, Francis, *Biosynthesis*, David McKay, Philadelphia, 1948.

10 Boadella, David, 'Between coma and convulsion', *Energy and Character*, 6, 1, 1975; 7, 1976.

11 Lowen, Alexander, *Physical Dynamics of Character Structure*, Grune & Stratton, 1958; reprinted as *Language of the Body*, Macmillan, 1969.

12 Keleman, Stanley, *Emotional Anatomy*, Center Press, 1985.

Chapter 7 Grounding as communication

1 Keleman, Stanley, *Somatic Reality*, Center Press, 1985.

2 Lowen, Alexander and Lowen, Leslie, *The Way to Vibrant Health*, Harper & Row, 1977.

3 Mott, Francis, *Biosynthesis*, David McKay, Philadelphia, 1948.

4 Ritter, Paul, *The Free Family*, Gollancz, 1958.

5 Lake, Frank, *Studies in Constricted Confusion*, Clinical Theology Association, Nottingham, 1981.

6 Winnicott, D. W., *Maturational Processes and the Facilitating Environment*, Hogarth, 1965.

7 Crisp, Tony, 'Yoga in childbirth', in *Relax with Yoga*, Sphere, 1977.

8 Linden, Millicent, *Stretch for Life*, New York, 1968.

9 Reich, Wilhelm, *Character Analysis*, Vienna, 1933; reprinted Farrar, Strauss & Giroux, 1969.

10 Lowen, Alexander, *Physical Dynamics of Character Structure*, Grune & Stratton, 1958; reprinted as *Language of the Body*, Macmillan, 1969.

11 Raknes, Ola, 'The orgonomic concept of health and its social consequences', *Orgonomic Medicine*, I, 1955.

Chapter 8 Facing and sounding

1 Gold, Philip, 'Orgonomic therapy of the ocular segment', *Orgonomic Medicine*, II, 1, 1956.

2 Lowen, Alexander, unpublished MS.

3 Stein, Leopold, *The Infancy of Speech and the Speech of Infancy*, Routledge & Kegan Paul, 1952.

4 Piaget, Jean, *Language and Thought of the Child*, Routledge & Kegan Paul, 1959.

5 Mott, Francis, *Biosynthesis*, David McKay, 1948.

6 Laing, R. D., *The Divided Self*, Penguin, 1965.

7 Fromm-Reichmann, Frieda, 'Some aspects of psychoanalytic psychotherapy with schizophrenics', in E. B. Brody and F. Redlick (eds), *Psychotherapy with Schizophrenics*, New York International University Press, 1952.

8 Roberts, Barbara, 'Exploration without intrusion', *Energy and Character*, 7, 2, 1976.

9 Foudraine, Jan, *Not made of Wood*, Quartet, 1974.

10 Pierrakos, John, monograph of Institute of Bioenergetic Analysis, New York, 1972.

11 Laing, R. D., *Knots*, Penguin, 1970.

12 O'Connell, Vincent, 'Crisis psychotherapy', in J. Fagan and I. Shepherd (eds), *Gestalt Therapy Now*, Penguin, 1970.

13 Krishnamurti, Jiddu, *The First and Last Freedom*, Gollancz, 1972.

14 McLeish, Archibald, *Poetry and Experience*, Bodley Head, 1960.

15 Winnicott, D. W., *Maturational Processes and the Facilitating Environment*, Hogarth Press, 1965.

Chapter 9 Borderline patients and boundaries

1 Waal, Nic, letter to D. Boadella, Spring 1952.

2 Keleman, Stanley, 'Bio-energetic concepts of grounding', in D. Boadella (ed.), *In the Wake of Reich*, Coventure, 1976.

3 Lowen, Alexander and Lowen, Leslie, *The Way to Vibrant Health*, Harper & Row, 1977.

4 Lowen, Alexander, *Physical Dynamics of Character Structure*, Grune & Stratton, 1958; reprinted as *Language of the Body*, Macmillan, 1969.

5 Reich, Wilhelm, 'The schizophrenic split', in *Character Analysis*, Vienna, 1933; reprinted Farrar, Strauss & Giroux, 1969.

6 Rosen, John, *Direct Analysis*, Grune & Stratton, 1953.

7 Willie, James, 'The use of a male dummy in the treatment of schizophrenia', *Orgone Energy Bulletin*, 1, 2, April 1949.

8 Seaborne-Jones, Glyn, 'Launching', *Energy and Character*, 7, 1, January 1976.

9 Rado, Sandor, 'Hedonic self-regulation in the organism', in R. G. Heath (ed.), *The Role of Pleasure in Behaviour*, Harper & Row, 1964.

10 Tausk, Victor, 'On the origin of the "influencing machine" in schizophrenia', in R. Fliess (ed.), *The Psycho-analytic Reader*, Hogarth Press, 1950.

11 Fulkerson, Mary, 'The language of the axis', *Theatre Papers*, 12, Dartington Hall, 1977.

12 Pesso, Albert, *Movement in Psychotherapy*, University of London Press, 1969.

13 Herskowitz, Morton, 'The treatment of an episode of catatonic mutism', *Journal of Orgonomy*, 2, 1, March 1968.

14 Reich, Eva, 'Emotional first aid', *Energy and Character*, 8, 3, Sept. 1977.

15 Perls, Fritz, 'Four lectures', in J. Fagan and I. Shepherd (eds), *Gestalt Therapy Now*, Penguin, 1972.

16 Bakker, Cornelius and Bakker-Rabdau, Marianne, *No Trespassing: Explorations in Human Territoriality*, Coventure, 1973.

17 Tinbergen, Nikolaas, *Early Childhood Autism*, London, 1983.

18 Foudraine, Jan, *Not Made of Wood*, Quartet, 1974.

19 Schiff, Jacqui Lee, *Cathexis Reader*, Harper, 1975.

20 Barnes, Mary and Berke, Joseph, *Mary Barnes – Two Accounts of*

a Journey Through Madness, Penguin, 1973.

21 Berke, Joseph, 'Anti-psychiatry: an interview', in R. Boyers and R. Orill (eds), *Laing and Anti-Psychiatry*, Penguin, 1972.

22 Esterson, Aaron, *Leaves of Spring: Schizophrenia, Family and Sacrifice*, Penguin, 1972.

23 Fischer, Ronald, 'Cartography of inner spaces', in R. Segal and Louis West (eds), *Hallucinations*, Wiley, 1979.

24 Laing, R. D., *The Divided Self*, Penguin, 1965.

25 Coles, Robert, Farber, Leslie, Friedenberg, Edgar and Kux, Kenneth, 'R. D. Laing and anti-psychiatry: a symposium', in R. Boyers and R. Orill (eds), *Laing and Anti-Psychiatry*, Penguin, 1972.

26 Lidz, Theodore, 'Schizophrenia, R. D. Laing and the contemporary treatment of psychoses', in R. Boyers and R. Orill (eds), *Laing and Anti-Psychiatry*, Penguin, 1972.

Chapter 10 Inner ground

1 Reich, Wilhelm, *Character Analysis*, Vienna, 1933; reprinted Farrar, Strauss & Giroux, 1969.

2 Pierrakos, John, 'The core of man', *Energy and Character*, 5, 3, 1974.

3 Boadella, David, 'Quenching, grounding and territory', *Charge of Consciousness*, Abbotsbury, 1979.

4 Freud, Sigmund, *The Ego and the Id*, Hogarth Press, 1950.

5 Lowen, Alexander, *Physical Dynamics of Character Structure*, reprinted as *Language of the Body*, Macmillan, 1969.

6 Keleman, Stanley, *Your Body Speaks its Mind*, Simon & Schuster, 1975.

7 Rajneesh, Bhagwan Shree, *The Book of the Secrets, Vol. II: Discourses on the Vigyana Bhairava Tantra*, Rajneesh Foundation International, 1975.

8 Reich, Wilhelm, *The Murder of Christ*, Orgone Institute Press, 1952.

9 Schatzman, Morton, *Soul Murder: Persecution in the Family*, Random House, 1973.

10 Pierrakos, John, *Human Energy Systems Theory*, Institute of New Age of Man, 1976.

11 Rajneesh, Bhagwan Shree, *And the Flowers Showered*, Rajneesh Foundation International, 1975.

12 Rajneesh, Bhagwan Shree, *The Book of the Secrets, Vol. III*, Rajneesh Foundation International, 1976.

13 Lowen, Alexander, 'George', unpublished case history, referred to in 'Energy and language', *Energy and Character*, 5, 3, 1974.

14 Lowen, Alexander, *Depression and the Body*, Collier Macmillan, 1972.

15 Rajneesh, Bhagwan Shree, *The Book of the Secrets, Vol. I*, Rajneesh Foundation International, 1974.

16 Philipson, Tage, *Kaerlighesdlivet: Natur eller Unatur*, Lund & Andersen, Copenhagen, 1952.

17 Raknes, Ola, 'Life and religion', in D. Boadella (ed.), *In the Wake of Reich*, Coventure, 1970.

18 Tillich, Paul, 'The depth of existence', in *Shaking the Foundations*, Penguin, 1962.

19 Keleman, Stanley, *The Human Ground*, Center Press, 1975.

20 Keleman, Stanley, *Living your Dying*, Random House, 1974.

21 Keleman, Stanley, *Lifetimes*, unpublished manuscript.

22 Ali, Hameed, *Essence*, Weiser, 1986.

Chapter 11 The womb, the tomb and the spirit

1 Boadella, David, *Baptism of Fire*, Abbotsbury, 1980.

2 Boadella, David, 'Incarnation', *Energy and Character*, 13, 1, April 1982.

3 Humphries, Nicholas, 'Four minutes to midnight', *Energy and Character*, 13, 2, August 1982.

4 Boadella, David, 'Regression, reversal and the loss of boundaries', in *The Charge of Consciousness*, Abbotsbury, 1979.

5 Bjornsson, Oddur, *Yolk Life* (translated from Icelandic by

Gudrun Tomasdottir, unpublished).

6 Bloom, Anthony, 'On death', address to the Fellowship Conference of the Greek Orthodox Church, 1978.

7 Pascal, Blaise, *Pensées*, Penguin, 1966.

8 Lifton, Robert Jay, 'On death and the continuity of life: a new paradigm', *Journal of Psycho-History*, V 1, 4, Spring 1974.

9 Stevenson, Ian, *Twenty Cases Suggestive of Reincarnation* (five vols), University Press of Virginia, 1973.

10 Burr, Harold, *Fields of Life*, New York, 1972.

11 Jeffries, Michael, 'The Kirlian camera beams in to hidden abnormalities', *British Medical Association News Review*, 7, 1, January 1981.

12 Andrade, Hernani, 'Psi matter', *Energy and Character*, 1981; 12, 3 and 13, 1, 1982.

13 Motoyama, Hiroshi, 'Experience and experiments of the chakras', *Theories of the Chakras*, Wheaton, 1981.

14 Hunt, Valerie, 'Electronic evidence of auras and chakras in UCLA study', *Brain Mind Bulletin*, 3, 9, March 1978.

15 Hodson, Geoffrey, *The Miracle of Birth: a Clairvoyant Study of Pre-natal Life*, 1929.

16 Bendit, Phoebe and Bendit, Lawrence, *The Etheric Body of Man*, Theosophical Publishing House, 1977.

17 Assagioli, Robert, quoted in Piero Ferruci, *What We May Be*, Turnstone Press, 1982.

18 Laing, R. D., *The Voice of Experience*, Pantheon, 1976.

19 Puharich, Andrija, *Beyond Telepathy*, Darton, Longman & Todd, 1962.

20 Crookall, Robert, *Out of Body Experiences*, Ballantine Books, New Jersey, 1980.

21 Muldoon, Sylvan, *The Case for Astral Projection*, Rider & Co., Chicago, 1936.

22 Davis, A. J., *The Physician*, 1850.

23 Reich, Wilhelm, *The Function of the Orgasm*, Orgone Institute Press, 1942.

24 Freud, Sigmund, quoted by Laing (see reference 18.)

25 Boadella, David, 'Styles of breathing', *Energy and Character*, 8, 1, Jan. 1977.

26 Kelley, Charles, *The Radix Journal*, Radix Institute, Ojai, Calif.

27 Keleman, Stanley, *Living your Dying*, Random House, 1974.

28 Tsu, Chuang, *The Inner Chapters*, Wildwood, 1974.

29 Reich, Wilhelm, *Cosmic Superimposition*, Orgone Institute Press, 1951.

30 Boadella, David, 'Organ systems and lifestyles', *Energy and Character*, 7, 3, September 1976.

31 Targ, Russel and Puthoff, Harold, *Mind Reach*, Granada, 1972.

32 Leshan, Lawrence, *Clairvoyant Reality: Towards a General Theory of the Paranormal* (new edition of *The Medium, the Mystic and the Physicist*), Turnstone, 1980.

33 Xavier, Chico, *Evoluçao em dos mundos*, Spiritist Federation of Brazil, Rio de Janeiro, 1958.

34 Lowen, Alexander, *Physical Dynamics of Character Structure*, reprinted as *Language of the Body*, Macmillan, 1969.

35 Boadella, David, 'Ego boundaries and brain gates', in *The Charge of Consciousness*, Abbotsbury, 1979.

36 Laing, R. D., *The Divided Self*, Penguin, 1965.

37 Boadella, David, 'Foetal life, dreams and the psychic frontier', in *The Charge of Consciousness*, Abbotsbury, 1979.

38 Guirdham, Arthur, *Obsession*, Neville Spearman, 1972.

39 Schatzman, Morton, *Soul Murder: Persecution in the Family*, Random House, 1973.

40 Guirdham, Arthur, *The Psyche in Medicine*, Neville Spearman, 1978.

41 Franco, Divaldo, *Obsession*, Salvador, Brazil, 1980.

42 Kardec, Allen, *The Medium's Book*, Psychic Press, 1971.

43 Wickland, Carl, *Thirty Years Among the Dead*, Newcastle Publishing Co., Van Nuys, Calif., 1974.

44 Reich, Wilhelm, 'The schizophrenic split', *Character Analysis*, Vienna, 1933; reprinted Farrar, Strauss & Giroux, 1969.

45 Long, Max Freedom, *Secret Science at Work*, De Vorss & Co., Marina del Rey, Calif., 1953.

46 Pierrakos, John, *The Core of Man*, Institute for the New Age of Man, 1974.

47 Payne, Phoebe and Bendit, Lawrence, *The Psychic Sense*, Faber & Faber, 1943.

48 Walker, Benjamin, *Beyond Death's Door*, Sheldon Press, 1974.

49 Tiller, William, 'Consciousness, radiation and the developing sensory system', *Proceedings of the Academy of Para-Psychology and Medicine*. Academy of Parapsychology and Medicine, 1972.

50 Boadella, David, 'The inner ground', *Energy and Character*, 10, 2, May 1979.

51 Laing, R. D., *The Voice of Experience*, Allen Lane, 1982.

Appendix 1

1 Breuer, Josef and Freud, Sigmund, *Studies on Hysteria*, ed. A. Richards and J. Strachey, Penguin, 1974.

2 Darwin, Charles, *The Expression of the Emotions in Man and Animals*, Chicago University Press, 1965 (first published 1872).

APPENDIX 3

A SELECTION OF BOOKS AND ARTICLES BY DAVID BOADELLA

Books and articles

Articles in *Energy and Character* since 1970 (two issues per year, Abbotsbury).

In the Wake of Reich, Coventure, 1976.

The Charge of Consciousness: Energy, Chemistry and the Brain, Abbotsbury, 1979.

The Spiral Flame: A Study in the Meaning of D. H. Lawrence, University of New York at Buffalo, 1981.

The Formative Process and the Organising Field: a Monograph, Abbotsbury, 1982.

Jesus the Heretic: a Study in Alternative Christianity, Abbotsbury, 1984.

Wilhelm Reich: The Evolution of His Work, Routledge & Kegan Paul, 1985 (originally published by Vision Press, 1973; Contemporary Books, 1975).

Processes of Life Energy (in Japanese), Bio-energy Centre of Japan, 1987.

Psicoterapia del Corpo fra Corpo e Mente (with Jerome Liss), Astrolabia, 1986.

Maps of Character (with David Smith), Abbotsbury, 1976.

Chapters in other books

'Biosynthesis', in John Rowan (ed.), *Innovative Therapies in Britain*, Routledge & Kegan Paul, 1987.

'Life, energy and blood', in Mark Kidell (ed.), *The Meaning of Illness*, Routledge & Kegan Paul, 1987.

'The return of the repressed: the pseudo-sexual revolution', in David Holbrook (ed.), *The Case against Pornography*, Stoddard, 1975.

'The Language of Bio-energy', in Gerald Kogan (ed.), *Your Body Works*, Transformation Press, 1987.

'Styles of breathing', in Beverley Timmins (ed.), *The Psycho-Physiology of Respiration*, Plenum, 1987.

INDEX

234

INDEX

Freud, Sigmund, xiii, 2, 32, 107, 153-5, 187
Fromm-Reichmann, Frieda, 115-16
fusion, 196-8

gestalt therapy, xiii, 107, 120, 155
Grant, Joan, 29
gravity, 56-9; *see also* grounding
grief, 174, 176-7
Grof, Stanislav, 31-2, 34, 41, 44, 48, 81, 200
ground, outer and inner, 214
grounding, xiv, 13, 15, 93-106, 125-6; and birth, 94-8; and falling anxiety, 102-3; positions, 98-102; sitting, 104; walking, 103-4
Guirdham, Arthur, 201-2, 204, 206-8

hallucination, 199
hara, 67-8, 73, 77-8, 164
Hardy, Sir Alister, 53
harmonisation, 87
Hartmann, Otto, xiv, 24
Hayashi, Moyotuka, 30
head, 64-6, 75; and heart, 165-9
heart, 67, 74, 78, 162, 164-9
Heidegger, Martin, 174
Herskowitz, Morton, 135-7
Hitler, Adolf, 202
huna, 203, 207-8
Hunt, Valerie, 179
hyperventilation, 80-3
hysteria, 79, 88, 217

id, 17, 126, 150, 152
institutionalisation, 149

Janov, Arthur, 34, 36, 38, 52, 124-5, 153
Jones, Glynn Seaborn, 117
Jung, C.G., 167

kahunas, 207-8
karma, 163
Keats, John, 189
Keleman, Stanley, xiii; on: brain, 168; character, 72, 156; contact, 160-1; death, 188-9; embryogenesis, 22; grounding, 11, 92, 100, 125; imaginary body, 105; psychosis, 130; regression, 173; somatic resonance, xv
Keller, Helen, 113
Kelley, Charles, 188
Kelsey, Denys, 29
kinaesthetic affect, 18, 94
Kitzinger, Sheila, 39, 42
Klein, Melanie, 20
Krishnamurti, Jiddu, 120

Laban, Rudolf, 2-3
labour, 38-49; baby's experiences of, 40-1, 44-8; mother's experiences of, 40-3, 47-9; *see also* birth
Laing, R.D., 142-3; on: birth transitions, 55, 183; cords, 183-4, 203; death, 187, 214; embryogenesis, 22-3, 30-1; schizophrenia, 115, 119, 145-6, 148; self-preservation, 145-6, 150; visions, 198-9
Lake, Frank, xiv, 20, 44, 96, 200, 202
Lamaze, Fernand, 38
language, 119-22; and brain damage, 117; and neurosis, 119; and schizophrenia, 115-16, 119, 149, 206
Lawrence, D.H., 12
Leboyer, Frederick, 31, 33, 35-6, 52, 55-7, 61, 182
legs, 11; *see also* standing; walking
Leshan, Lawrence, 192
Lidz, Theodore, 150
life progress, 174-8; *see also* energy
lifestreams, *see* streamings

and embryo, 18–19; and
  embryogenesis, 22, 178, 180–1;
  and orgasm, 102, 131; and
  schizophrenia, 89, 131–4
stress, 5, 200, 216–17
sub-cortical/extra-pyramidal
  nervous system, 70–1
suckling, 59–61, 85, 93
suicide, 189–90
super-ego, 17
superimposition, 196
sympathetic nervous system,
  13–14, 71

Tausk, Victor, 131–2
tension, 5–6, 165–6; body
  segments, 6–11, 65–9; rings of,
  67–9; and speech, 117
territoriality, 137–42, 144, 149–50
therapy: biosynthesis, xiv (*see also*
  centring; facing; grounding);
  gestalt, xiii, 107, 120, 155; and
  embryology, 13–19; vegeto-, xiii,
  89, 124–5, 131
thinking, 113–15, 156
Thomas, Dylan, 180
Thorpe, W.H., 85–6
throat, 9, 65–6, 74
Tiller, William 212
Tillich, Paul, 170
Tinbergen, Nikolaas, 138–9
transitions, birth, 50–63

trauma, 20, 38, 45–6, 62–3, 173
trunk, 10, 68
Tsu, Chuang, 189–90

umbilicus, 31, 55–6, 59, 182;
  umbilical affect, 18, 87;
  umbilical castration, 23, 182–3
uterus: during labour, 38–42; life
  in, *see* birth; foetus

vegetative identification, xv, 107
vegetative nervous system, 4–5, 13–
  14, 71
vegeto-therapy, xiii, 89, 124–5, 131
Vellay, Pierre, 42
visions, 198–201
voice production, 117–19

Waal, Nic, 3, 89, 125
Walker, Benjamin, 209
walking, 103–4
Wickland, Carl, 205
Willie, James, 128
Winnicott, D.W., 97, 121
womb, *see* uterus

Xavier, Chico, 192

yoga, 100
Yunker, Barbara, 44

zygote, 22

Also by David Boadella:

WILHELM REICH THE EVOLUTION OF HIS WORK

WILHELM REICH THE EVOLUTION OF HIS WORK

Wilhelm Reich is a figure who presents extraordinary contrasts. He has an international reputation as a scientist of integrity, but was publicly slandered as a racketeer and a quack. His productive work covered forty years, across six countries, and spans many disciplines, including psychiatry, sociology and biology.

During the last decade, in a climate that has become more sympathetic to Reich's ideas, the seminal importance of his work in, for example, the fields of alternative medicine and humanistic psychology had been increasingly acknowledged. In this clear and comprehensive account of what Reich actually did, David Boadella surveys the development of this thoughts, the main objections to his findings and the principal research since his death that supports them.